99

LATHES AND TURNING.

A TREATISE

ON

LATHES AND TURNING

SIMPLE, MECHANICAL, AND ORNAMENTAL

BY

W. HENRY NORTHCOTT

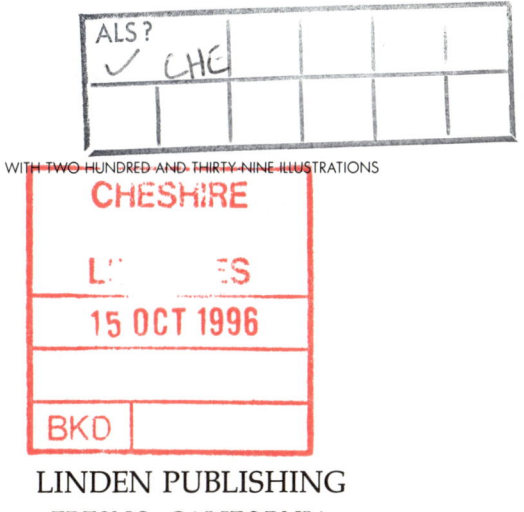
WITH TWO HUNDRED AND THIRTY-NINE ILLUSTRATIONS

LINDEN PUBLISHING
FRESNO, CALIFORNIA

Produced in co-operation with the
Museum of Ornamental Turning, Ltd.
1661 S. Research Loop
Tucson, AZ 85710

Originally published in 1868 by
Longmans, Green, and Co.
London

2nd Edition published in 1876

24689753

Library of Congress Cataloging-in-Publication Data

Northcott, W. Henry (William Henry), b. 1846.
    A treatise on lathes and turning, simple, mechanical, and
ornamental.

    Reprint. Originally published: London: Longmans, Green, 1868.
    1. Lathes.   2. Turning.   I. Title.
TT201.N67   1987   684'.083   87-3618
ISBN 0-941936-10-4

Linden Publishing Co. Inc.
3845 N. Blackstone
Fresno, California 93726

In memory of
S. Linden
33 Craven Street
Strand, London

CONTENTS.

PART III.

PART IV.

ix

ILLUSTRATIONS.

PART I.

PART II.

HAND-LATHES AND THEIR USES.

PART III.

PART IV.

FOREWORD

THE YEAR WAS 1868. William Henry Northcott, a young engineer from Exeter was just 21 years old. He saw the need for a "handbook" on lathes and turning and set about applying his efforts to the task. He had in mind a book that contained the latest information on lathe development, was readily comprehensible, and modestly priced. He accomplished his goal with this offering. His success has been born out by it remaining a classic reference on the subject long after Mr. Northcott's death at age 71 in 1914.

By a "handbook" Northcott sought to put in the hands of the lathe operator a text that first explained the different lathes extant in the mid 19th century. It was a time when man was enthralled by his own genius at developing things mechanical. Today's reader is treated to several drawings of that genius at work at the mother of all tools – the machine lathe. Next Northcott explains hand or simple turning, an art that is practiced mainly by the hobbyists. He goes on to explain the more complex operations achieved by the more mechanical "self-acting slide lathe", used for the heavier duty work of metals. This too is rapidly becoming a lost art as modern computer programmed lathes replace the skilled mechanic of a former era. Lastly, Northcott treats us to the truly lost art of Ornamental Turning, practiced by only a few artisans at that time and even fewer today.

It is necessary to put the year of writing, 1868, in the context of the literature on turning and related mechanical endeavours. By 1850 Charles Holtzapffel had completed the first three of six promised volumes of the epic series "Turning and Mechanical Manipulation". His early death created a vacuum in the mechanical world and there was a lapse of nearly 30 years until his son, John Jacob Holtzapffel, the second, resumed the series. The writings and drawings of the Holtzapffel family are still respected as unparalleled classics in the field. Into this vacuum stepped the young and perhaps brash Northcott to offer in his treatise a condensed and precise explanation of lathe operations. It too, remains a classic reference work.

The late 20th century has witnessed a revival of turning as an art. Organizations such as the Museum of Ornamental Turning, Ltd. have prompted a re-education of lost practices by encouraging works such as this. It is hoped that the reader will enjoy this re-publication of the first edition of "On Lathes and Turning".

Richard I. Miller
The Museum of Ornamental
Turning, Ltd.
Spring, 1987

PREFACE.

———•◊•———

FOR SOME TIME I have been expecting to see the publication announced of a book on the subjects of which the present work treats, and also the completion of Holtzapffel's unfinished but long-promised 'Mechanical Manipulation.' Such a volume not having appeared, I have endeavoured to write, in as small a compass as practicable, a work which, I hope, will be found of service to the many who desire an acquaintance with these useful arts.

I have myself found considerable difficulty in acquiring information—otherwise than by practice—concerning the multiplicity of operations that can be conducted by the aid of the lathe ; and judging from the numerous letters and enquiries on the subject appearing in the Mechanical papers, I believe such a work as the present to be greatly wanted. For, although there are many books on Turning already in existence, they are either too old to be now of much value—too expensive to be within reach of all—or their information, being confined to but one branch of the art, is too limited to be widely useful.

This work being designed to supply in some measure the existing deficiency, the information given is correspondingly comprehensive. All branches of Turning are noticed, and a good deal of practical information is given upon each.

Many operations and apparatus are described which do not properly come under the head of Turning, but as they are to a great extent performed by means of the Lathe, and as they are also exceedingly useful, I think the book is rendered more complete by including them.

No historical disquisition is introduced, from the opinion that it is unnecessary. It is very certain that the invention of the Potter's wheel—from which it is supposed the lathe has been derived—is lost in pre-historic ages. It is equally certain that the lathe proper is quite a modern contrivance. What matters it, therefore, whether the crude principle upon which is remotely founded its present efficiency, is derived from the Greek or North American Indian? The enquiry would appear to concern the Mechanic but little. Suffice it therefore—especially as this part of the subject has before been frequently entered upon—to treat of the lathe in the present work as it at present stands. Our great concern in this, as in all other mechanism, is not with its ancient history, but its present and future condition, and our main solicitude would be how best to develope the resources we have in hand.

The lathe can be applied to such a large number of purposes, that some of the operations performed by its aid may have been overlooked and omitted.   Probably in some of those described there is still room for improvement.   I shall therefore be glad to receive additional information and suggestions respecting new or amended processes from anyone whose practice is in advance of that here indicated, and who will kindly communicate it.   This supplementary matter shall be inserted at the first opportunity, and due credit given to those who contribute it.

My thanks are due to the Whitworth Engineering Company, and to Messrs. Fairbairn, Kennedy, and Naylor, of Leeds, for the fine photographs of lathes, from which the illustrations given were taken, and to Henry Perigal, Esq., F.R.A.S., for having furnished much information on the Geometric Chuck, and for having given the chapter on that instrument the benefit of his revision.

W. Henry Northcott.

Exeter: 1868.

SAFETY PROCEDURES FOR LATHE USE

All readers are advised that this text is intended to show how lathe operation was practiced at the time of original publication, 1868, it is not intended as a work of educational instruction in lathe work. This is a book of historical interest only. Always use good judgement and standard safety procedures with all tools.

LATHES AND TURNING.

PART I

DEFINITION OF TURNING.

TURNING is the art or operation of shaping bodies by means of the lathe ; and the lathe is an instrument by which substances are rotated upon an axis under such arrangements that they may be cut and smoothed by a stationary tool. In its simplest form a lathe consists of two fixed points or centres, between which the object to be turned is rotated, and a chisel or other cutting tool is so held that all the portions of the material projecting beyond the plane in which the point of the tool is moved are cut away as the object rotates, leaving a smooth and cylindrical surface. Lathes, however, are now often made of a very complex configuration, and many operations besides that of simple turning are now performed by their instrumentality. These different forms of lathe will be described hereafter.

There can be no doubt that the lathe in its simplest form is a very ancient instrument, and it probably consisted merely of two fixed points, or centres, between which the object to be turned was placed, and it was

then probably moved first in one direction and then in
the opposite, by means of a bow, the string of which
passed two or three times round the object, so as to
give it the requisite hold. This action is precisely the
same as that which we see in the case of the bow-drill;
and lathes upon this principle are up to the present day
in use, not merely in the far East, but in Spain, Portu-
gal, and some other European countries. The application of the crank and flywheel to the turning lathe is
not of very ancient date, and before the introduction of
that improvement, bow-lathes must have been the kind
exclusively employed. In the East, the turner sits on
the ground and holds the chisel with one hand, while
with the other he moves the bow backward and forward, so as to put the object into revolution first in one
direction and then in the other. The chisel is guided
and steadied upon the rest by the workman's big toe.

In some modern lathes, instead of the tool being
kept stationary and the object rotated, the object is
kept stationary, and the tool, by suitable mechanism
is made to travel round it, removing in its course all
asperities. But whether the tool or the object is
moved, the object is equally said to have been turned.
If, instead of the fixed tool being applied to the
revolving work, so as to produce a solid cylinder, it is
used to cut out the interior of the article, or make a
cylindrical hole, the article is still considered to have
been turned, unless a special tool be used to produce
the hole, when the operation is called drilling or
boring, as the case may be. But by far the greater
number of operations in turning are conducted when
the work is revolving and the tool stationary. When

the hole is produced by a revolving tool, the work itself being stationary, the operation is almost always called boring or drilling, and not turning.

The principal parts of the lathe are the bed or bearer, which is the most massive part—and to which the other parts are *fastened*—the cone-poppet, or headstock, to which motion is first communicated, and which in turn sets the work in motion through the medium of chucks. This headstock is generally at the left hand of the workman, and the screw-poppet, or headstock for holding and supporting long work, at the right hand. Then in hand-lathes we have the rest-holder and rest, which supports the tools; and in self-acting lathes, the slide-rest, which carries and guides the tools. Lathes for long work must have long beds or bearers, and for large work the lathe-spindle must be raised high off the bed. The distance the lathe-spindle is from the surface of the bed is called the 'height of centres,' and is the term generally used to express the size of the lathe. Thus, a lathe having its spindle raised six inches above the bed-surface would be called a six-inch centre lathe, and lathes of ordinary construction will turn articles double the height of centres in diameter, or articles equal in radius to the height of centres. The length of articles of that diameter—however long the bed—is limited to a few inches, as but few lathes are capable of receiving long cylinders of that size.

It would be difficult to imagine what we should now do without the lathe. There are few arts or manufactures that can dispense with machinery, and few machines can be constructed without the lathe. No contrivance yet invented is capable of more varied or valuable applications. It is made in every conceivable form, for every conceivable purpose. We now use lathes specially adapted as dentists' lathes, lapidaries' lathes, osteological lathes, gunstock lathes, rocket-stick lathes, shoe-last lathes, and copying lathes of various sorts.

We have lathes for drilling, boring, for turning shafts, for turning railway axles, railway tyres and wheels, rolls for rolling iron, and for cabinet-makers' work, billiard-ball turning, slight ornamental work, for cutting screws either singly or many at a time, and slide and screw-cutting lathes for ordinary engineers' work, with a multitude of others, to describe the whole of which would require a rather extensive volume. The last-mentioned species of lathe is the one most used by mechanics; it contains the principles of most of the other lathes, and is capable of doing nearly all the work in usual request. Those thoroughly acquainted with its action will have little trouble in learning the use of *most* of the others.

I shall here give a brief explanation of the varieties of lathe in most general use, and shall explain in detail certain lathes which are types of all the rest, many of which are of such limited application as to be interesting to but few. The hand-lathe was at one time the only lathe used by mechanics, but since the introduction of the improved forms of lathe it is not now used in workshops of any pretensions. Still, however, it may be found in country blacksmiths' shops; and schoolboys of a mechanical turn are commonly well pleased to be possessed of one of the lighter forms. One of these is shown at Fig. 1. (a) is the bed; (b) cone-poppet or headstock; (c) screw-poppet; (d) tool-rest; (e) treadle. These lathes can be bought anywhere, and at prices varying from 2*l.* to 20*l.* Their capabilities are rather limited, but they are well adapted ' to teach the young idea how to turn.'

A better constructed lathe, of similar properties, as made by Messrs. Easterbrook and Allcard, is shown at Fig. 2. In this lathe (a) is the bed, which is of metal; (b) is the cone, or fast headstock, also of metal, with a steel mandril and gun-metal bearings; (c) is the moving or screw head-stock, with a hand-wheel and tightening lever; (d) is the tool-rest and holder; (e) the treadle for the feet; (f) is the chain connecting the treadle to the crank (h); (g) is the gut band passing over the driving pulley (i) on the crank-shaft, and communicating motion to the cone of the lathe-spindle; (k, k) are handles for fastening

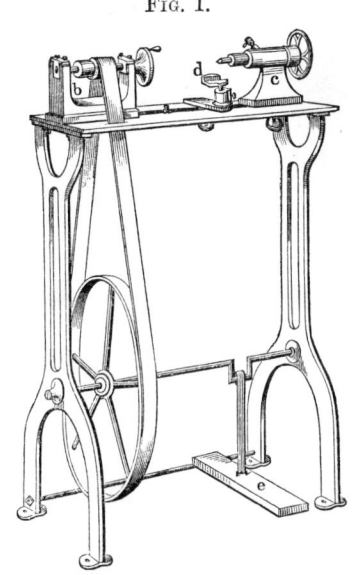

Fig. 1.

the headstock and rest-holder firmly on to the bed in a convenient position; (l, l) are the two standards or supports for the lathe-bed; (m) is the back-board, or shelf, for placing tools and instruments upon within reach of the workman's hand.

In these lathes, whether driven by the foot or by

steam, it is impossible to produce work requiring much
force. Although ample power may be available, the
strap is insufficient to transmit it to the lathe-spindle,
and the capability of varying the speed is but small,
and unsuitable for any but small variations in the diameter of the work. Lathes are therefore fitted with
double or back gearing, which enables them to be used

FIG. 2.

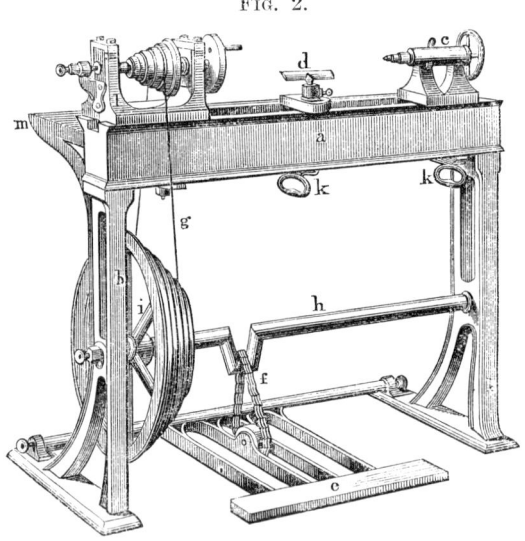

upon much heavier work, and of course renders the lathe
much more serviceable. This double gear accomplishes
its object by diminishing the speed and increasing the
power in a corresponding proportion. It is variously
arranged, but is usually set at back of the lathe-spindle,
as shown in several of the lathes illustrated. The neatest
arrangement is that in which the wheels are enclosed
in the cone; but this is not so powerful, nor is it so
accessible as outside gearing.

The capabilities of these lathes can be still further increased by the addition of a slide-rest, but then they can scarcely be considered ' hand-lathes,' as that term is used to denote those lathes with which the work is performed by hand-tools, or tools held in the hand.

The slide-rest (Fig. 3) is a sort of mechanical hand, or instrument to be used instead of the hand, for holding the tools and applying them to the work. The example given in the figure is of plain but convenient construction. The part (a) bolts down upon the bed

Fig. 3.

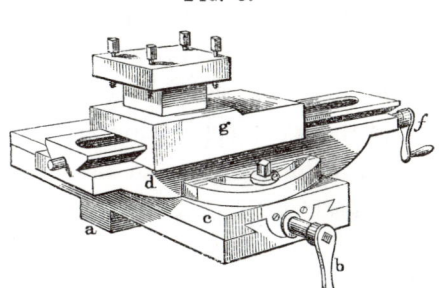

with the projecting piece between the bars of the bed ; (b) is a handle, by moving which the slide (c) is caused to move upon (a); (d) is well fitted upon (c) and is moved around a central pin, and adjusted at any required angle, by the screw (e); by moving the handle (f) the slide (g) is caused to traverse along (d). The tool is placed in a convenient position on (g) under the screws, two of which are tightened down to hold the tool firmly in place. By the use of the slide-rest, the operator is enabled to turn plane surfaces, parallel bars, articles of regular taper shape, true curves, &c., far better and faster than when the tool is held in the hands.

Some varieties of work, however, can be turned better by hand than by slide-rest tools.

When using these mechanical hands, it is only necessary—after they are properly adjusted—to turn a small handle, and the tool is caused to move along in the required direction. Even this small amount of hand-labour may be rendered unnecessary by making the slide self-acting—that is, causing the motion of the lathe itself to move the handle and work the slide, so as to cause the tool to move. This can be done in many different ways. The slide-rest, when in use, is fastened on the lathe-bed, just opposite that portion of the work it is desired to turn—a finger being fastened to the work, and a star-wheel to the handle of the screw—and the work set in motion. This finger in revolving strikes against the teeth of the wheel, and causes it and the screw to revolve slowly; and, consequently, the slide, upon which the tool is mounted, is caused to advance. This, however, is a clumsy method, but seldom used. The most convenient plan is by means of an eccentric on the lathe-spindle, the motion of which is communicated by a wire or cord passing overhead to a lever and ratchet-wheel on the screw of the slide-rest. The neatest, but not so convenient a plan as the last, is to have an eccentric, and a small rocking-lever shaft in front of the lathe, fastened to the bed. This lever, being caused to oscillate by the eccentric, moves the slide-rest screw by a small ratchet-wheel and catch motion.

The beds of hand-lathes are frequently made of wood, either beech or mahogany. For the larger sizes, the top part of the bed is covered with iron. Wood is not a good material in any case, however ; as, besides being clumsy for the purpose, it is affected by damp and by variation of temperature ; and in course of using the wood gets bruised and chipped off. Iron is infinitely to be preferred for many reasons, especially as regards durability.

There is another species of hand-lathe, called bar-lathes, from the bed being a triangular bar of iron, to which the poppets and rests are fitted. These are chiefly used by watchmakers, and are generally very small.

Self-acting slide-lathes are used almost wholly by mechanics for turning plain cylinders, or shafts of iron, and similar work. In these lathes the use of hand-tools is dispensed with altogether ; and, instead of the slide-rest being fastened immovably to the bed, it is made to slide along it lengthwise, generally by a rack and pinion movement, the pinion being attached to the slide-rest, and driven through a long shaft from the lathe-spindle, the rack fastened to and forming part of the bed. Cylindrical shafts, or bars of metal of almost any length, are thus turned without the workman being required to move the rest at all. He has only to adjust the tool so that it will take the required depth of cut, and to throw the self-acting mechanism into gear. The rest, and consequently the tool, will then tra-verse or slide along the bed without further manual assistance.

A lathe of this sort is shown at Fig. 4, which is taken from the lathes made by Messrs. Fairbairn, Kennedy, and Naylor, of Leeds. The cone-spindle carries a supplementary cone-pulley, for giving motion to the self-acting mechanism. This lathe is automatic

10-inch Centre Self-acting Slide and Surfacing Lathe.

FIG. 4.

Fig. 5.

21-inch Centre Slide Break Lathe.

on both the longitudinal and transverse motions—that is, the motion of the slide-rest along the bed is automatic, and also the motion of the tool along the slide of the rest is self-acting.

These lathes are seldom made smaller than with ten or twelve-inch centres, and the bed is usually made very long; but as in some cases the whole length of bed is not required, it is customary to utilise the unemployed length by placing one or more headstocks upon the bed. These are removed when very long shafts have to be turned.

Self-acting surfacing-lathes are for turning up large plane surfaces, and are generally made very massive and heavy. The beds of these lathes are seldom made of any great length, but their centres are raised very high, so as to admit articles of large diameter. The slide-rest is not required to travel any great distance along the bed parallel to the line of centres, its chief motion being required parallel to the face-plate across the bed, at right angles to the line of centres. In large surfacing-lathes there is some little difficulty in getting the proper variation of speed. The best are constructed so that the number of revolutions diminish as the tool travels from the centre, so as to keep the cutting speed constant.

Many lathes are constructed for both surfacing and traversing. They have the beds of moderate length, and moderately high centres, and are adapted to turn articles of small diameter and good length, surfaces of moderately large diameter, and also cylinders of moderate size and length. Such a lathe is illustrated at Fig. 5, which is a Slide Break Lathe, 21-inch centres,

made by Messrs. Fairbairn, Kennedy, and Naylor.
These are only used by mechanics.

The lathe in greatest request is the self-acting screw-
cutting lathe. This is able to perform all the work of
those described, and, in addition, is capable of cutting
screws of any inclination or pitch. In some of these
the rack and pinion for traversing are done away with
altogether, and the saddle of the rest is caused to travel
along the bed by means of a screw called a leading screw.
When this is the case, the screw is used alike for ordinary sliding up or traversing and for screw-cutting, the
variation in relative speed of traverse being gained by
means of wheels termed ' change-wheels.' By changing
the wheels connecting the lathe-spindle and the leading screw, any required relative speed is obtained
between these two. Thus, for ordinary plain turning
or traversing, the lathe-spindle would run very much
faster than the leading screw. For cutting fine screws
or screws of fine pitch, wheels would be put on which
would cause the screw to run somewhat faster than for
traversing. To cut a moderately coarse thread, say,
the same pitch as the leading screw itself, the lathe-
spindle would be connected to the leading screw by
such wheels as would cause the two to revolve at the
same speed, or at the same angular velocity; and for
cutting screws or spirals much coarser than the leading screw the lathe-spindle must be caused to revolve
much slower than the screw. For most lathes the
leading screw is made with two threads to the inch—
that is, it has to revolve twice to cause the saddle and
tool to traverse one inch along the bed. Other numbers of threads are also used, but two is the most

convenient for general work. If other numbers be used they should be even—such as 4 to the inch, and 8 to the inch, unless the pitch be 1 to the inch. Such pitches as $\frac{3}{8}$ths or $\frac{5}{8}$ths should be avoided.

It is obvious that, to cut a perfect screw in the lathe, the leading screw must itself be perfect. This, however, is not always the case, even in these days of 'perfection of mechanism.' And even should the screw be perfectly true in the first place, it does not long remain so, especially in those lathes in which the ordinary traversing motion is derived from the screw ; as the screw soon gets out of truth and unequally worn. In most lathes the greater part of the work is done within a foot or two of the cone centre, or, in other words, there is more short work done than long ; and, as only a few inches of the leading screw are used to obtain the required traverse of the rest, it follows that these few inches are much more used and consequently more worn than the remainder. With a screw thus injured it is utterly impossible to originate or cut a perfect screw of any pitch. This cause of deterioration is obviated to some extent by using the screw only for screw-cutting, and having a separate rack and pinion motion for the ordinary traverse of the slide-rest.

Although it is impossible to cut a perfect screw in a lathe from an imperfect leading screw, by far too much faith is placed in that one article alone. Many clever mechanics appear to imagine that if they have a perfect leading screw nothing further is required. This, however, is a mistake, as, although such a screw is indispensable, it is still very easy to cut a screw of irregular pitch with the best of leading screws.

To cut a good screw in the lathe, not only should its leading screw be perfect, but the change-wheels should be equally so ; yet but few care at all about the state of their changes, although they may be fully alive to the value of having a good leading screw. Even with a good leading screw and accurate change-wheels, it is not always that a long screw can be cut with its pitch mathematically uniform ; indeed, at the best of times, this is a very delicate operation. The change-wheels made by Mr. R. Lloyd, of Birmingham, as specimens of casting, if not unequalled, are certainly unsurpassed.

The *sun's rays* passing through a window or skylight, and falling on a leading screw, will cause it *to expand*, and for some feet *the pitch will be coarser*; and this irregularity will be reproduced in the screw cut in the lathe. If the screw to be cut is of coarser pitch than the leading screw, the irregularity will be increased ; but if the screw be of finer pitch, then the irregularity will be diminished.

It is obvious that when a separate traverse motion is employed, and the screw of the lathe used only for screw-cutting, that if a great deal of short screw-cutting has to be done the leading screw must be worn unequally, although not nearly to so great an extent as when the screw is used for both screwing and traverse turning. The larger and heavier screw-cutting lathes are employed solely by mechanics; there are many different designs, but that given at Fig. 6, which is the Whitworth Company's Duplex Lathe, embodies, perhaps, the latest improvements.

The Whitworth Company also make an excellent form

Fig. 6.

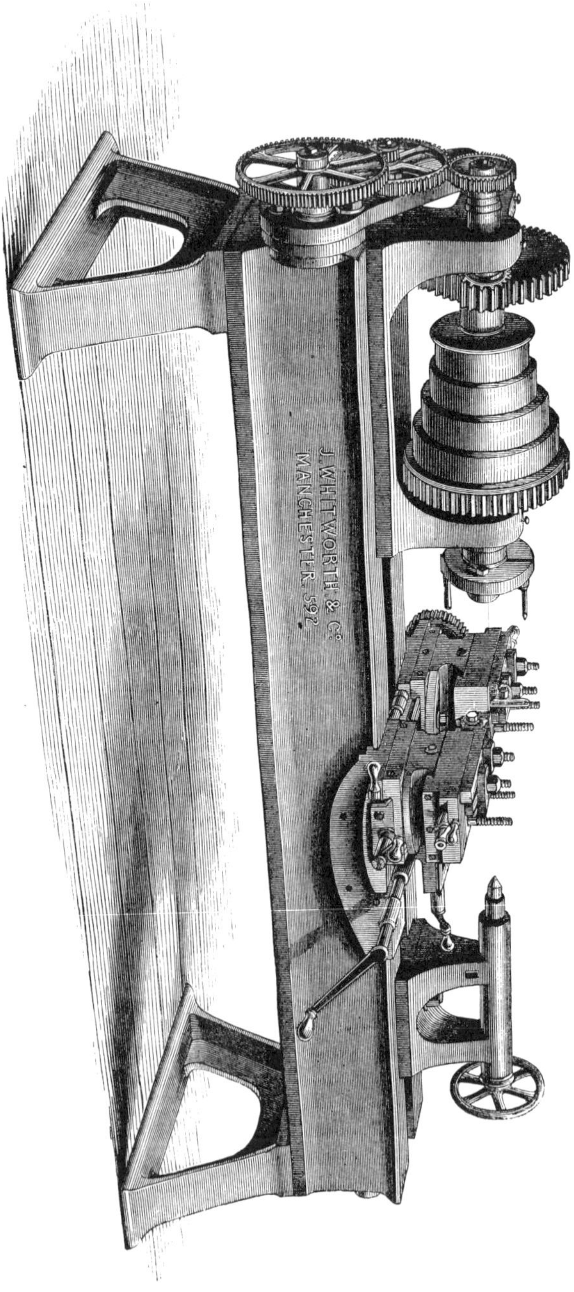

10-inch Duplex Self-acting Lathe.

FIG. 7.

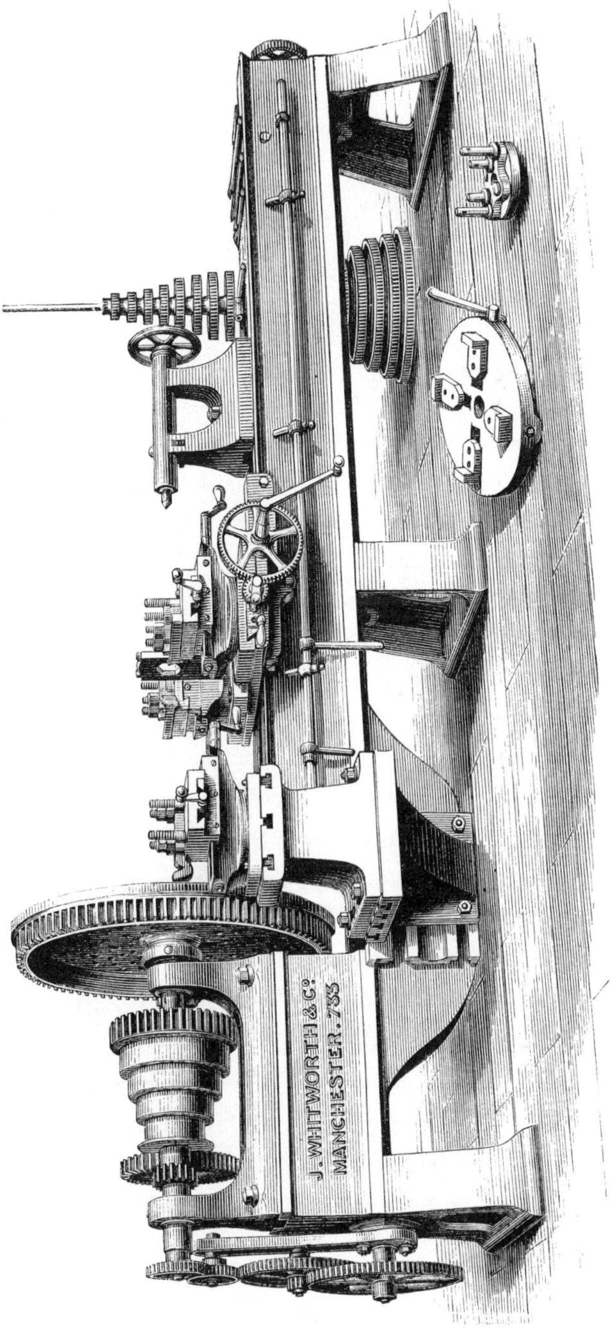

Duplex Self-acting Gap Lathe, with Additional Rest.

of Duplex Lathe (Fig. 7), which differs from the last
mainly in being adapted to turn large short articles.
The bed has an opening, or gap, which increases the
height of centres, and provision is made for bolting on
an additional slide-rest. Screw-cutting lathes of smaller
size and lighter make are employed by mechanics and
also by gentlemen amateurs. One of this class of good
design is given at Fig. 8.

The slide-rests for screw-cutting and other lathes
are made of many varieties. Some are made to slide
along the bed past the headstocks, which is very
convenient. The headstocks are fastened down as
usual, but the slide-rest is fastened to the front side
of the bed. The Messrs. Muir, of Manchester, have a
patent for a neat plan of lathe of this sort, in which
there is a double bed, or bed formed of a casting,
having three longitudinal bars or faces, the centre one
being rather wider than the others. The headstocks
slide upon one of the outside bars and half the inside
bar, and the slide-rest travels upon the other half of
the middle bar and the other outside bar.

Ornamental lathes are the ones chiefly used by
amateurs; as, although the work to be done in them
is not so large and substantial as that to be done in
screw-cutting lathes, yet it is far more ornamental,
delicate, and beautiful. Ornamental lathes are also
used by ladies; and, as a great deal depends upon the
taste and lightness of touch of the operator, it is not
unfrequent to see work produced by lady and gentle-
man amateurs which equals, if not surpasses, in beauty
that produced by the professional turner. These lathes
are made very light, but very accurate; they are

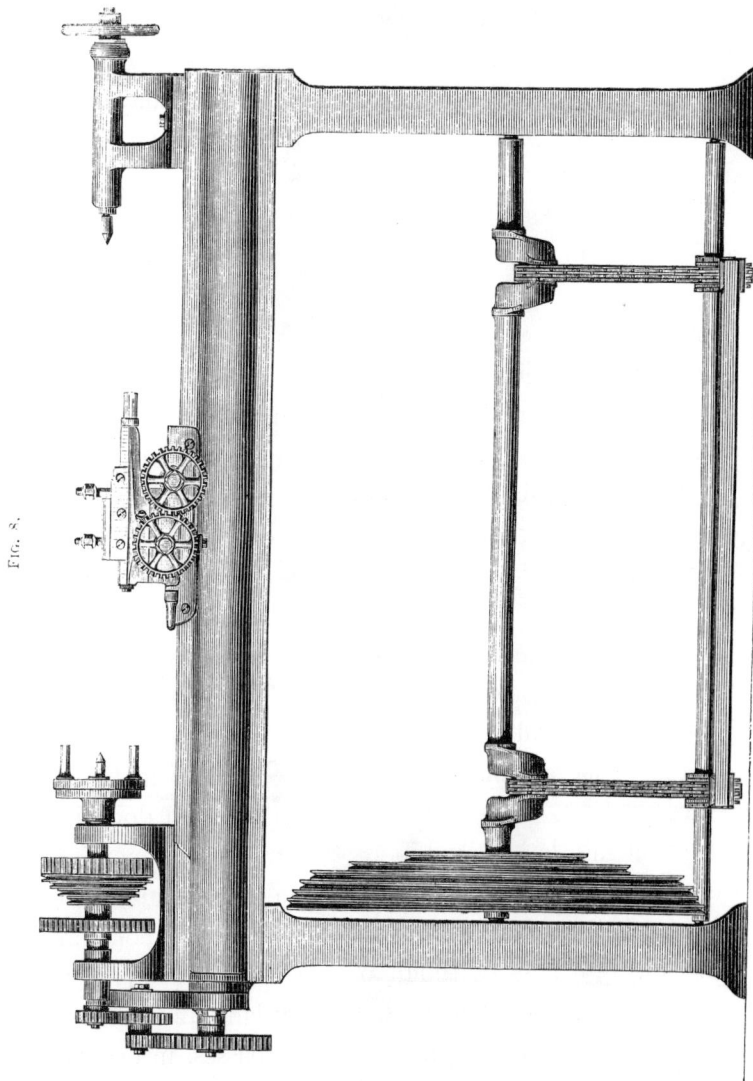

Fig. 8.

5-inch Self-acting Lathe for Foot-power.

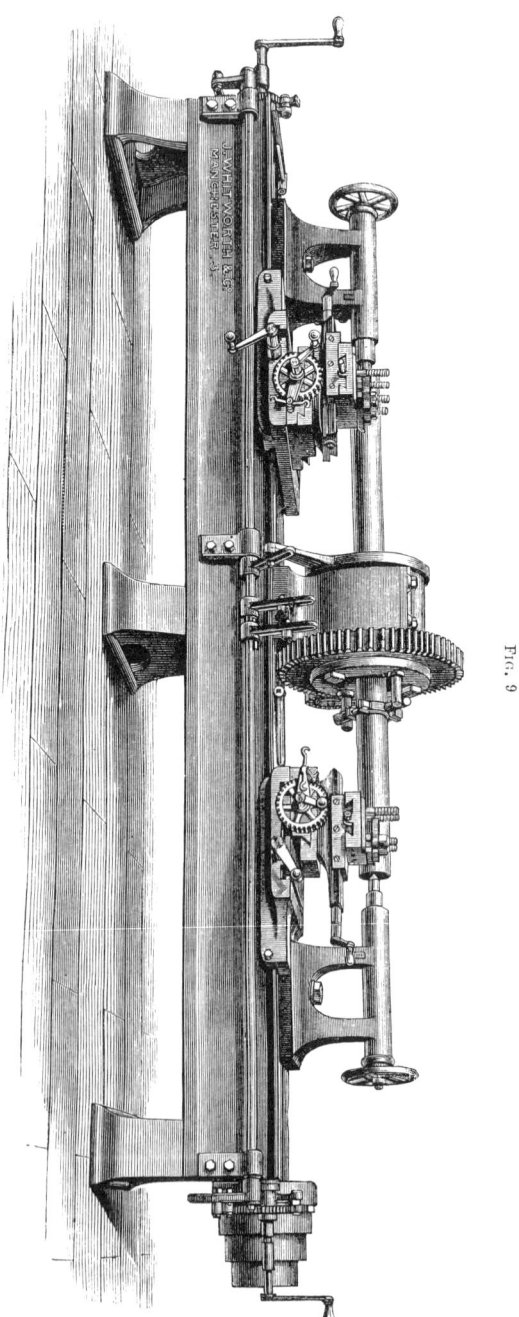

Fig. 9

Self-acting Railway-axle Lathe.

Fig. 10.

Duplex Railway-wheel Lathe.

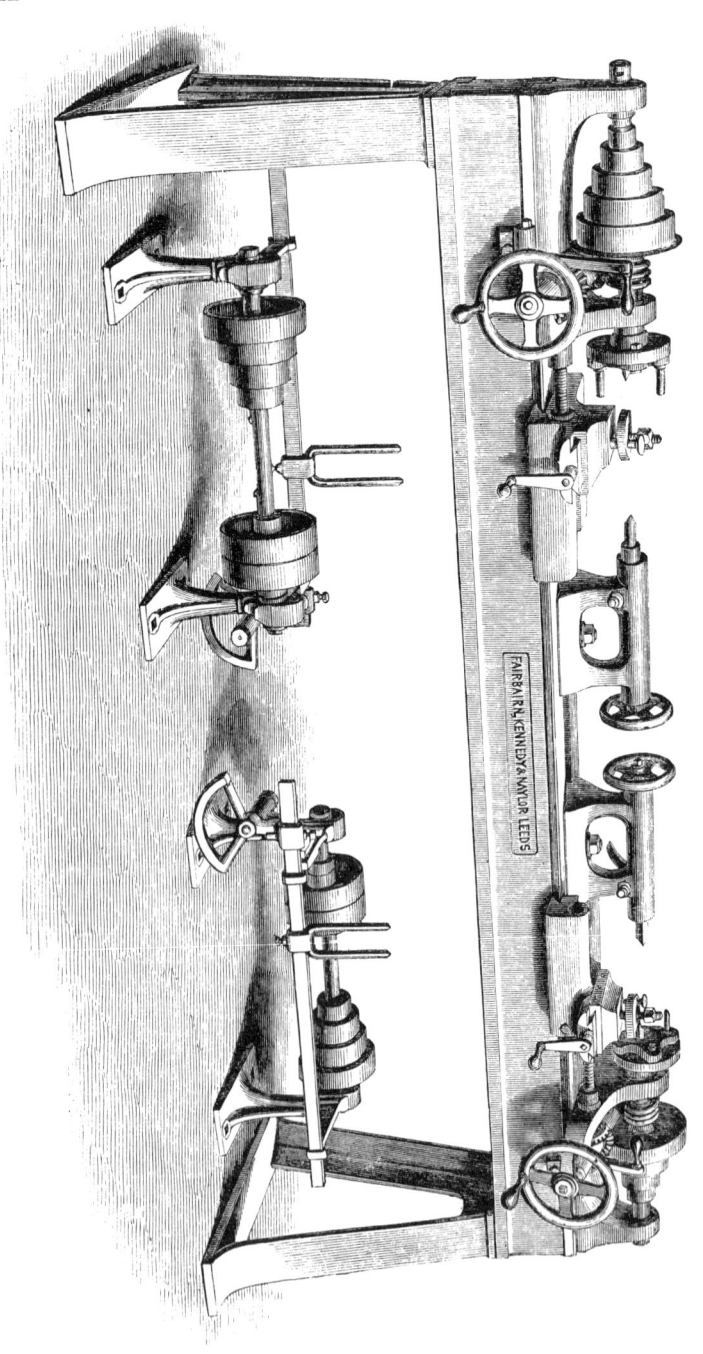

6-inch Double Lathe for Bolts and Studs.

FIG. 11.

FAIRBAIRN, KENNEDY & NAYLOR, LEEDS.

similar to the hand-lathe without back gear, the ornamental work being produced more by the aid of independent instruments than by the lathe itself, although the lathe has to be fitted up in a peculiar manner to allow of these instruments being applied and conveniently used.

In addition to these there are many lathes designed for special work, or the manufacture in large numbers of one article of peculiar shape. Fig. 9 is a lathe made solely for turning railway axles. The ends only of the axle having to be turned, it is put in the lathe, as shown, and both ends are turned at the same time by separate tools. This lathe is also shown as made by the Whitworth Company.

Fig. 10 is a lathe made by Fairbairn, Kennedy, and Naylor, for turning railway wheels on their axles. Both wheels are turned at once, two tools being employed on each wheel.

Fig. 11 is a neat lathe, by the same makers, for turning bolts and short work. There are two complete lathes on the same bed, and the saddle having only to traverse a short distance, is moved in a simple manner, as will be seen.

The lighter sorts of lathe are frequently driven by the operator's foot. This, of course, renders the work somewhat more laborious, and until one becomes accustomed to the unsteadiness of the motion it is more difficult to produce good work with lathes of this kind. The inconvenience wears off to a great extent after practice and use; but of course this unsteadiness does not affect tools held in the slide-rest.

For many sorts of ornamental work, professional

turners prefer to drive their lathes by the foot, because
of the delicacy with which they can adjust the pressure
and speed. There are many plans for driving by foot,
but in all the power derived from the pressure is communicated to a shaft underneath by a treadle and
crank. Sometimes the treadle and crank are connected
by connecting rods, and sometimes by flat chains passing
over the trucks or pulleys. The latter plan is preferred,
owing chiefly to its having less friction. If connecting
rods or links be used they must be hooked on to the
crank or treadle pins, so that, should anything get
under the treadle—the operator's foot, for instance—
when being pushed down, the treadle being stopped
by the obstacle, the link shall unhook ; otherwise, if
the connection were rigid, the momentum of the flywheel would urge the treadle down with such force as
would crush the operator's foot, or, if the obstruction
were of a harder nature, would fracture or strain some
of the mechanism.

In working with foot-treadles of ordinary construction, when the treading ceases, the weight of the treadle
and connecting rods, or chains and cranks, causes the
crank to take such a position that no pressure whatever on the treadle will cause the crank to again move.
This position is known as the 'crank being on the
centre.'

In order to again start the lathe, the operator must
move the crank off the centre by hand before commencing treading. Now, as in ornamental turning it is
not unfrequently the case that both hands are engaged
and cannot well be moved, it is very annoying to find
that the lathe cannot be started without having to move

it by hand; this inconvenience can be obviated in so simple a manner, that the wonder is that the plan is not more frequently adopted. By balancing the weight of the treadle and crank (*c c*), by a counter weight, the crank can be made to stop at any point in its circle of revolution. That point or position should be chosen which is the most convenient for starting from. This arrangement has another advantage—it lessens the vibration, and reduces the power required to drive the lathe.

The power to be obtained by the treadle is necessarily small; but the Messrs. Muir, of Manchester, have patented and brought into use a method of driving by many treadles and many feet. The power obtained in this case of course increases with the number of men employed in treading. Lathes of considerable size can thus be driven; and the plan is obviously of great value on board ship, where men to tread can be had without any extra expense, and where, perhaps, owing to a break-down of the engines, no other power is obtainable. When steam or other motive power is to be got, no one would think, except in the cases before stated, of driving by foot power.

Slide and surfacing lathes are continually driven in one direction, and generally from a small shaft, called a counter-shaft, placed over the lathe, and driven from the main shaft by a belt. This shaft is either stopped or started by means of a pair of pulleys on the counter-shaft, one fastened to the shaft, and the other, termed the loose or idle pulley, free to run around upon it: when the belt is slipped on to the loose pulley, that pulley is set in motion upon the shaft, but the shaft itself remains still. When, however, the belt is slipped on to the fast pulley, not only does the pulley revolve, but, it being fastened to the counter-shaft, the shaft revolves also. This motion is then communicated from a cone-pulley on the counter-shaft to the cone-pulley of the lathe-spindle, by a belt passing over both. In self-acting lathes the direction of motion is the same ; but when the saddle of the rest has travelled the whole length of the bed, or as far as is required, it is reversed, or caused to go back again, without either reversing or stopping the lathe itself.

Frequently, however, these lathes are constructed to cut or traverse only in one direction ; and when the saddle has travelled as far in that direction as the nature of the work requires, the mechanism connecting it with the lathe-spindle is thrown out of gear, and the saddle moved back along the bed by the workman himself. Screw-cutting lathes are also driven from a counter-shaft, but in a different manner. When the rest and saddle require to be reversed, it is usually done by driving the lathe-cone in the opposite direction, the tool being thrown out of cut until the motion is again reversed, and the saddle is travelling in the original direction. The lathe-cone is reversed by reversing the counter or auxiliary driving-shaft. There are a number of methods for doing this, but the most general is to have two straps or leather belts, one passing straight around the two shafts, the other crossing midway between them. The main shaft is furnished with a pulley wide enough to take both straps, and the counter-shaft has on it three pulleys. Of these the centre one is fastened to the shaft : the other two are idle or loose pulleys, and are wider than the inner one. When the counter-shaft is not required to be driven, these two belts are on the loose pulleys, one on each, and as one of the belts is crossed the pulleys will consequently revolve in opposite directions. There is a slide having two forks or guides engaging these belts. This slide is worked by a lever, hanging down within easy reach of the workman.

Now when the lathe is required to move in one direction, the lever is moved so as to cause the slide to carry one of the belts on to the fast pulley, which is then driven in the same direction as the pulley whence the belt was taken. The other belt is, by the motion of the slide, caused to run nearer the outside of its own pulley, and this pulley revolves as before, without influencing the motion of the shaft. By moving back the lever to its former position the belts are also brought to their former positions, and the counter-shaft is stopped. By moving the lever in a contrary direction the other belt is carried on to the fast or driving pulley, which is then driven in a contrary direction to what it was previously. As the lathe takes its motion from this counter-shaft it follows that its motion is changed in direction by shifting the belts.

This reversing motion is commonly used for screw-cutting lathes, and as the tool does not generally cut both ways, being withdrawn from cut during the return stroke, it follows that the time occupied by the return of the saddle is time wasted. It is a good plan, therefore, to make the pulley on the main shaft of two sizes, that size which drives the lathe during its return stroke being made larger than the other. This has the effect of causing the return of the saddle to be accomplished in less time, and consequently less time is wasted.

The belt-guide having a considerable distance to travel, the motion of the lever-handle which actuates the slide is much too great for ease of manipulation. The belt employed also, if worked hard, gives some little trouble by stretching and breaking ; nevertheless, the motion is very noiseless, and is communicated and reversed without any injurious shock.

In order to do away with the inconvenience arising from the length of travel of the reversing lever, a plan has been devised which effectually and in a simple manner accomplishes that object, and which is especially applicable to those lathes in which starting, stopping, and reversing, are effected by self-acting means, or through the motion of the lathe itself. In this plan the use of two straps is retained, and the two loose pulleys on the counter-shaft are also used, together with the driving pulley on the main shaft of either one or two sizes. The loose pulleys on the counter-shaft are, however, only half their usual width, and no belt-guide is used, the straps always remaining in one place on their respective pulleys. For the fast pulley between the others is substituted a friction-clutch, caused to revolve with the shaft by being fastened thereto by a feather and groove, which, however, permits it to have a slight sliding or longitudinal motion on the shaft. The inside rim of the pulley is turned taper to fit the tapering parts of the friction-clutch. The clutch is moved by a lever to gear with either of the pulleys, or into a position between the two and out of contact with both. In the former case the clutch, and consequently the intermediate shaft, partakes of the motion of that pulley with which it is in contact. In the latter case the shaft remains still. In this plan the motion of the lever handle is not more than one-third or one-fourth of that necessary in the other plan with shifting belts.

In addition to these, there is also a method for driving and reversing, by means of a single belt, three bevel wheels and a double clutch. It is, however, much inferior to the two plans described.

Amateurs are advised to purchase their lathes of a respectable maker, and not attempt to make one for themselves. It may always be considered that when an amateur makes his own lathe—although he himself may consider it a remarkable work of genius—in reality it will be found to be of little value. This may be an unwelcome truth to many mechanical aspirants, but it is not the less inexorable; and I am constrained to intimate it from having been a spectator of many such miscarriages. I have even heard of a wooden slide-rest and wooden elliptical chuck having been thus constructed. But these I have not seen.

In purchasing a lathe, the tyro must not suppose that all those made for the same purpose are necessarily alike. Each maker has his own peculiar style, and although lathes differ much in design and workmanship, each maker probably considers his own make the best. The design of a lathe more especially affects its convenience and usefulness, and the workmanship the quality and accuracy of the articles manufactured in the lathe. With regard to the workmanship there can be but one opinion, and that is that it cannot be too good or too accurate. Money spent in burnishing, or otherwise uselessly ornamenting a lathe is money wasted; but money spent in procuring accuracy of workmanship is well invested.

There is a vast difference between good work, or mechanical ornament (if I may so express myself), and useless or tawdry ornament. A good mechanic will leave those edges sharp which form joints, so that the joint can scarcely be seen, whilst terminal edges he will chamfer or round off, to prevent them hurting the operator, or being bruised or broken off, and left ragged themselves. By judiciously shaping the component parts of a machine, he will contrive to give the whole a graceful, finished, and mechanical appearance, which would otherwise be wanting, and this he does without extra expenditure, and without impairing the usefulness of the machine ; whereas another will cut a number of beads and mouldings on his work, burnish a great portion of it, make as much of the machine as possible ' bright,' and paint the unpolished or ' black ' portion of some flaming colour, and daub it with gilt or bronze. This he does imagining he improves the appearance of his work, whereas he impairs it. The beads and sharp edges and angles weaken the article considerably, and, in course of working, they are certain to be bruised and indented in some way, and the hand *seems always* to be knocking against them, and being cut or scratched. They also serve as receptacles for dirt. Burnishing machinery usually has the appearance of being done to cover defects, and the style becomes what is known amongst mechanics as ' deep scratch and high polish.' Gaudy colouring soon loses its bloom, but in whatever state it may be it imparts to the mechanism such a tawdry appearance as to excite the ridicule of every man of common sense.

As to the design of a lathe, that depends so much on the fancy of the user, and is so much a matter of opinion, that it is difficult to lay down many arbitrary rules. When one is accustomed to use a lathe of any peculiar design—even though it be in reality a bad arrangement—being familiarised with its defects and inconveniences, one is apt to overlook its bad features, and be prejudiced in its favour. The following may, however, be mentioned as a few of the main points of a good lathe :—

1. It should be constructed wholly of metal, for although some are of opinion that the introduction of wood is advantageous, as preventing that injurious jarring or 'chattering' which frequently annoys the operator, and renders it difficult for him to produce good work, I believe the notion to be almost exploded amongst mechanics—the chattering being always caused by the inattention or the unskilfulness of the operator.

2. The various parts should be as strong and massive as possible, without clumsiness.

3. The bed should be thoroughly unyielding, and stand immovably firm and level.

4. The spindle should be of good size, and its bear-- ings not too close together.

5. Conical bearings hardened are perhaps as good as any. When well made, with proper care and occasional regrinding, they will last a long time, and give but little trouble ; but if left unlubricated, screwed up too tight or improperly, or if the metal of the headstock

yield to the pressure of the screw, then in either case the necks 'bind,' get hot, abrade, and cause great trouble and annoyance.

6. The starting and reversing handle should be within easy and convenient reach of the operator.

7. The slide-rest should have a motion independent of the ordinary screw, for throwing the tool in and out of cut. For screw-cutting this motion is very valuable.

8. The tool-holder should be one of those allowing the tool to be placed at any angle or convenient position on the tool-plate.

9. All wearing or working surfaces should be provided with oil holes for lubrication, and those holes likely to get filled with dust or grit should be furnished with proper stoppers.

10. All sliding surfaces should be scraped to a good bearing, and without grinding.

There are certain technical terms and expressions used by turners which should be understood by learners. These terms vary according to the locality, but I believe the meanings here given to them are those most generally received.

'Traverse turning,' 'traversing,' and 'sliding-up,' are the expressions variously used to denote those operations in which the tool is caused to move along the length of the bed, the tool being set either parallel or nearly so to the line of centres, and by which the work produced is of the same size throughout, or nearly so.

'Surface-turning,' 'surfacing,' and 'facing-up,' are used to denote those operations in which the tool does not slide along the bed, but across it, at right angles to the line of centres, and in cutting produces a plane surface.

'Burr,' 'fash,' and 'raw-edge,' are generally used to denote the edge or angle of junction of two cuts, at right angles, or less than right angles, to each other. Such edges are usually rather sharp, or wire-edged, and frequently inflict serious cuts and gashes in the workman's hands, should he happen to touch the edge whilst the work is in motion. When cutting holes in metal the orifices of the hole, and especially that one from which the point of the tool makes its exit when cutting, are frequently exceedingly sharp and dangerous to touch.

'Trueing up' is the expression used to denote turning up an article for the sake of having a smooth surface, and without regard to size, and would be accomplished when the rough casting or forging had all the black or scale turned off.

'Hold up to size,' or 'Not to hold up to size.' When an object has to be turned to certain dimensions, if all the black or scale is turned off, it is said to 'hold up to size;' but if when the proper dimensions are attained, patches of scale are still seen, the article is said 'not to hold up to size.'

'True,' 'out of truth.' Surfaces are said to be 'true' when smooth and level, cylinders when perfectly cylindrical, and so with other shapes. Articles are said to 'run true' when in the case of a surface the surface revolves in a plane at right angles to the centre of lathe spindle, and in the case of a cylinder when it revolves concentrically.

'Chattering,' or 'shattering,' is the characteristic term applied to a peculiar noise, made generally by

the rapid vibration of the article turning. The noise is
very unpleasant. When once heard it is not soon to
be forgotten, and it is a tolerably sure sign that something is wrong. Work produced while this chattering
is going on is usually ' out of truth ' and wavy.

' Thread ' of a screw is that part raised above the
surface of a cylinder upon which the screw is cut.
Screws may have several threads.

The ' pitch ' of a screw is the distance from thread
to thread, or the longitudinal distance which the thread
advances in one revolution of the spindle upon which
the screw is cut.

' Drunken pitch ' is the term used to denote a badly
made screw. When the thread advances faster during
some portions of a revolution than at others, or a screw
has an uneven pitch, or one not uniform, it is said to
be drunken.

' Centres ' are the indentations made at the ends of
articles, for retaining them in place whilst being
turned.

' Catch in ' is the expression used when the tool in
cutting suddenly jerks deeper into cut, and either digs
out an irregular hole in the material, or throws it out
of the centres, or jerks the tool out of the operator's
hands. This occurrence is very frequent with beginners.

' Loss of time,' or ' backlash,' is the distance through
which the first motion must travel, when the direction
of motion is reversed before the action will commence,
in the case of wheels in gear, such as the change-wheels
of a lathe. After the lathe has been running, and
the saddle of the rest travelling along the bed, when

the direction of the motion is reversed, the reversal of the saddle does not take place immediately, but the saddle remains stationary, while the lathe-spindle moves a considerable distance. This is called 'loss of time,' and in the case of wheels is caused by the necessary slack or clearance of the teeth. In the case of a screw alone, such as the screw of the surfacing slide of the rest, it will be found that after moving the slide in either direction by the screw, the handle of the screw must be reversed, and moved part of a revolution before the saddle will commence its motion in the reverse direction. This is owing partly to the slackness of fit or 'play' between the screw and nut, and partly to the screw having slight 'play,' or longitudinal motion between its collars. In the case of ordinary turning, this loss of time is of no consequence, but for screw-cutting it is sometimes inconvenient, and for ornamental turning much more so. This will be seen, and the method of counteracting it will be explained hereafter.

PART II.

PLAIN TURNING WITH HAND-TOOLS.

In order to describe the simplest operations first, I shall commence with instructions for plain turning with hand-tools in the simple lathe. It is necessary that the operator should have a good knowledge of the use of these tools before he can become a good workman at either the slide and screw-cutting lathes, or the ornamental lathes. In the working of the slide-lathes, and others of that sort, it is frequently necessary to make use of a hand-tool to touch out some corner or curve which it is difficult to come at properly with the tools in the slide-rest. It is also far easier to judge of the correct shape and method of using tools in the slide-rest when one thoroughly understands the cutting action of hand-tools. As these tools are held in the operator's hands, and guided by him, he very soon feels when they are out of order, or applied in the wrong position. But when tools do not cut aright in the slide-rest, the workman has to rely on his sight alone to inform him of the fact, and this to the inexperienced is seldom sufficient.

In ornamental turning, hand-tools are still more frequently required, and for this work especially, should the operator be able to use them with dexterity and certainty, as the slightest slip or clumsy touch would result probably in the work being spoiled. The primary lessons should be learned upon a rough or strong lathe of some sort, as, although it may appear the easiest thing imaginable to use these tools, it is, nevertheless, generally found upon trial that some of them—unless carefully used—are extremely apt to play awkward tricks.

I do not mean to say that the difficulty is very great, because it is not: with cautious handling no mishap need occur. But it is, however, desirable to guard against accidents, which, if they were to happen, would perhaps damage beyond repair the delicate mechanism of the ornamental lathe. Those who are totally unacquainted with turning should at first take a few lessons from a proficient in the art, acquiring by this means much rudimentary but necessary knowledge, which could scarcely be gathered from a book. There are many professional turners who make it their business to teach amateurs in all branches of the art, and also to procure for them the necessary fancy woods, and any instruments they may require. I think the present work will furnish the reader with most of the information these gentlemen could communicate; but I would, nevertheless, advise beginners to attentively watch the movements of a good turner, as, by this means, they will best be able to form an idea as to how they should proceed themselves.

The lathe itself having been previously described and illustrated at Fig. 2, I shall proceed to describe the chucks or instruments for communicating the motion of the lathe-spindle to the work. These chucks or drivers are screwed either on to the male

screw on the spindle end or 'nose' of the lathe, or
into the female screw of the spindle.   Chucks are not
only necessary for giving motion to the work, but in
some cases for firmly fastening and holding the material
in a convenient position for allowing the tools to be
applied to it.   As the articles to be chucked vary
greatly in size, shape, and material, the chucks must
be constructed variously.   Many will, however, answer
equally well for hard and soft woods, and ivory.   A few
can be used indiscriminately for these materials and
metals, but, as a rule, metals require chucks of greater
strength and different construction.   The drill-chuck,

FIG. 12.   FIG. 13.

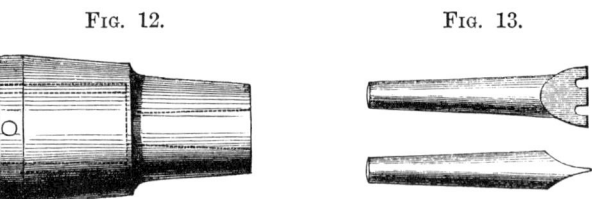

Fig. 12, is made either of brass or cast or wrought iron.
The dotted lines denote that it is fitted with a female
screw for screwing on the spindle end.   It also has a
taper square, or taper round hole to receive a set of
drilling tools, and also the two drivers, Figs. 13 and 14.
Fig. 13 is the prong for the softer varieties of wood.
Fig. 14 is the cross kerf driver.   It is made of steel,
and is used mostly for the hard woods, ivory, bone,
and small work in metals.   When these drivers are
used, the work is always supported at the other extremity by the screw centre.   The taper-screw chuck,
Fig. 15, is made of metal, and screws on the male
screw of the mandril.   The taper-screw itself is made

of steel, and is fastened to the body of the chuck by a screw thread, so that if the screw be broken off or damaged, another can be substituted. This chuck is used for either soft or moderately hard woods. It is not well adapted for hard wood or ivory, although it is occasionally made to answer for them. Any attempt to chuck metals with it would result in the breaking or spoiling of the screw. Generally, this chuck is used for holding pieces of wood from half an inch to six inches in thickness. Thinner pieces have not sufficient substance to give the thread the requisite amount of

FIG. 14.   FIG. 15.

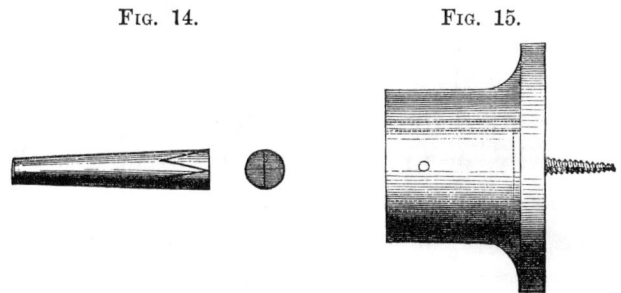

holding power. When the wood exceeds six inches in length, it must be supported at the other extremity by the centre, or by a proper bearing or stay. This chuck may be very conveniently used when it is required to turn any recesses in moderately thick pieces of wood ; but when this has to be done in the case of very long pieces, it is inconvenient to support the other end by the screw centre, as that centre would then be in the way of the tool. In cases such as this, the exterior should be turned, whilst the end is supported by the centre. This, of course, can be done without inconvenience ; the centre is then removed, and the work supported by a wooden bearing, whilst the interior is being operated upon, and the required recess or cavity turned out. A piece of wood is then made to fit the mouth of this cavity, and to form an abutment for the centre while the outside is being finished. If the cavity be sufficiently large to allow the centre and the spindle to enter, the former may be forced into the wood at the bottom of the cavity. In this case no stopper is required.

Sometimes, after the cavity is made, it is required to remove the work from the chuck, and change ends with it, in order to get at the end which hitherto has been against the chuck. In this case, remove the work, and on to the same chuck screw a piece of thin flat wood, which turn down to the size of the mouth of the cavity, or to fit the cavity rather tightly. The article being then gently pushed on to this stopper, and the centre forced into the hole made by the taper-screw may be finished with ease. When this plan is followed, the end of the article on the stopper or chuck, as well as the cavity, is certain to run as 'true' as may be required.

The five-pin or plate-chuck, Fig. 16, is also of metal. It screws on the mandril end, and its body or 'boss' is of the same shape as the chuck last described, only instead of being furnished with a taper-screw, it has five steel pins or points projecting from its face. These pins are arranged as is shown in the figure. This chuck is used almost wholly for holding thin pieces of soft wood.

The cone-chuck is made of metal, and screwed on the spindle end. Its construction will be understood by referring to Fig. 17. The projecting pin (*a*) is of steel, and has a screw cut upon it to receive the nut (*b*). The cone (*c*) is also of metal, but sometimes for temporary use it is made of hard wood : it slides on the pin (*a*). This chuck is used for turning pieces of wood of large diameter, and having a hole through them. Articles of this sort are by its means chucked true or concentric with their central holes. The universal mandril, Fig. 18, is used for the same description of object as the last, than which for many purposes it is somewhat better.

FIG. 16.　　　　　　　　FIG. 17.

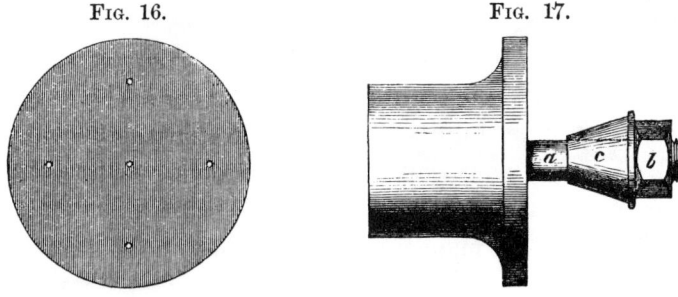

The mandril (*a*) is of steel, the ends are carefully hardened, and are furnished with centre holes for running between the ordinary lathe centres. It is driven by means of a carrier or driver. The mandril is screwed throughout almost its whole length, and is fitted with a nut (*b*), and washers (*c c*). When it is required to turn any article having a hole through it of a size for which the operator has no mandril, a piece of hard wood is taken and bored through with a hole rather smaller than the mandril thread. This wood being then twisted on the mandril, a thread is formed in the hole

D

which holds the piece firm enough to allow the wood
to be turned, to the size required to fit the hole in the
article requiring the mandril. This
wooden socket should fit the hole
nicely, otherwise the work turned
out on it will be 'out of truth,' or
eccentric with its hole—the article
is forced on the wooden socket, and
the nut (*b*) screwed up so as to hold
it firmly between the two washers.
It is, of course, necessary that the
length of the wooden socket should
be somewhat less than the length of
the hole in the article to be turned
upon it; otherwise the washers will
tighten up against the *socket*, and
will not exert any holding or gripping
power on the article itself.

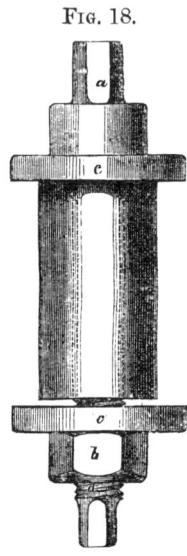

Fig. 18.

The double or male and female screw-chucks, Fig. 19,

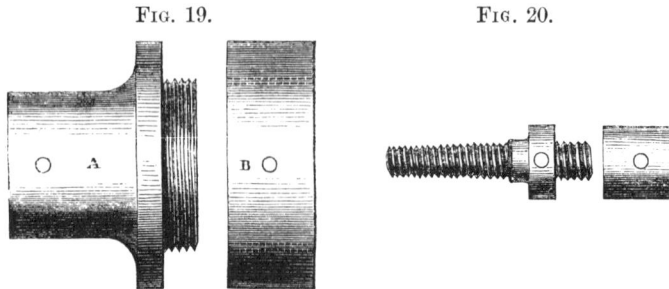

Fig. 19.   Fig. 20.

are of metal : (A) is the male, (B) the female chuck. The
male chuck is made to screw on the mandril end. The
projection in front is cut with a fine screw-thread, such
as is used for the covers of fancy boxes. The female

chuck is merely a ring or nut, having a screw cut through it to correspond with the male screw. The male screw-chuck is used alone. The female can only be used in combination with the other, upon which it is screwed. They are both alike used for hard woods, ivory, and metals. A smaller pair of these useful chucks is shown at Fig. 20. They are both used in the same manner, and for similar purposes and materials as the last. The only difference is in their mode of

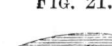

FIG. 21.

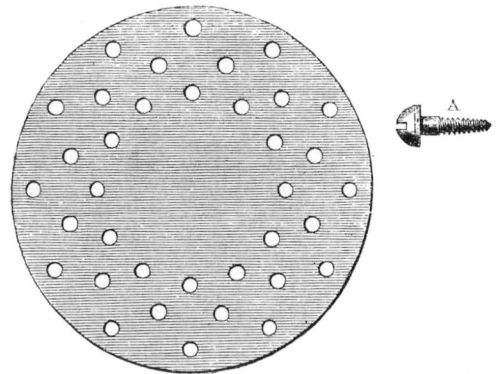

attachment to the spindle, the first being fitted to the screw on the spindle end, whereas in the latter the male part screws into the centre-hole of the spindle.

The chuck-plate, Fig. 21, is of metal, and with a boss the same as that of the others described. It screws on to the mandril. The plate part, or surface, is larger than that of the others, and is drilled through with a number of small holes. It can be used either as a surface chuck, to which to attach thin pieces of wood by means of turners' cement, or as an attachment for rough chucks of temporary service. For this latter purpose especially it is very useful. Four or five screws, such as are shown at Fig. A, are made to fit in common all the holes in the plate.

Any rough piece of wood which it is wished to fasten to the plate is laid on its face, and two or more holes, in convenient positions, are made in the wood by a gimlet passing through the holes in the plate from behind. The screws are then used to fasten the one to the other. These should be inserted in such positions that they may take into those parts of the wood which do not require turning, and not into any place where they would project and be in the way of the tools. The holes being made all over the plate give every chance of the screws being properly arranged.

The temporary chucks, for which this plate is used as an attachment, are merely cavities turned out of a solid piece of wood fastened to the chuck-plate, as explained. The recess or cavity—or it may be a projection to take into a cavity—is turned so that the article may fit it rather tightly. Such chucks as these are frequently required :—they are principally used for holding half-turned articles whilst they are being finished.

The work to be chucked may be of either hard or soft wood, or ivory, &c.; but the chucks do not possess sufficient holding power to answer well for metals, although a chuck of hard wood is sometimes used to hold small spheres of brass whilst being turned. Wooden cup-chucks are very inexpensive, are easily and readily made, and do not damage the tools should they inadvertently be allowed to come in contact with them. The great objection to their use lies in the

liability, or rather certainty, of their shrinking, warping, and getting out of truth and out of shape. For
this reason chucks of universal use are made of metal ;
but when, as is frequently the case, a peculiar chuck is
needed for only one or a few articles, and, these done,
it is of no further service, the wooden chucks are far
preferable.

Spring chucks are made of either box-wood or
metal, and screw on the spindle-end. They are formed
in several parts or staves, something like a cask. These
staves, having considerable elasticity, spring open ; so
that an article to be held by one being inserted in its
mouth, and the staves compressed upon it by means
of rings which encompass the staves, is held whilst
being turned. These rings are sometimes made to
compress the staves by being slid towards their largest
diameter.   And sometimes the outside of the staves is
screwed, and the ring is also cut with a corresponding
screw ; the staves are then compressed by twisting
the ring around so as to advance it towards the largest
diameter of the chuck. In some cases these chucks
are very convenient, but as they have only little power
of variation in size or expansion, their use is necessarily
limited. Some turners, however, have such a great
liking for them that they keep them in all sizes.
In most cases, a chuck turned from a solid piece of
wood fastened to the chuck-plate will be found to
answer just as well. Split chucks are used for wood
and ivory, and occasionally for metals.

There are a number of other chucks used by turners
in wood and ivory, but those described are probably
amongst the best and most generally useful. Many lathes

are furnished with chucks in great number and variety, but, as a rule, one half of them are utterly valueless, and never come into requisition. It is a bad plan to buy too many chucks with a lathe. Turners will find it much to their advantage to purchase at first only those which are of great use and extended application, and to add other chucks as they find they require them.

Most good lathe-makers make all their work to standard sizes, and use standard Whitworth screw-threads; so that any chucks purchased even years after the lathe, can generally be relied upon to fit the spindle and ' run true.'

As before mentioned, chucks are usually made of metal;—for the larger sorts cast iron is the best material, but for some of the smaller ones, wrought iron is to be preferred. Brass is frequently used for both large and small chucks; but, beyond its non-liability to rust, it possesses no advantage over iron. On the other hand, it is much more costly, it is more easily bruised and indented, and is much more troublesome to keep clean. The hands of the workman are also somewhat soiled by touching brass, and this does not conduce to the production of clean and unsoiled work.

Chucks are generally put on by hand, the threads of the screws being well fitted, but not made so tight as to prevent this being done. The usual mode is—after removing the centres and clearing away all dirt from the spindle-end and also from the chuck itself—to hold the mouth of the chuck against the nose of the spindle by the right hand, the left hand being at the same time applied to the driving-strap, and the cone and spindle caused slowly to revolve in the same direction as for turning. After a chuck has been used for any but very light work, it will be found to be jammed up against the collar of the spindle too tightly to allow of its being started by the hands. The chucks, therefore, are all furnished with some means for applying the power of a lever to unscrew them. Those described are shown with a small hole in the bosses, in order that they may be removed by the pin and circle wrench, as shown at Fig. 22. This method is as neat and convenient as any.

Some turners are in the habit of taking up a drill or old piece of iron and forcing it into the pin-holes; but

FIG. 22.

this is a very bad practice, and is only followed by careless workmen. When this slovenly method is resorted to, the pin-hole soon becomes bruised out of shape, and so much enlarged, that the proper instrument is rendered useless. Taper-pins are not good instruments to use for this purpose, and they should be discarded, except in those cases where but little force is required, and that not frequently.

The tools required for turning soft woods are very few and simple. The professional turner seldom uses more than half a dozen, and with these he can manage to produce a great variety of work. The bobbin or spool turner, with the aid of one tool only—the gouge, and occasionally the gouge and chisel—will turn out twelve dozen or more of the bobbins used in spinning and other factories in one day. That number is generally considered a day's work. It can therefore be readily imagined that there is no time to waste in putting down one tool and taking up another ; but, although a workman does so much, he seldom appears to be in any violent hurry, but continues his work almost with the easy celerity and regularity of a machine. These tools, besides being so few, are frequently very rough, but they are usually surpassed in that respect by the lathe ; yet an amateur, with the best of lathes and any number of tools, would scarcely succeed in doing that quantity of work. Indeed, I am inclined to think that he would consider it a very good day's work if he had completed one dozen or one twelfth the number.

It will be understood that the above refers only to turning in soft wood. Turners in hard woods and ivory require a much more extensive collection of tools; and the number is never complete, but requires continual additions for the variation in the nature of the work to be done. Many sorts of work require tools of such peculiar shape that they are only useful for that purpose for which they were designed. As, however, these differ only in shape but are alike in cutting principle, it would be unnecessary—if it were possible —to describe all those used. When the operator becomes acquainted with the peculiarities of a few of the principal tools, he will seldom have much difficulty— supposing him to be possessed of a due amount of common sense—in contriving tools which will enable him to satisfactorily execute any description of work he may have in hand. The tools most generally in use for soft woods are those shown; namely, the gouge Fig. 23, chisel Fig. 24, scraping chisel Fig. 25, diamond-point or V tool Fig. 26, cranked chisel Fig. 27, cranked point Fig. 28, cranked round Fig. 29, and parting tools Fig. 30. The gouge and chisel are those in most frequent use. These differ altogether

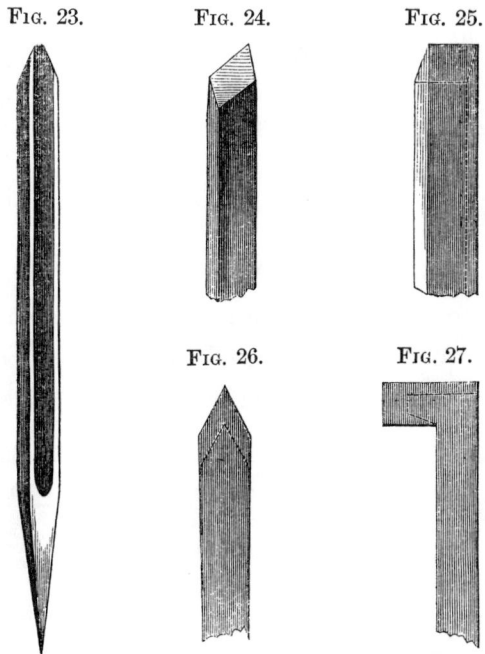

FIG. 23. FIG. 24. FIG. 25.

FIG. 26. FIG. 27.

from those used for hard woods and ivory; but the others do not differ so much, being of similar shape but ground somewhat differently.

The hard-wood tools are shown at Figs. 31 to 50. The uses of these tools will be spoken of presently. I may, however, mention here that, although to the inexperienced eye the tools may appear to be so very much alike that they may be used indiscriminately for

hard and soft woods, that is not the case. In use they
do differ materially. If the soft-wood tools be used for
hard materials, their edges will very soon not only be
blunted, but knocked off altogether; and they will

Fig. 28.   Fig. 29.   Fig. 30.   Fig. 31.

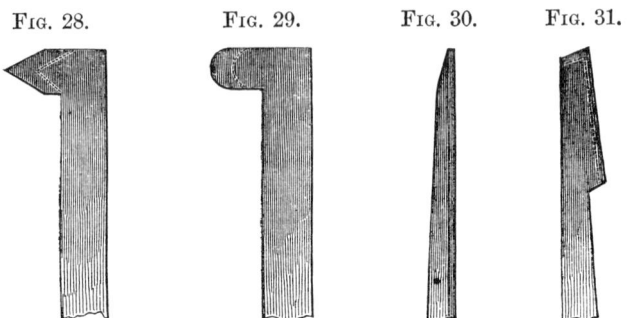

require considerable regrinding before they can again
be applied to their legitimate use. On the other hand,
when hard-wood tools are used upon soft substances,
although the tool may not get damaged the work does,

Fig. 32.   Fig. 33.   Fig. 34.   Fig. 35.

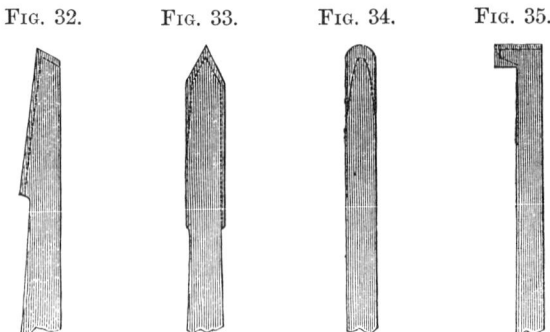

as it cannot be done nearly so smooth as with the proper
tools. The woody fibres do not get cut or shaved off,
but are pulled off in large pieces; and the work is
without truth, regularity, or polish.

The cutting edges of the two sorts of tools being

ground to a different angle, this angle must be preserved within a shade or two, if the user would wish
them to do their work well. When they become dull
from use and require grinding, care must be taken to

FIG. 36.　　FIG. 37.　　FIG. 38.　　FIG. 39.　　FIG. 40.

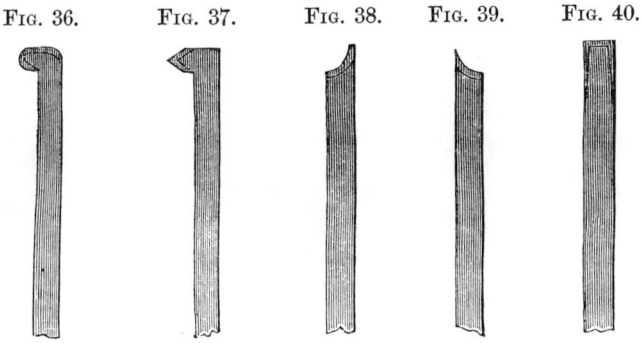

retain the proper cutting angle as closely as can be
judged, and that angle should not be destroyed by the
subsequent operation of honing or oil-stoning. It is

FIG. 41.　　FIG. 42.　　FIG. 43.　　FIG. 44.　　FIG. 45.

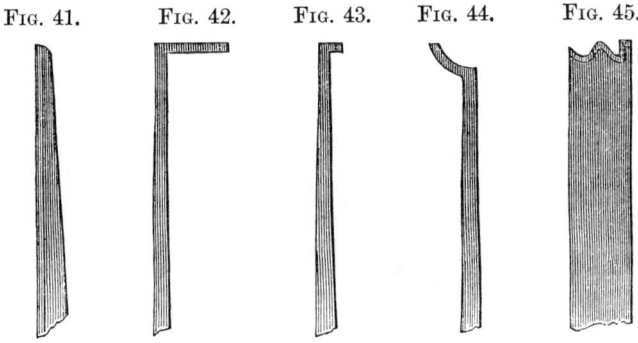

not unfrequently the case that even professional turners
will say that their tools 'won't stand,' 'won't make
good work,' when in reality the fault lies with them
entirely, and is the result of their own careless and
slovenly grinding. On examining the tools, it is found

that, instead of the cutting edges being formed of two
straight surfaces, or one straight and the other concave, as it should be, it is ground with convex surfaces,
or surfaces formed of such a collection of curves that I
am not sufficiently a geometrician to give a name to

Fig. 46.   Fig. 47.   Fig. 48.   Fig. 49.   Fig. 50.

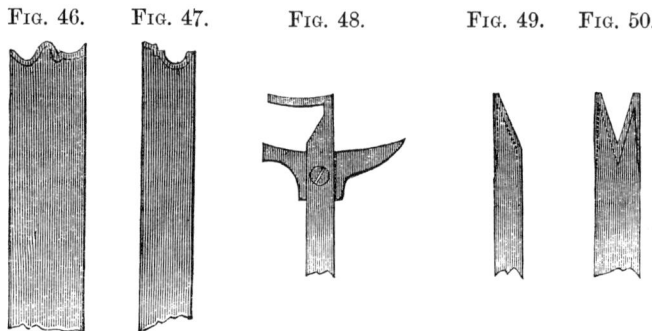

them.   The same tool, ground by a careful person,
will work as well as can be wished.

Should the operator be unable to judge of the proper

Fig. 51.

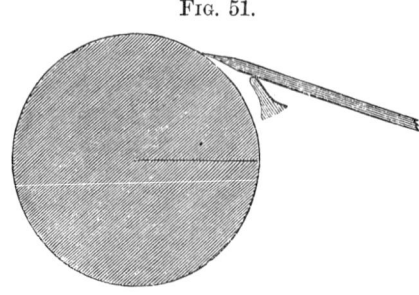

angles by the eye, it will be better for him to cut out
a piece of thin sheet-iron or brass to fit the tool when
properly ground, and to grind the tool to this gauge
when it gets out of order.

The angle for soft woods is from 25° to 40°, for hard
woods from 60° to 80°.   The angles for various hand-

tool edges, as well as the positions of the tools, are shown in Figs. 51, 52, 53. An attentive examination and comparison of these will be useful to the reader. The tools illustrated are those mostly in use. Only one

FIG. 52.

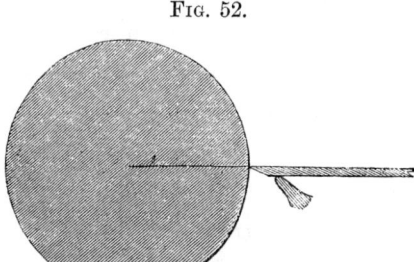

size of each is shown, but most of them should be had in many sizes, for both right and left hand work.

In addition to the chucks and cutting tools, other instruments are required; some of which—such as

FIG. 53.

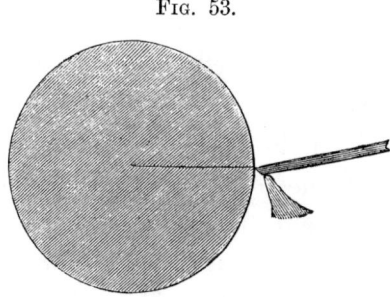

tool-rests—vary with the sort of lathe with which they are used. The chucks and tools are the same, how-ever, for almost all lathes. The tool-rest, or tee (Fig. 54), seen in the lathe at Fig. 2, is necessary as a support for the tool when cutting. If the lathe be a simple hand-turning lathe, such as that shown, and adapted only to

that kind of work, then no alteration of rests is required.
If the lathe be one with a slide-rest, and we wish to execute any hand-turning, it is generally the better plan to
remove the slide-rest altogether. But if the lathe be a
slide and screw cutter, the slide-rest cannot at all times
be removed so easily. It is not, therefore, worth while
to be at the trouble of removing it, unless absolutely
in the way, or the turning to be executed will occupy
a considerable time. When this is the case, the
moving or screw headstock should be taken off, and
the slide-rest altogether traversed along the bed until
past the place where the headstock is to be fastened.

FIG. 54.

The headstock is then replaced, and a
rest-holder and rest placed on the bed
between the headstocks, and fastened
down in any convenient position. This
rest-holder and rest is similar to the
one shown in position on the lathe-bed
at Fig. 1, and needs no separate illustration. It can be moved anywhere along the bed
of a lathe between the headstocks, can be placed at
any distance from the line of centres to accommodate
differences in diameter of the work, and can also be
placed at any angle to the line of centres. The rest, or
tee, can also be raised to any height, for the better ac-
commodation of any of the tools, and can also be set
with the edge of the rest either parallel to or at an
angle with the line of centres, as is found most convenient for the work in hand.

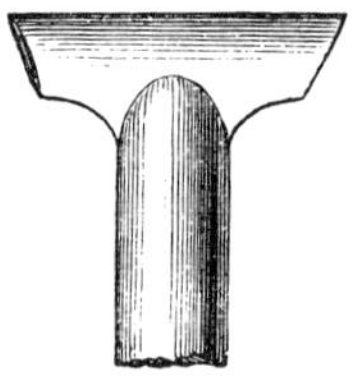

Care must always be taken that the rest-holder be
firmly bolted to the bed of the lathe and the rest, and
fastened tight in its socket before the work is com-

menced. It may otherwise result in a serious smash of
the tools, of the work, or of the operator's fingers.

A pair or two of different sized callipers are also an
indispensable part of a turner's collection of tools. Those
shown at Fig. 55 will be found of convenient construction. They are used as gauges for turning to any particular size, and the same pair answers equally well for
measuring either internal or external work. In Fig. 55
they are set for internal and at Fig. 56 for external
measurements. Those illustrated at Fig. 57 are of

Fig. 55. Fig. 56. Fig. 57.

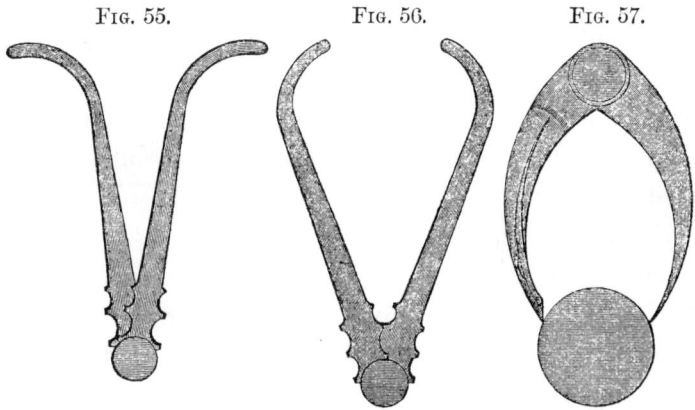

capital construction, but they are not well adapted to soft
woods—indeed, they are seldom used with woods at
all, but principally for metal. The peculiarity of these
consists in one of the legs being formed to act as a
spring, so that when applied to any article which is
not turned small enough, the spring leg opens.

Attached to the lower part of the leg is a pointer
extending up the side of the leg as shown; the extremity of this pointer is made—by the springing out
of the leg—to indicate the extent the article is above

the required size. I speak from memory, but I believe I am correct in stating that these callipers were first used at the establishment of the Messrs. Penn at Greenwich, and am inclined to think they would be much more used were they better known.

The gauge is formed of a graduated slip of steel sliding in a stock of either the same material or brass. This is used to measure the depth of holes, cavities, or recesses, and for other purposes. Another convenient instrument is the temporary tool support, or arm-rest, which is simply a piece of steel with its end cranked up for about half an inch. It is set in a handle, and is used with the cranked part up, on the ordinary hand-tool rest, as a temporary or moveable support for the tool, and to obviate the continual necessity of shifting the rest itself.

The woods chiefly used for plain turning are alder, apple wood, box, beech, holly, lignum vitæ, mahogany, and pine. A great many other woods are used, but chiefly for ornamental purposes, and then more for their rarity and colour than for any other superiority they possess over those above mentioned. Amongst the more beautiful sorts are the African black wood, black and green ebony, cam wood, Spanish yew, king wood, &c. These, and a multitude of other sorts, can be procured of dealers in foreign woods in wholesale quantities. They can also be purchased in small lots, prepared for the lathe in various sizes, of almost any small-lathe and tool maker. Many of the sorts, however, are rather expensive; and therefore the tyro will not find it advantageous to learn turning with them, but is recommended to have considerable practice on

the cheaper sorts, before attempting to exhibit his skill
on expensive hard wood and ivory.

Woods for turning should be thoroughly dry, and
well seasoned ; it is great folly to use wood just as it
comes from the tree, even when it appears dry. It is a
good plan—when it can be followed—to partially turn
out an article and let it remain in a dry warm place
before finishing it ; as it is very annoying to find, after
having completed a very fine specimen of turning, that
in a day or two it shows signs of cracking in all
directions, which, however, is the almost certain result
of using wood not seasoned.

If the wood be bought in the log, a piece should
be cut out somewhat near the required size, the waste
corners being sawn off and preserved for future use,
either for portions of turned articles or for inlaying.
The shavings of some of the ornamental woods are very
good for dyeing and staining.

These woods differ much in density, and theoretically
should have tools ground differently for each difference
in hardness. Practically, however, this is not necessary,
they being divided into two classes—soft and hard
woods. Alder, apple wood, pine, mahogany, and
beech belong to the former class, and are turned with
the soft-wood tools.

Nearly all the woods used for ornamental work and
lignum vitæ belong to the class of hard wood, and are
turned with the hard-wood tools. Box wood and holly
occupy an intermediate position, and can be worked
equally well with either sort of tool. Ivory is very
similar in texture to some of the hard woods, and
is easily turned by the same tools, and in a manner

E

similar to hard wood ; but being more expensive than even the fancy woods, care should be taken that there is no unnecessary waste of material in working it.

Besides these substances, there are others used by the ornamental turner. Amongst them may be mentioned jet, cannel coal, bone, glass, Derbyshire spar, cocoa-nut shell, coquilla nut, ivory nuts, and india-rubber—the latter both in its usual state and vulcanised. These can be turned with the tools used for the various woods and metals, but they each require peculiar treatment. Woods differing in density, besides requiring different tools, require different treatment in other respects. In the matter of speed lies one great point to be observed of the turner : but this is a point whereon authorities differ greatly. For instance, when turning soft wood, some advise that it should be run at a few hundred feet per minute, and others, at as many thousand. Many also are of opinion that it cannot be rotated too rapidly ; but this is a mistake. It is very well known that when a tool is applied for some time to wood in rapid motion, the tool gets hot from the friction, and the extreme edge becomes of a blue colour, which indicates that its temper is reduced, and its cutting power is damaged. We judge from this that the motion is too rapid, and we reduce it accordingly. If the tool be applied intermittently, that is, applied to the cut for a few seconds, then removed for a short space and re-applied, the wood may be revolved much faster than if the cutting were made continuous. This obviously arises from the fact of the tool being partially cooled during the time of its withdrawal from cutting.

Again, some turners can run their work faster than others without injury to the tools, which is to be accounted for by their holding the tools in such position as to cause less friction, and consequently to develope less heat. The two positions may vary from each other to an extent so very slight as to be quite inappreciable to the eye, and yet we can judge from the heating effects which is the better, and which gives out the most work for the power expended in driving the lathe. It will, therefore, be understood from the foregoing remarks that no arbitrary rule for the speeds can possibly be laid down, and a great variation may be made without alteration of efficiency : 2000 feet per minute has been found to answer well, but experience with observation is the safest guide. For hard woods and ivory, a speed of from 300 to 800 feet is usually given the work per minute.

The term 'feet per minute' may require some explanation to enable certain readers to understand the meaning intended to be conveyed. By it is meant that so many feet must pass the tool in one minute. Thus, if the article be one foot in circumference, it should revolve 2000 times if of soft wood, and from 300 to 800 if of hard wood or ivory. The tyro should ascertain by calculation the circumference of the object he wishes to turn, until he gets sufficiently experienced to tell by simple observation. This power of judging is soon acquired by a careful observer, and, when once gained, is scarcely ever lost.

Having now described most of the appliances and instruments, I will endeavour to give fuller information as to the method of using them in actual practice. To this end it will be as good a plan as can be adopted if a few examples be chosen, and the various steps to be taken and course to be pursued in turning them be fully detailed and explained. In order to communicate as much information as possible, these examples shall be of as varied a nature as can be chosen from amongst those of any use, and I will endeavour so to describe the *modus operandi* that even those persons who have not had the advantage of seeing such work performed, shall still be able to form a tolerably correct idea of the method of proceeding.

The First example shall be very elementary. We will suppose that we require to turn a cylindrical piece of wood, say 12 inches long and 4 inches in diameter, the wood to be one of those in the class of soft woods. First, select a piece of the required sort of wood, large enough to contain the cylinder, but as little above that size as is obtainable. If this piece have any rough projections or corners, they should be chopped off with a hatchet. The inexperienced turner will find it easier to judge of this if he take a pair of compasses and find the rough centre of each end of the wood, and from that centre draws a circle rather larger in diameter than the cylinder is to be turned. By roughly chopping away the wood outside the circle at each end he will bring the wood somewhere about the required shape. This chopping is not absolutely necessary, but the shaping is more quickly done in this manner, whilst the chances of knocking off the edge of the tool are much lessened.

If the centre be fixed in the hole of the lathe-spindle, it must be taken out, or if any other chuck be on the spindle-nose it must be removed. The drill-chuck can then be screwed into its place, and the prong-driver, Fig. 13, put into the hole of the drill-chuck. The centre of one end of the wood is then placed against the centre of the driver, and held there by the left hand, whilst the right hand pulls the shifting headstock along the bed up to the work, and then fastens it down on the bed. The hand wheel of the headstock is turned so as to force the centre point of the spindle into the centre of the end of the wood, the pressure at the same time forcing the prongs of the driver into the other end of the wood. The greater the depth to which the driver is embedded in the wood, the more power it will drive, or the heavier the cut it will take without slipping. Unless forced in tolerably deep, a heavy cut, or sudden jerk caused by the tools ' catching in,' will cause the prong to slip and act as a drill, cutting a round recess, instead of a simple indentation. Occurrences of this sort should be avoided as much as possible, as, although no great injury is done to the lathe or chuck, the work is rendered untrue, and would probably require re-turning. After the centre and the driver are properly forced up, the pressure should be taken off, and the centre just removed from that end of the wood to allow of a drop of oil being put into the indentation of the centre. The lathe should then be pulled round a few times by hand, whilst the rest-holder and the rest are adjusted conveniently in position and height. By moving the lathe in this way an accident of otherwise frequent occurrence is prevented, as if the wood be at all irregular in shape, or run out of truth, and the rest be adjusted close to the place in the wood having the least

radius, it is obvious, that on starting the lathe, the part
of greater radius will come around into contact with
the top of the rest, and the belt driving the lathe will
either slip, or the wood be burst from its centres, and
projected with force into the operator's face, or perhaps
through a window, if one be near. This occurrence
should be avoided even more carefully than the last.

Take a pair of callipers, Fig. 55, and set them by a
graduated straight edge or rule to the required diameter, namely four inches. Set the lathe in motion, at
the right speed, and apply the gouge, Fig. 23, to the
wood, until the whole length is reduced nearly to the
right size, as indicated by the callipers. When down,
the rest will probably be too far from the work, and
require re-adjusting. The chisel, Fig. 24, or the scraping
chisel, Fig. 25, is then to be applied till the callipers
will just drop over the work.

It must be remembered that, for a pair of callipers
to gauge properly, they must be applied to the work
precisely at right angles with the line of centres. If
held ever so slightly across, the indications will be in-
correct, as the work will necessarily have to be turned
too small, to allow the calliper legs to pass over; the
hypothenuse of a right-angled triangle being greater
than its base.

And now a few words to explain the manner of
holding and applying the tools whilst turning the wood
down to size.

The tools being placed in suitable handles—Fig. 58
is a good shape—they are grasped by both hands, the
left being placed on the tool itself, not far from the
cutting edge, and the right upon the end of the handle

farthest from the edge. The cutting end is then placed on the rest, and inclined upwards, something like Fig. 51. The left hand is pressed down upon the tool so as to keep it firm upon the rest, and sufficient pressure is put at the end of the handle by the right hand to keep it steady in cut. The tool is traversed or guided along the rest by the left hand, but the point is forced into the cut, and raised or lowered by the right.

Fig. 58.

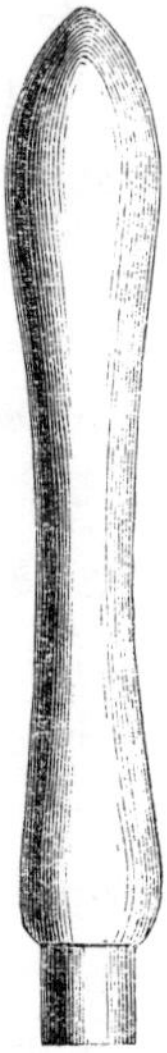

All the tools — whether for scraping or cutting—are held in a similar manner, but those for scraping are placed upon the rest and applied to the work horizontally, as shown at Fig. 52. The chisel, Fig. 24, should not be used as a scraping instrument, not being adapted to that work; but the scraping chisel, Fig. 25, may be used in that manner with good effect if the edge be kept very keen and smooth. When using the scraping tools, the rest must be lowered to allow the top of the tool to come level with the centre. The chisel, Fig. 24, should be held inclined as at Fig. 51, with its cutting edge oblique to the axis of the work.

The work in hand is not yet finished, however, as it yet requires to be made of the right length. Take the gouge, lay it on its side on the rest, with its bottom towards the end to be cut off, and its point inclined rather above the centre of the work. Grasp the end of the handle firmly with the right hand, if turning down the right-hand extremity of the wood, but with the left hand if turning the left extremity, and gradually push

the cutting edge towards the centre, lowering its point
as it approaches.   It requires some little skill to use the
tool in this manner, as if it be allowed to turn over
to its usual position, a terrible 'catch in' and a con-
sequent smash is the frequent result.   Care should be
taken not to allow the edge of the tool to come against
the steel centre, or against the chuck.

If the end thus turned requires to be very true it
may be touched over with the diamond point or V-tool,
Fig. 26, held flat on the rest with its cutting edge in
the position shown for soft-wood scraping tools at
Fig. 52.   One end of the example having been turned,
its length, 12 inches, should be marked off, the super-
fluous length turned away, and the end finished in the
same manner as before.   The rest should never be
allowed to remain too far from the work, as that
lessens the workman's command over his tool, and
renders it far more likely to 'catch in.'   The trouble
of adjusting the rest is not very great, nor does
it take much time.   The beginner should more especially be careful about the position and stability of
his rest.   Although the experienced turner is also
careful, it is more from habit than necessity; as to
him, it makes but little difference whether the rest be
rather too far from the work, or even whether it be
firmly fastened to the bed or not.

The great difficulty beginners have is to hold the
tool still upon the rest, as, when the work happens to
be irregular in shape, they cannot prevent the tool from
going in and out with the irregularity.   But this should be
overcome as soon as possible, because every movement
of the sort is fatal to the production of true work.   A

good workman, however rough the wood may be, can manage to hold his tools as firmly as if held in the slide-rest. By firmness is not meant rigidity, but a sort of elastic steadiness of the tool on the rest, which produces good work with little damage to the tools, and little exertion on the part of the workman. The reader may find it somewhat difficult to understand the difference here indicated, but he will soon discern it, if he carefully observe two turners, one good and the other bad at work. Soft woods are rendered somewhat smoother than when only turned, either by holding a sheet of glass cloth against the wood whilst it is in rapid motion, or by taking a handful of fine shavings, and pressing against the revolving surface. Curved portions are smoothed over beautifully by pressing the flat part of the gouge against them, whilst in motion in the lathe. The gouge must be firmly held, so that, although not cutting at all, it is nearly on the point of cutting, and when moved along carefully over the surface of the wood has the effect of burnishing the work, or compressing those fibres just on the surface. Such polish is generally more lasting than that obtained in other ways. It is possible that the absolute truth of the work may be somewhat impaired, but not to any appreciable extent.

The rest of the soft-wood tools are used in the same manner as those for hard wood, and I will therefore choose the next example of the latter material. Let the example selected be the stem of a vase or pedestal, of the shape given at Fig. 59; its extreme dimensions being, say, 6 inches long and 1 inch in diameter. Choose a piece of wood, and cut it out roughly

to a cylindrical shape, as previously explained. The
prong-driver can be used, but perhaps it will be better
Fig. 59. to use the driver shown at Fig. 14, called the
cross-driver.

This driver is one of the neatest and most
convenient I have ever seen, although it does
not appear to be much used. It holds more
firmly than the prong-driver, is not so likely to
split hard wood or ivory as the other, and
turned work driven by it will run true if
frequently taken from the lathe, and again returned
to its place. Knock out the prong-driver from the
chuck, and replace it by the cross-driver. If the
wood be not very hard, both driver and centre may
be forced into the wood in the same manner as
was explained in the last example for soft woods.

Fig. 60. Very hard woods, ivory and metals, to be
driven by it, require two grooves or saw-
kerfs being cut in their end at right angles
to each other, see Fig. 60, and also the indentation for the centre should be produced
by a centre-punch. The work is put into
the lathe, and the headstock and tool-rests adjusted
precisely as before described in example First. Set
the lathe in motion : for that size of work it should
revolve about 2000 times per minute, and with the tool
at Fig. 34, roughly turn the wood until nearly of the
right size. Then, with either of the tools at Figs. 31,
32, or 33, square off the ends, and bring the piece to
the proper length. Set the callipers to the size of
the largest place, and turn that place to its right
size, making the whole length of the wood nearly the

same size or parallel. Set the callipers to the next largest size required, and with a pair of compasses measure the distance that place is from one of the ends of the pedestal. Then apply the compasses to the work, so as to draw a line around the wood at the place required to be made of a less diameter. Apply the tool to the line, and turn this place down to its size, and so with the other principal parts of the work. After this, turn the intervening parts in such order as is convenient, occasionally using the callipers to make sure of the right sizes. For turning any of the beads or mouldings it is better to use a beading tool, such as is shown at Figs. 45, 46, 47. These tools are to be procured of almost any shape or moulding, and where many beads or mouldings of the same shape are required, such tools should always be used, as with them the work is certain to be uniform, and all the beadings of the same shape. If the operator has not got a suitable bead-tool for his work, he must turn one portion of the bead at a time, and use such tools as will enable him to do this best. These beading tools are not indispensable—although very convenient—as almost any shape of bead can be made with the ordinary tools. The general position for all the hard-wood tools when in use is shown at Fig. 53. Hard woods are polished with very fine glass cloth, and with their own fine shavings held in the hand and pressed against the work when in motion. A little clean oil put about the shavings much improves the appearance of the work, by giving it a better polish, brightening the colour, and bringing up the grain of the wood.

Our Third example shall be a small plain box, such as

is shown in Fig. 61, and we may suppose it to be made in hard wood. Take any suitable piece of wood, put it

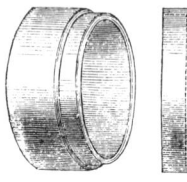

FIG. 61.

in the lathe, and turn down one end of it parallel for a length rather more than the length of the proposed box, and of a slightly larger diameter. True off the end of the piece so turned, and cut the length off from the remainder of the piece.

Take off the drill-chuck and the driver, put on a spring-chuck of suitable size, and fasten the piece of turned wood into this, allowing rather more than the body of the box to project from the chuck. With the requisite tools square off the edges of the projecting end, and hollow out the wood to the depth and size required for the interior; the depth is best measured by using the turning square, and the diameter of the cavity by setting the callipers as shown at Fig. 56.

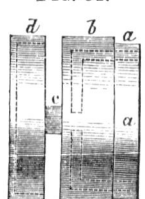

FIG. 62.

Take a pair of dividers, and make a line around the wood showing the width of the rim or ledge (*a*) Fig. 62, and turn that portion down to its proper size. Then mark off the width of the part (*b*), and turn that to its intended size. Take the parting tool, Fig. 44, and make a groove such as (*c*), so as to cut off that part of the box and leave the piece of wood for the cover in the chuck. Now turn a cavity or recess in that to allow the rim (*a*) to fit into it 'hand tight' and to the proper depth; push the two parts closely together, and then touch off the bottom of the box, making it quite flat or slightly concave.

Remove the wood altogether from the chuck and re-

verse it, that is, place the *bottom* of the finished part into
the chuck, taking care not to bind it in tight enough to
injure it, and also, before touching the work with the
tools, taking care to adjust it so that the turned part
runs perfectly true.   The outside of the cover can now
be completed, and the box is then finished.

It is necessary that the inside of the box be taken
out before the rim or ledge (*a*) is turned, because the
removal of the interior wood allows the ring remaining
to contract.   If, therefore, the rim were turned first it
would contract and become smaller on the removal of
the core.   If the wood be not of a very expensive sort
this core can be removed in shavings, and the shavings
used for polishing the box; but when such boxes are
made of expensive woods or ivory the core should be
removed entire, so as to save the material for another
smaller box, or to be otherwise useful.

To remove the centre entire a set of interior parting
tools such as Figs. 42, 43, is required.   A groove is first
cut parallel to the sides of the box, as shown by the
space between the two dotted lines in Fig. 62.   That
tool of the set of parting tools having the shortest point
is then inserted carefully, and is followed by the others
of the set, until a groove parallel to the bottom of the
box is cut out.   This groove is shown by the space
between the two other dotted lines.   When these grooves
are cut it is obvious that the core of the box will fall out,
and the inside can be finished to its proper size by the
ordinary tools.   In some cases, when the box is large,
the core must be removed from two places, by making
a hole of the depth of the cavity in the centre of the
core, and inserting the parting tools both from this hole
and from the circular groove as before.

The Fourth example is that of a sphere in ivory or hard wood—we will suppose it to be a billiard or bagatelle ball.

Take any suitable piece of ivory, put it into the lathe to be driven by the cross-chuck, and turn one end of it as nearly to the spherical shape as you can judge. Take a piece of thin metal, and drill a hole through it of the same diameter as the sphere required. To drill a perfectly circular hole in sheet metal is a difficult matter, the better plan therefore is to drill the hole rather smaller, and then to broach or ryme it out to its full size. Carefully cut the sheet iron or metal across the hole, so as to leave one perfect half circle, or it may be slightly less than half the circle. This is for a gauge. Fasten the rough ball in a spring-chuck, leaving not less than half outside the chuck's mouth, and carefully and gently turn down the part immediately outside the chuck *nearly* to the diameter of the required sphere. Remove the work from the chuck, and replace it so that one half of this ring is inside the chuck and the other half outside. Carefully turn down the projecting part of the article to fit the sheet metal gauge, remove it from the chuck, replace it in a reversed position, and again turn the projecting part to fit the gauge. The ball *should* now be a perfect sphere. But not many workmen are able to bring it nearly to that shape without many more changes of position, and even then it is not absolutely spherical. But balls can be thus turned sufficiently perfect for most purposes, if great care and patience be exercised.

For a Fifth example the vase Fig. 63 may be selected. Take a flat piece of the required wood, saw off the corners, so as to roughly bring it to a circular shape, and plane off one side. Put the taper-screw chuck, Fig. 15, on

Fig. 63.

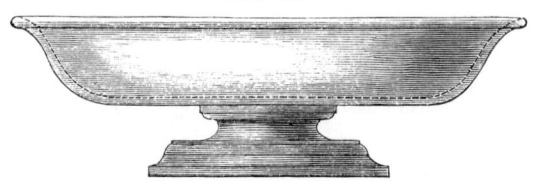

the spindle of the lathe, make a small hole in the centre of the wood, but no deeper than is required, and twist the wood on to the screw of the chuck, taking care that the planed surface beds well against the face of the chuck. Set the lathe in motion (the shifting headstock is not now required), true up the edges of the wood, both on the surface and the side, making the latter nearly of the right diameter. Rough out the interior of the vase, rough down the exterior nearly to its proper shape, after which finish turning out the interior, and then also complete the turning of the edge and exterior body of the vase; and remove the work from the lathe. Take a rough piece of any common wood rather larger than the edge of the vase, and not less than 1 inch thick. Screw this upon the same chuck, and turn in it a ring or groove of such a shape as will allow the mouth of the vase to fit it, both inside the mouth and outside the rim of the mouth. Rub a little good chalk about the groove of this wooden chuck, and gently tack the mouth of the vase on to its place, care being taken that it beds well down on the chuck; and that no particle of dust or grit be allowed to get between the surfaces of the work and the chuck, as that, of course, would cause the article to run out of truth, and the turned portions to be of unequal thickness.

These wooden chucks will generally hold work sufficiently fast to withstand a good-sized cut being taken off, but it is safer to work gently—especially at first—and not to subject the work to any jerk from pushing the tool suddenly into cut. Should the work slip, a little more whiting will generally improve the holding power of the surfaces.

For the present case, as the substance of the turned work is very thin, and the surfaces in contact are not of good angles for fast holding, it will be as well to bring up the shifting headstock, and to put on a little gentle pressure, and the support of the centre—the mouth of the screw hole in that end of the wood being previously turned out a little to fit the centre. The remainder of the vase can now be finished without again shifting the work.

The centre screw hole can be stopped up either with coloured putty, or by a plug of the same sort of wood as the article is made of. The vase can be turned without this hole being made, but as it is in the bottom and out of sight it is no disadvantage.

For our Sixth example, let us take the piece of work usually termed Chinese balls. In this there are several balls contained one inside the other, and without any joint, so they must be turned out of the solid piece of ivory.

First turn the outside sphere, as explained in our Fourth example. The tools for turning the interior balls are sold in sets suitable for the work, of the shape shown at Fig. 44, but of various sizes. Two or more holes must be turned to admit these curved tools. The smallest one of the set is then inserted in the hole, and worked sideways, so as to turn a portion of the groove which forms the inner sphere. The work is then removed from the chuck, and replaced so that the tool can be introduced through another hole. Another portion of the groove must then be cut out as before, and so on until the innermost sphere is detached. The next in size of the tools is then taken, and the next sphere turned in the same manner, the operation being continued until the whole of the balls are completed. By the addition of a guide to the tools, as at Fig. 48, the difficulty of turning is much reduced, but to turn these balls properly requires great care and patience. The amateur must not, therefore, let a few failures discourage him. I have seen some balls in ivory brought either from China or India which were magnificently cut out and carved. There may have been a dozen or more, one inside the other, yet the exterior one was, from what I can recollect, only about 2 or 3 inches in diameter. The thickness of the shell was of course but small, and the spaces between the balls were so narrow that I cannot imagine how any tools could have been introduced into them.

Besides balls being turned in this manner, with other balls inside them, spheres, cubes, and solids of almost any number of sides can be turned having spikes and other shapes inside them, as at Figs. 64, 65, 66. Most of these things require tools especially adapted to the work, but cutting on the same principle as those already described. It will not be necessary to give more examples, as those already chosen are

F

sufficient to indicate the general mode of procedure for almost any article that the lathe is called upon to make.

When turning out articles the interior of which cannot well be seen, the amateur will find it a good

FIG. 64.   FIG. 65.   FIG. 66.

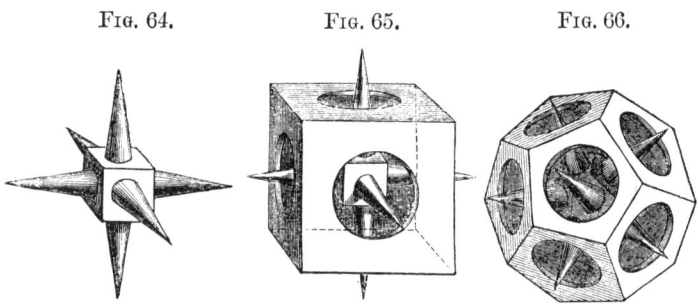

plan to lay down a section of the required shape on paper, and arrange in his mind the shaped tools he will require, the portion of work to be executed by each tool, and the order in which the various parts of the work can be the most safely and conveniently performed.

HAND-TURNING IN METALS.

The materials hitherto spoken of are comparatively soft and easily worked; but the metals, being much harder, require different treatment and different tools.

Amongst the metals, however, there is as much variation in texture and density as amongst the woods. The difference is not only between dissimilar metals, but, even in the case of the same, the density varies so much that whereas some parts can be turned almost as easily as wood, other parts cannot be satisfactorily turned even by the most powerful and best tempered tools. The metals chiefly used are wrought iron, cast iron, malleable cast iron, steel, and brass. Other metals, such as copper, lead, zinc, &c., sometimes require to be turned, but as their application to articles which have to be turned is very limited, and they can be cut well enough for most purposes with the tools used for the other materials, it will suffice if I explain the methods adopted for turning the metals first mentioned.

Some specimens of wrought iron—Low Moor, for example—are very easily worked in the lathe, the shavings coming off in lengths, having one side of great brightness, and with a peculiar metallic click, well understood by the experienced mechanical turner.

Although this description of wrought iron is so easily cut, the tools soon lose their keen edges, but the points are seldom broken off. When, therefore, a large quantity of this iron has to be turned, it is a good plan to temper the tools slightly harder than for other work. There are other descriptions of wrought iron, which turn only with great difficulty; as the tools are continually being broken off, although their keen edges are not materially blunted. Other sorts again contain veins of vitrified oxide, so hard that the tools are blunted immediately they are applied to the work, and if not soon removed, their edges are cracked away in such a manner as to require much grinding to again fit them for use. These hard veins do not always arise from the description of iron, but from imperfections in its manufacture. Iron is also sometimes met with containing numerous hard patches, and small pins of steely iron; this is known by the term 'pinny iron,' and is, equally with the last, the utter abhorrence of the turner.

Sometimes, but not often, iron of this sort may be turned by running it very slowly : at other times no manœuvring on the part of the workman will enable him to turn it, as when the tool is applied, its edge is quickly ground, or rather rubbed away, without its cutting the metal, and if the tool be pressed with more force to its work, the friction is so great that sufficient heat is generated to quickly reduce the temper of the tool to a deep blue colour. When this has been done, the tool usually has to be not only re-ground, but re-tempered before it can again be used. These hard pins may sometimes be removed, or generally softened somewhat, by two or three heatings and quenchings in water or oil, followed by a careful annealing.

Steel is turned by the same tools, and in the same manner as wrought iron. If carefully annealed no difficulty whatever is found in turning it, nor are the tools much damaged or soon blunted.

Most amateurs, and many professional turners, do not pay that attention to the softening of their steel that they should do ; but they either put it into the lathe just as it is cut from the bar, or, if heated at all, it is generally considered sufficiently annealed when thrust in the ashes of the forge, and allowed to get cold. Sometimes, indeed, it is not even allowed to do that ; but directly it ceases to be red hot—still hot enough severely to burn the hands when touched, it is immersed in the cooling trough. All these practices are to be condemned, as it is bad policy to attempt to turn steel that is not properly and thoroughly annealed. The labour expended in annealing it is far from being thrown away, as, when well annealed, the steel may not only be turned with greater ease and with less damage to the tools, but it may be driven much faster and turned with greater certainty of being ' true ' or perfectly circular.

Cast iron is generally rough-turned by hand with the same tools as wrought iron and steel, but it is finished by tools differing altogether from those used for roughing. Some sorts of cast iron are so soft that they can be turned like cheese (I must, however, admit I have never turned this latter material). Other sorts are very hard, and for rough turning require tools ground to an angle much less acute than that used for wrought iron. But the same tools are used for finishing both hard and soft cast iron.

The outside skin or scale of cast iron is frequently so very hard that the tools will not touch it. It is therefore a good plan either to chip off or grind away a small portion of the scale, so that the tool may be applied to its cut first at the place so cleared of scale, and worked away from it. When once the tool is under the scale, it will seldom be much injured by it, but if the article be rather out of truth, and will not admit of a cut of sufficient depth being taken off it to get below the scale, then the workman has a great deal of difficulty in getting his tools to stand and in finishing his work perfectly true.

The edges and corners of castings—especially when small—are frequently hard or ' chilled,' not only at the surface or scale, but for some depth in the metal. It is

not often that annealing will soften or remove this
'chill,' nor do I know of any simple process whereby
this may be done effectually. Ordinary turning tools
will not turn these chilled portions, but an old file or
piece of grindstone forced against the part will generally
remove them. The operation is rather slow, however,
and no dependence can be placed on the truth of the
work so done.

Malleable cast iron occupies a position midway between cast and wrought iron. When thoroughly malle-
ableised—which, by the way, is not often the case—the
iron may be turned as easily as ordinary wrought iron,
the tools being perhaps blunted rather sooner. When,
however, the cast iron has been but imperfectly malle-
ableised, half the turner's time is taken up in grinding
and repairing his tools. There is now far greater
chance of getting good malleable iron than there used
to be ; the art of converting cast into malleable iron
being better understood.

Brass and gun-metal are also to be obtained of every
degree of hardness ; but for articles to be turned the
metal is usually of medium density, and then it is cut
without much difficulty. These metals are turned with
tools similar to those used for cast iron, but at a
greater speed. When turning them care should be
taken that the bright rays of the sun are not allowed
to fall directly on the work, otherwise the light reflected
from the shining metal surfaces will so much dazzle
the operator's eyes, as to greatly inconvenience him,
and in time to permanently impair his visual powers.

In metal turning of all sorts, but especially brass
turning, the shavings fly off from the tool with force

sufficient to project them many feet from the work, and as, when detached, the shavings are of a high temperature, when they fall upon the naked skin the sensation produced is far too warm to be agreeable. A hot shaving falling inside a workman's shirt sleeve, or down his neck inside the collar, will usually cause him to drop his tools and commence shaking himself with considerable vigour and earnestness. These shavings appear to have a peculiar knack of finding out all the most tender and sensitive parts; projected into the eye, I have known a steel shaving to produce blindness; projected around the eyes, metal shavings will often raise a blister, and cause the most exquisite pain, which is only to be thoroughly appreciated by those who have experienced it.

With regard to the rotation of objects in the lathe, the metals are treated in the same way as wood and ivory, the work being set in motion, and the tools applied to those parts to be reduced; but the manner in which motion is communicated to the work is somewhat different from that for woods. Whereas long pieces of wood are usually driven by a driver or chuck, and supported by one centre, long pieces of metal are supported by both centres and are rotated by a driver. The centres used for ordinary metal turning are very much the same as those for woods, the angles only differing, as will be seen on referring to Figs. 67 and 68. Fig. 67 is best adapted for wood, or very small metal work. The angle of its point is 60°. Fig. 68 has an angle of 80°, which is a good angle for ordinary metal-turning. Both centres are of steel, with their points carefully hardened and tempered. The part under the shoulder

is made to screw into, and nicely fit the centre hole
of the lathe spindle. The wrench or instrument for

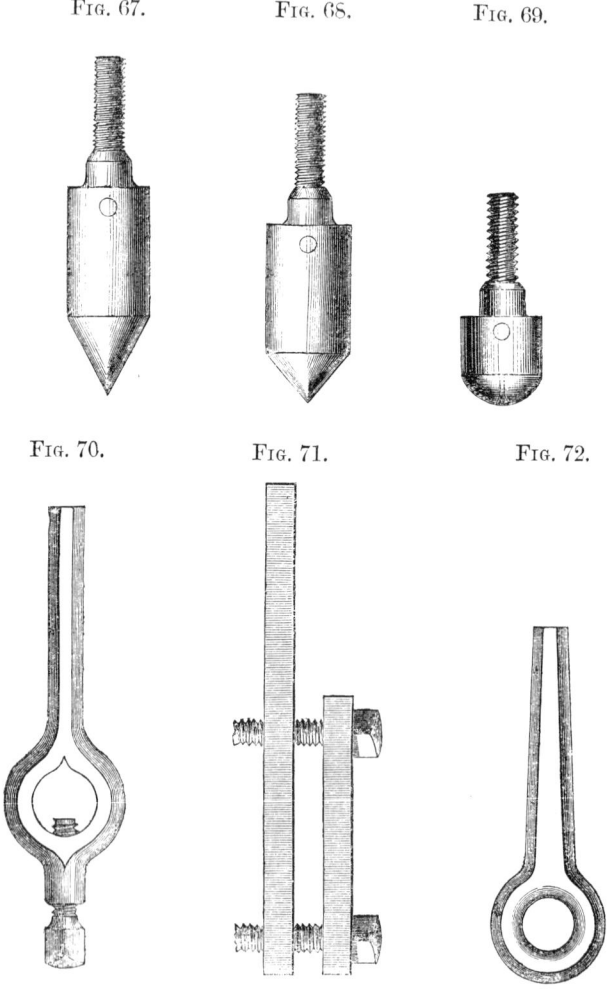

Fig. 67.   Fig. 68.   Fig. 69.

Fig. 70.   Fig. 71.   Fig. 72.

screwing and unscrewing them is shown at Fig. 22
in position for use. The internal reverse or female
centre, Fig. 69, is of steel, and made to fit the lathe-
spindle in the same way as the last; but instead of

being formed with a coned point, it has a coned recess, as shown by the dotted lines. The ordinary carrier

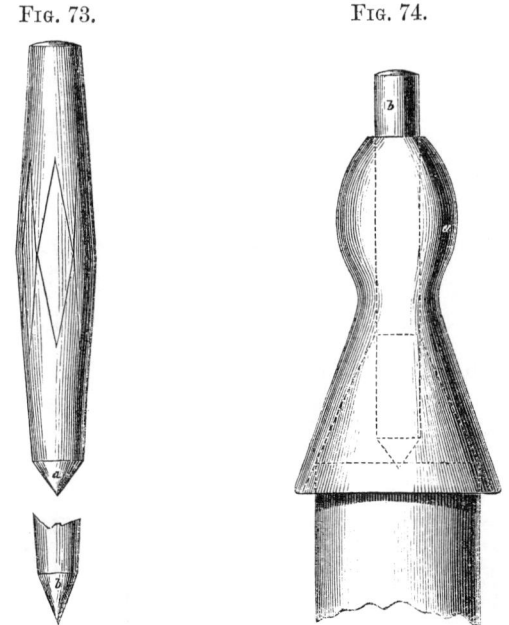

Fig. 73.　　　　　　Fig. 74.

or driver for round iron is shown at Fig. 70 : it is made of iron, and with a steel screw.

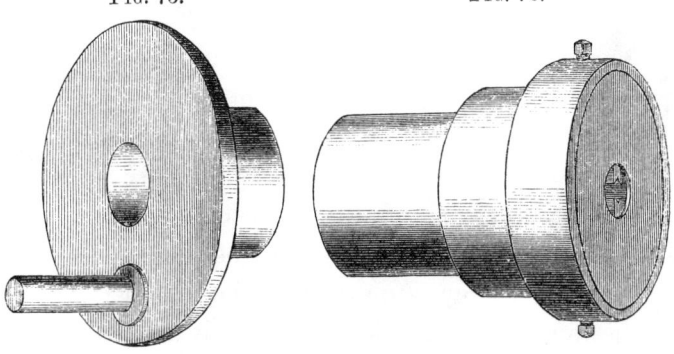

Fig. 75.　　　　　　Fig. 76.

The carrier, or driver for flat and square iron, is shown at Fig. 71 ; it is made of two pieces of flat iron, and with

the tightening screws of steel. The carrier for screwed
work, at Fig. 72, is of either iron or steel; the hole
FIG. 77. shown through it is tapped with a screw thread
of the same size and pitch as the article to be
driven by it. Various sizes of each sort of carrier
are in very frequent requisition, and are indispensable to the turner in metals.

The centre-punch, Fig. 73, is of steel: its
point (*a*) is made with the same angle as the
lathe-centres, and is carefully hardened and
tempered. The indent-punch is similar to the
last, but its point (*b*) is ground to an angle much
more acute than the last. The centering cone,
Fig. 74, is in two parts, the box or cone (*a*)
and the sliding punch (*b*). The former is made
of iron or brass, and the latter of a straight
cylindrical rod of steel, pointed with the same
angle as the lathe-centres, and carefully hardened. This rod is free to slide up and down
the hole in the cone box. The illustration will
sufficiently explain the instrument.

The driving plate at Fig. 75 is usually of
cast iron: the driving pin or arm is of wrought
iron or steel, and is fastened to the plate by
passing through a hole and having a nut behind. The plate has a boss fitted with a screw
thread for screwing on to the spindle of the lathe.
The die-chuck, Fig. 76, is made of iron, with steel
screws. It is screwed on to the lathe-spindle.

The round mandril, Fig. 77, is merely a round bar of
steel, carefully turned to a standard size; its ends
are drilled with small holes, countersunk to fit the

lathe-centres, and afterwards carefully hardened. The shape of the mandril end is shown enlarged at Fig. 78. It must run perfectly true, and should be either quite parallel or *very* slightly tapered. Many sizes are required. The screw mandril, Fig. 79, is of steel, and has a true standard thread cut upon it. This thread may be either right or left handed, or both, as seen in the figure. The mandril ends are made of the same

Fig. 78.

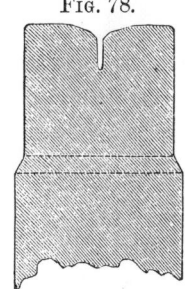

shape as the last, and are hardened. Screw mandrils of various sizes and pitches of thread are in frequent request. The tool-rest, Fig. 81, is of wrought iron,

Fig. 79.

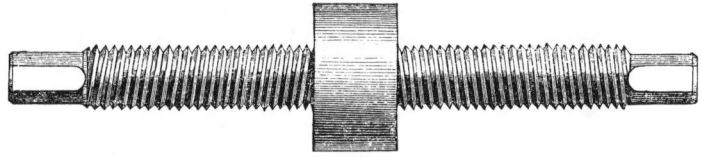

and its shank is turned to fit the socket of the rest-holder of the lathe. Other shapes than that shown are occasionally required for peculiar work.

Fig. 80 is the ordinary hook tool used for roughing wrought iron, steel, cast iron, and malleable iron; (*a*) is the holder and (*b*) the tool, which, fitting a groove the whole length of the holder, can be slid farther out as the tool wears away. It will be noticed that the tool passes through a sort of staple, so that by twisting the handle (*c*) in one direction the tool is firmly fastened between the staple and the bottom of the groove in the holder; and by twisting the handle in the contrary

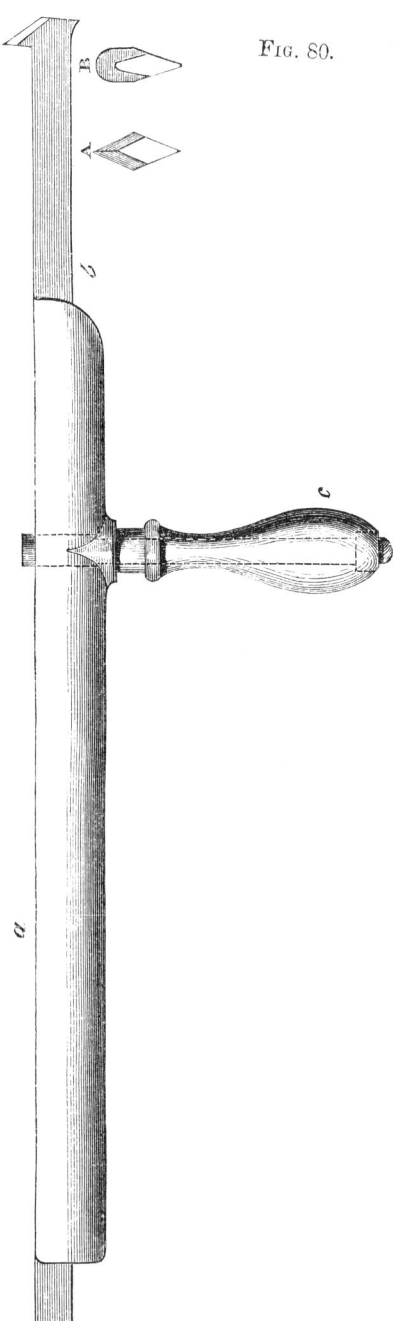

Fig. 80.

direction, the tool is released and can be withdrawn entirely from its place. There are two sorts of this hook tool: one has its cutting edge ground off to a round shape as at B, the other has a pointed or angular cutting edge as at A. The tool having a round cutting edge is used entirely for roughing; the angular tool is used for roughing down any small works in metal, and for trueing up the ends of articles, the sides of collars, and flat shoulders. Both tools are held in the same manner, and the position in which they cut is shown at Fig. 82, (a) being the work, and (b) the tool. The rest or support for the tool is that shown in Fig. 81.

The handle (c) of the tool-holder is grasped by the right hand of the operator;

the extremity of the holder farthest from the point of
the tool is laid on the shoulder, the left hand being
placed upon the holder between
the handle, (c), Fig. 80, and the

FIG. 81.

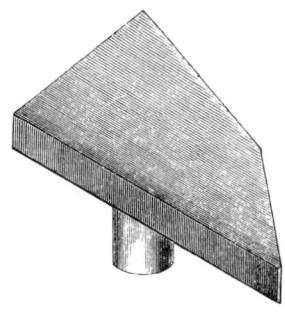

shoulder, and the point of the
tool held about level with the
centre of the work.

This is a very effective tool,
but its use is not easily learnt
by amateurs ; as beginners find
it very difficult to prevent the
tool ' catching in ' and taking a much deeper bite out
of the metal than is necessary or desirable. When
this occurs, the work, the tool, or the lathe-centre is
certain to receive some damage;

FIG. 82.

and in certain cases the operator is lifted off his feet before he
knows what the matter is. After
the use of the tool is learned,
it is one of the easiest to manage ; it will cut off the
metal in large deep shavings, and may be held and
guided by a couple of fingers. All workmen should
be able to use this tool from either shoulder.

These hook-tools should vary in shape according to
the height of the user, as will be evident to all who
examine the illustration, Fig. 82. The difficulty of
using increases with the angle of the tool ; the tool
being a lever of the first order, of which the ' heel'
or point bearing on the rest is the fulcrum. The
weight is applied at the cutting edge, and the power
at the other end of the handle. It will therefore be
understood that the nearer the cutting edge is to being

in a vertical line passing up through the fulcrum or heel
of the tool, the less will be the force required at the
other end to counterbalance this weight on the cutting
edge. The weight, of course, is the resistance of the
metal to being cut.

There are other varieties of this tool in which the cutting part is shaped so that the handle has to be placed
under the shoulder, instead of on it; they are used in

Figs. 83.   84.   85.   86.   87.   88.   89.

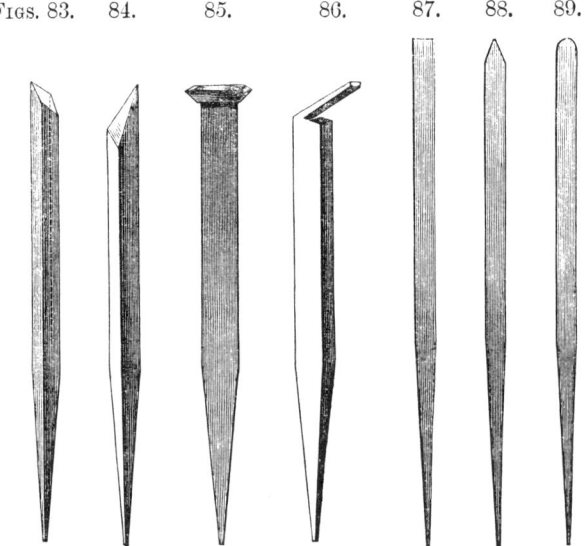

the same manner as the others, but I do not consider
them equal to the others in efficiency and facility of
using. Both sorts, however, may be manipulated with
very little exertion, the workman only having to guide
the tool, all the weight of the cut being borne by the
tool rest. I have nevertheless seen illustrations of a
workman using a tool of this sort, and hanging on it
as though his life depended on the amount of force he
could expend upon the tool. Such illustrations are not
true to good practice.

The other tools for roughing iron are the graver, Fig. 83, the side tool Fig. 84, bolt head tool Fig. 85, and cranked tool Fig. 86 ; there are numbers of others, but these are amongst the best. The graver is almost of universal application, and is used by watchmakers for all sorts of work. It is merely a square rod of steel, ground off to a diamond shape, and hardened at the end—the point and the two projecting sides forming the cutting edges.

Fig. 90.

The side tool is made of a triangular rod of steel, ground off as seen by the figure; the point, and the side of the triangle proceeding from the point form in this case the cutting edges. As its name implies, it is used for side work, such as turning the sides of collars, the ends of cylindrical rods, &c.; which it will do, either to the right or left hand.

The bolt head tool is only used for tolerably heavy work ; it has four cutting edges, and will take off a very heavy cut. The cranked tool has two cutting edges. It is used principally for turning the sides of collars, or parts at an angle to the centre line of the work, which it does with greater truth than the other tools sometimes used for that purpose.

The chisels, Figs. 87, 88, 89, are used for smoothing and sometimes finishing articles of wrought, cast, and malleable iron and steel. They are all used in a handle as shown at Fig. 90, and are generally made with three shapes of cutting edge, flat as in Fig. 87, angular as in Fig. 88, and half round as at Fig. 89. This difference however is only in the grinding, their sections being alike.   The under edge of all these tools is serrated, so as to give them a better hold on the rest, and prevent them from slipping about.   The position for holding them on the rest will be seen on referring to Fig. 91.

FIG. 91.   FIG. 92.

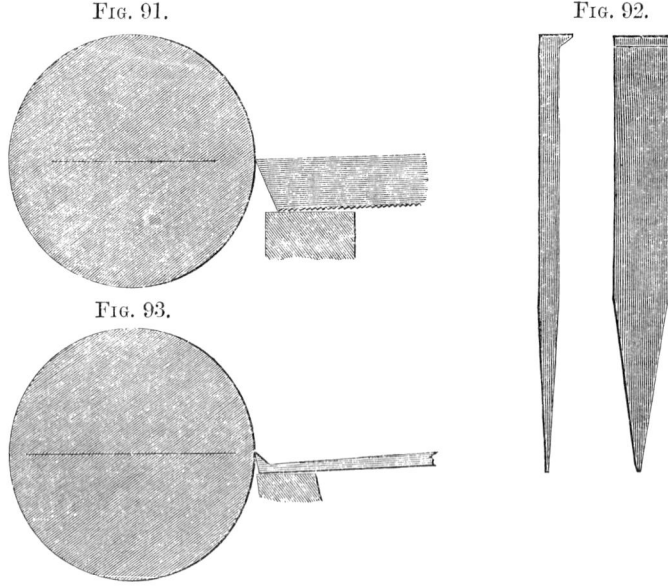

FIG. 93.

Fig. 92 is the tool used for polishing wrought iron and steel.   Its bottom is laid on the rest, so that the cutting edge is just level with the centres (see Fig. 93): it is then moved carefully along the rest, and only a very slight cut or scraping of metal is taken off by it. Meanwhile the surface of the work is kept well moistened with oil or water.   This tool requires considerable care and caution to prevent its ' catching in,' but, when it is properly used, a very bright smooth surface is given to the work.

Cast iron is smooth-turned by the tools or scrapers shown at Figs. 94 to 102. These are of various shapes for various kinds of work, but they are all of the same side section as Fig. 103; and their cutting edges being all ground off at right angles, they may be used either side up. They are placed flat upon the rest, with the cutting

Figs. 94. 95. 96. 97. 98. 99. 100.

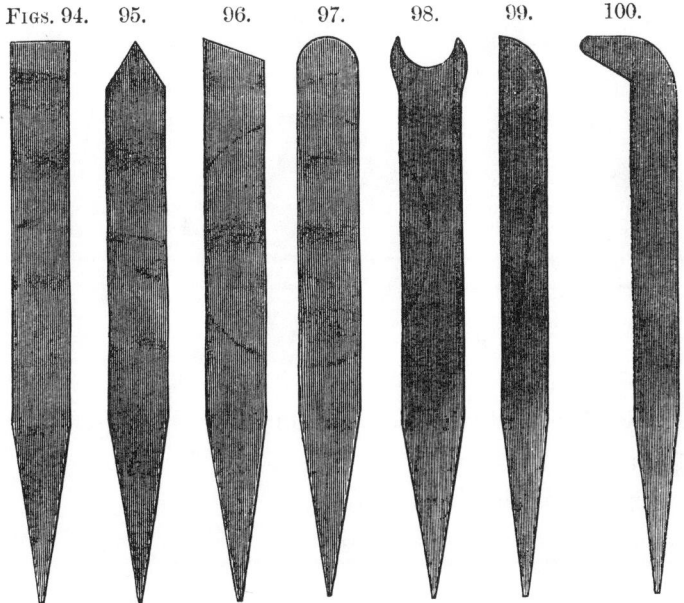

edge about level with the centres (see Fig. 104). The tools for wrought iron, cast iron, and steel are made with a cutting angle of between 60° and 80°; and for polishing cast iron and brass, with an angle of 90°.

The clamps, Fig. 105, and the glazing stick, Fig. 106, are used for polishing cast iron, wrought iron,

G

malleable iron and steel. The clamps are lined with lead, as shown in the figure.

With regard to the best tools for turning brass and gun-metal, there is a great diversity of opinion. Some maintain that the ordinary hook-tools are the best, when they are *blunt*; others prefer tools of circular sections which they roll along the rest; others use tools of square

Figs. 101.   102.   103.

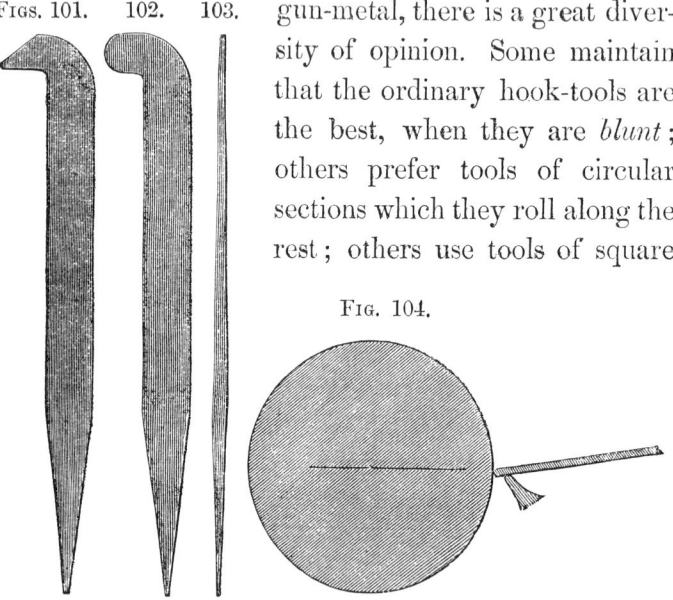

Fig. 104.

section, and cut with all four sides. When one is dull the others are used in turn : this tool is effective, and when dull is easily ground.

Fig. 105.

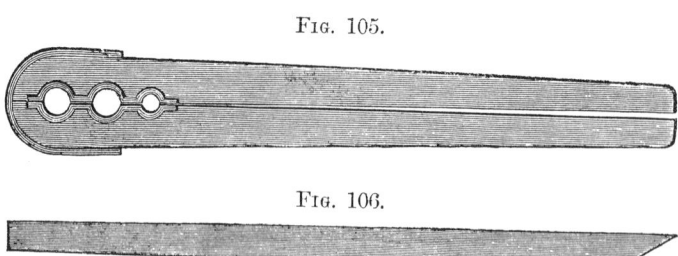

Fig. 106.

Without, however, being able to lay claim to a long lifetime of experience, I have, nevertheless, turned some hundredweights of brass and gun-metal, and, having tried all the tools, have found the hook-tools very liable to ' catch in ' ; the round-section tool liable to slip off the rest, and to require a deal of forcing to make it take a good cut ; the square-section tool to be good, but only applicable to straight work ; but the ordinary round-nosed chisel, Fig. 89, to be well adapted for roughing every sort of brass. It can be used either upon straight or curved work, it is not liable to ' catch in,' does not require violent forcing, will take a light or heavy cut, does not easily lose its edge, and when dull is easily ground. It should be ground with a cutting angle of about 80°, and placed upon the rest, as shown at Fig. 107. For fin-ishing or smooth-ing brass and gun-metal, the same scraping tools are used, and in the same manner as for

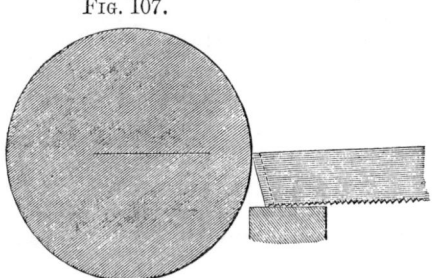

FIG. 107.

cast iron. With regard to these tools, some prefer them to be thick and clumsy, and use them upon the ordi-nary rest, others use very thin scrapers, and to prevent ' chatter' place a piece of hard leather between the rest and the tool, to act as an elastic cushion and to deaden the vibration. The best-formed scrapers are those thin at the cutting edge, but increasing in thickness and strength gradually towards the handle ; and these can be used upon the naked rest without chatter. The chasing or wood-turning rest is the best for use with these tools ; it should not be too far from the work, and should be adjusted so that the tool edge will come just level with the line of centres.

With regard to the proper speed for turning metals, it will at once be seen that owing to their being harder than wood, they should be driven at a lower speed whilst being cut.

For wrought iron a speed of from 18 to 22 feet per minute is found to answer well. Veiny iron or pinny iron must be turned at a much slower speed.

Steel well annealed will turn well at 18 or even 20 feet per minute, but if improperly annealed a speed of 14 or 15 feet can seldom be exceeded without damaging the tools.

Brass of medium or usual density should be driven at about 100 feet per minute; if very hard, the speed should be about 40 feet, and for very soft about 150 feet per minute.

Lead is usually turned when being driven at about 200 feet per minute.

It will be understood that these speeds apply only to hand-tool turning, and then only for small diameters. When the diameter of the work exceeds $1\frac{1}{2}$ or 2 inches the circumferential speed for turning must be slightly reduced; this necessity arises from the tool being longer in contact with the metal and having less time, comparatively, to cool between the cuts. Whenever, in turning, the tools get much or quickly blunted, or their edges become of a yellow or blue tint, the workman may conclude that he is driving his work too fast; and he must then regrind his tools, and reduce the speed of the work. When polishing metal work it is driven much faster than when turning it. Wrought iron and steel are sometimes smoothed over after the tools with a fine file; but the practice is not to be recommended, as work is rendered untrue by much filing. Some workmen have a great horror of files, and will not allow one to come near their work, others scarcely take a piece of work from the lathe without its having been filed to excess. The former is prejudice, and the latter is laziness and want of care.

Work requiring great truth should not be touched with a file, other work may be rubbed over once or twice with a smooth file without being injuriously affected. When a file is used it should be either a ' smooth ' or a ' dead smooth' and not a new file; its surface should be moistened with oil, and all 'pins' or particles of iron jammed between the teeth removed before using. The file should be gently pressed upon the work, and pushed slowly forward as when filing work in the vice, the article being revolved about double the speed used when turning it. After this filing the work is polished in the usual way.

When the polishing tool, Fig. 92, is used as before-mentioned, no filing nor further polishing is required, the surface being left very smooth and bright; but for polishing these shapes in wrought iron and steel where the polishing tool is not admissable, and for polishing filed work, emery cloth of various degrees of coarseness is pressed against the rapidly revolving work. A little oil is generally used on these metals, but for cast iron and brass the emery cloth is used dry. For polishing curved work in iron and steel the glazing stick is also used; there are two sorts of these tools, but both are of the same shape, and made of soft wood cut to the shape shown at Fig. 106.   One, however, is dipped in glue and then into emery powder, and allowed to get dry before using. This is used mostly for cast iron: the other is dipped into a mixture of emery and oil, and pressed against the work wet. This latter is chiefly used for wrought iron and steel.

The clamps, Fig. 105, are perhaps the best means for polishing parallel bars of iron and steel.   Some emery and oil being placed in that groove of the clamps which will best fit the work, the instrument is placed over the work, so as to hold it between the grooves or notches, the handles are then pressed tightly together, and the clamps moved slowly backwards and forwards upon the rapidly revolving metal, until the tool marks are obliterated, and the surface of the work is bright and smooth. In course of using, the oil dries up, and the emery gets wasted; it is necessary therefore to frequently supply a little more emery and oil to the grinding surfaces. Brass is left tolerably smooth by the scraping tools, but if a little extra polish be required it is given it by means of very fine well-worn emery cloth used dry. New emery cloth does not answer so well.   When either iron, steel, or brass has to be very brightly polished, a little crocus, rottenstone, or rouge powder on a piece of soft wash or chamois leather, is applied to the work and gently pressed against the rapidly revolving surface.

Let us now take an example or two to illustrate the usual mode of procedure in turning metal by hand-tools.   Our first example shall be the same as in wood, namely—a plain cylinder, say, 6 inches long and 1 inch diameter, but in wrought iron.

First cut off a piece of rod iron, about $1\frac{1}{8}$ inch diameter and $6\frac{1}{8}$ inches long, and if the ends be very rough, slightly smooth them over with a rough file or by putting them against the grindstone.

With the centre punch, Fig. 73, knock in a centre mark at each end of the piece, as nearly in the middle of the end as can be managed. The cone-centre box, Fig. 74, is the best instrument for the beginner to use for this purpose, as with it he is more likely to centre his work correctly. When using it, to ensure centrality it is only necessary to place the work in a vice, and apply the cone to its end, as shown in the figure, taking care to hold it upright, and then give a smart blow to the sliding punch with a hammer.

Put both centres in the lathe, and adjust the head-stock to receive the required length of work; then run the hand over the iron so as to revolve it and to see whether it is truly centred. If it be not, hold a small piece of chalk steadily on the rest, and against the work, so as to just touch those parts which are farthest from the centre. Remove the work from the lathe and knock the centre-mark sufficiently towards that side touched by the chalk, as to counteract the eccentricity; replace the wood in the lathe, and if it do not then run true, continue chalking it and forcing the centre towards the chalk marks until it runs as true as required. Absolute truth is not necessary, but no part should be as much out of truth, as the rough iron is larger in diameter than the finished size required, otherwise some portion of the black scale will be left unturned, and the work will not ' hold up to size.'

Now knock in a deeper indent or mark with the indent punch ; put the driving plate on the lathe-spindle, and see that the pin or arm is fastened on firmly, as, if loose, it may fly out and do some injury. Put a carrier of the right size on one end of the piece of iron, and put the iron between the centres with the carrier towards the driving-plate, and so that the arm and not the screw end of the carrier engages with the driving-pin. A little oil being then dropped about the other centre, the work is ready to be put in motion.

The moving centre should be kept well oiled, as, if allowed to get dry, the surfaces will abrade and cut each other so as to throw the work out of truth, and also to wear away the extreme point of the lathe centre. The deeper point made by the indent punch acts as a cavity for holding the oil, and it also prevents the work touching the point of the centre; the deeper cavity should always be made when much has to be done to the work.

In using the carriers, it is a bad plan to make a large carrier do for small work, as it is very clumsy, and in revolving rapidly the unbalanced momentum of the carrier causes the slight work to vibrate, so that the turned parts are not true. The tightening screw of the carrier is also liable to be broken off when thus used.

The rest, Fig. 81, is to be put into the rest-holder, and adjusted so that the point of the round-nosed hook-tool, Fig. 80, will just be on a level with the centre, when the tool is held in position on the shoulder. The rest must be firmly fastened in place, as it has to bear considerable pressure.

Set the spring-indicating, Fig. 57, or other callipers, to the required size—1 inch. With the point hook-tool or a side tool, turn off the end of the iron, either quite flat, or slightly rounded, or convex, as required. Reverse the work in the lathe, and turn off the other end to shape, and so as to make the work of the proper length. Then commence anywhere in the length of the work, and with the round hook-tool held as directed, rough down the metal nearly to its proper diameter. It is best to do this first in several narrow bands at intervals of an inch or so along the rod ; as these turned portions then act as a guide in roughing down the other parts without having to use the callipers. When all that portion is roughed down, again reverse the work in the lathe, and rough down that portion of the work previously covered by the carrier. Now take the flat chisel, Fig. 87, and turn down several bands to the finished size, or very nearly so ; and finish turning the whole length in the same manner as before, carefully using the callipers at short intervals to see when the right size is attained. In putting a carrier on to work which has been smooth-turned, in order to prevent the point of the tightening screw jamming against the bright work and disfiguring it, a piece of sheet brass or copper should be bent to a ring to encircle the work and come between it and the carrier. The work being turned to size can now be polished by any of the methods previously explained. The relative positions of the tools and work of various materials, are shown at Figs. 91, 93, 104, 107. The figures explain themselves to a great extent.

For a second example, take a brass ring, say, of 1'-inch diameter, 1 inch wide, and having a hole through it $\frac{3}{4}$ of an inch diameter. Such a piece of brass would be obtained by casting it from a wooden pattern slightly larger than the finished size. The hole having been made—the method of doing this will be explained hereafter—take a $\frac{3}{4}$-inch standard mandril, Fig. 77; put the ring on this, and hammer it well on.

To knock work on or off mandrils, a mandril-block should be used, the work placed with its hole just over the hole in the die of the block, and the mandril put through both holes, and, if a small mandril, it should be knocked in with a mallet or soft iron hammer. If an ordinary steel hammer be used, it must on no account be struck direct on the end of the mandril, as that would probably cause a piece of the hammer or the mandril end to fly off, and so injure the mandril, or if the mandril end be rather soft it would be hammered out of shape, so that when placed between the centres it would not run true. A piece of lead or copper should therefore be placed upon the mandril end, and the hammer struck upon that.

If the work be very heavy, it may be driven on or off without any hammer, by lifting the mandril with the work off the ground, and allowing it to fall with its end on to a block of wood or lead; the motion of the mandril being thus suddenly destroyed, the momentum of the collar will generally suffice to drive it either on or off the mandril as the case may be. In driving a collar on in this manner, the small end of the mandril must be held uppermost, and the large end be brought down against the wooden block; in driving the work off the ends must be reversed.

The practice of striking out mandrils with a centre punch is to be strongly condemned, as also is that of using the ordinary steel-faced hammer direct upon the mandril end.

In hammering such articles as wheels or pulleys with arms, on and off mandrils, they should not be rested upon the rim, but upon the boss or the metal nearest the hole ; and if the rim project in the way, a collar should be put on the mandril between the boss and mandril block, to transfer the force of the blow to the boss.

To return to the example which is now on the mandril :—put a carrier on the end of the mandril, and let the point of the tightening screw jam against the flat, cut on the mandril end. Place the mandril between the centres, and put a drop of oil about the centre previous to screwing the spindle tight up. I may mention that the centres should be screwed up only just *so* tight as to hold the work between them without looseness ; so tight that when the end of the carrier is taken in the fingers, and the work pulled round, the workman can just *feel* a slight resistance.

Now adjust the rest for using the round-nose chisel, Fig. 89 ; and with this tool rough the work all over, and reduce it nearly to its right size. Remove the rest, and put in that one which is shown at Fig. 54 ; adjust this for using the scraping tools. With Fig. 94, finish the edge of the collar, and, with Fig. 95, finish the sides and polish the whole, if required, by any of the methods described. These scrapers should be kept very keen and smooth ; after grinding they should be rubbed on a good oil-stone until the stone marks are removed, and the cutting edges are smooth and bright. They should not be allowed to get very dull ; but whenever they become slightly so, a few rubs on the oilstone will restore the edges. A good keen scraper, properly used on brass, will produce a surface beautifully bright and smooth.

Surfaces are turned in the same manner, but with the rests facing the work, the truth or flatness of the surface being judged by a straight edge, which is merely a piece of thin steel with its edge brought to a perfectly straight line.

SCREW-CHASING.

Besides the work already described, screws can be cut in the hand-lathe by means of suitable tools; and this method can frequently be conveniently followed in other lathes, and those especially constructed for screw-cutting, owing to the mechanism being required for purposes which renders it inconvenient to alter its arrangement.

Fig. 108. Fig. 109.

The hand operation of cutting screws is termed chasing, and the tools used are called chasers or combs. The tool shown at Fig. 108 is the outside chaser, and Fig. 109 is the inside chaser. These tools are the exact shape of the grooves of the screw, and are also inclined to the same extent; they are to be procured of standard threads of all tool makers, and the method of making them will be hereafter explained.

One of these tools will answer for cutting a screw upon any diameter of work, and a skilful workman can cut a thread of double or quadruple the pitch; but this is an operation that not many can manage satisfactorily.

For cutting left-hand threads, the chasing tool must be inclined in the other direction, although for a makeshift the right-hand tool is occasionally used to cut threads of reverse inclination. This is not difficult to do, but there is not the same certainty of producing a true thread. With the proper tools it is equally easy to cut right or left hand threads.

The method of using these chasing tools is extremely simple, but is not easily acquired. A short explanation will give the reader a good idea how to proceed, but practice alone will enable him to cut a screw with truth and certainty.

The work upon which the outside screw is to be cut having been turned somewhat larger than the diameter of the outside of the required thread, it is held in the lathe precisely as for turning, but if driven by a carrier, the tail of the carrier should be tied to the driving arm of the lathe, to prevent any 'stopping about.' The ordinary hand-tool rest for iron can be used, but the rest used for wood-turning is the best for the purpose. Whichever is used, the top edge must be quite smooth and free from ruts or grooves, and its edge should also be parallel with the line of centres. It should be fastened at such a height as will bring the edge of the chasing tool just level with the centres; also it must be near the work.

The chasing tool is held in one of the ordinary handles, and applied in a very similar manner to the metal-turning chisels, being for heavy screws pressed against the work by the workman's shoulder. The tool is not, however, held stationary, since that would only result in cutting as many grooves around the work as the tool had teeth ; but it is pressed against the work, and traversed or pushed along the rest at a speed depending on the speed of the lathe and the pitch of the screw. To push along the tool thus appears to be very easy, but it must be considered that for every fractional part of a revolution of the work, the same fractional part of the pitch of the screw must have been traversed by the tool, otherwise the pitch is 'drunken,' and the screw is useless.

The best way for beginners is to take the graver, Fig. 83, and first make a deep scratch with the point on the work, and, at about the inclination of the thread. This scratch then acts as a guide for the chasing tool, and makes it far easier to 'catch' the thread of the screw.

With bad iron no workman, however good, can make sure of getting a true and good thread, as the chaser cuts deeper into the soft places than it does into the hard ; but, with good metal, threads can be chased by hand almost as correctly as by any other method.

For chasing brass the tools should be thinner than for iron. Chasers which have been used until ground too thin for iron are better than new tools for brass.

When cutting a thread on wrought iron or steel, the surface of the metal should be kept moist by soapsuds, or oil and soda water ; but brass and cast iron do not require this treatment. Screw threads are cut internally, by means of the other chasing-tool, Fig. 109. The same rest is used, but it is fixed across the line of centres at the same height as before ; and the work being put in motion, the chasing tool is pushed along the surface inside the hole, until the thread is properly cut. The hole to receive a thread should be turned out rather smaller than the thread is required to be, so as to allow of the removal of any scratches made when starting the chaser.

Both of these chasing tools are ground on the face, so that the correct shape of the thread is always retained, and the tools are only made somewhat thinner. This is easily compensated for by raising the tool-rest rather higher.

DRILLING AND BORING.

When holes are required to be made through various materials, it is frequently more convenient to cut them out with special tools than with the turning tools ; indeed, with hand-tools it is difficult to cut out holes or recesses of any great depth, but this may very easily be done by means of tools called drills or borers.

Sometimes these operations are performed with the work in motion, and the tool still ; and sometimes with the tool in motion, and the work a fixture. Whatever the material of the article through which the hole is to be made, the mode of making the hole is very similar ; but the tools differ—as in the operation of turning. The tools for woods are shown at Figs. 110, 111, 112 ; Fig. 110 is the gouge, Fig. 111 the centre bit, and Fig. 112 the spiral bit.

The tools for metal are shown at Figs. 113 to 119 ; Fig. 113 is the common drill, Fig. 114 the spiral drill, Fig. 115 the pin drill, Fig. 116 the cutter drill, Fig. 117 the countersink drill, and Figs. 118, 119 are rhymers or broaches. All these drills are made with a tapering square end, as will be seen, to fit the hole of the drill-chuck, already described and used for other purposes.

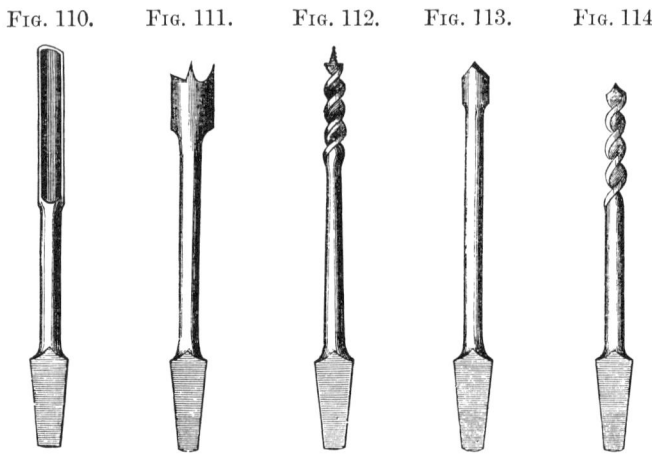

Fig. 110.   Fig. 111.   Fig. 112.   Fig. 113.   Fig. 114.

The spiral drills are sold in sets, under the name of American drills, and are accompanied by a special holder or chuck. They are used much more in America than here, but are now coming into very general use.

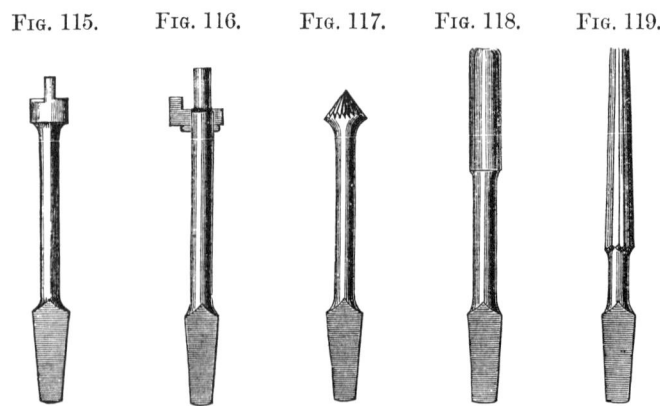

Fig. 115.   Fig. 116.   Fig. 117.   Fig. 118.   Fig. 119.

They are not, however, an American invention, although mostly made there. The spiral is made with a gradually-increasing pitch or rise. All the other drills can also be bought at the tool makers; but it will frequently be found convenient to make them, as they are not difficult to manufacture.

The article through which the hole is to be made is centered, as for turning, or, at any rate, a centre mark knocked into the place where the hole is to be commenced. The drill for use is then put into the drill-chuck, on the lathe-spindle, and set into rapid motion; one centre-mark is then put against the point of the drill, and the other against the centre of the moving headstock. This headstock being fastened down conveniently on the bed, the hand-wheel is moved around so as to force the article against the point of the revolving drill. It will be understood that the article itself must be prevented from revolving with the drill, otherwise, of course, no hole will be made.

For holes of the ordinary size, the article is held stationary by the hands, and then the workman is enabled to ascertain the amount of strain there is upon the drill, by the amount of force he has to exert in keeping the work still. When the strain is too much for the drill, the workman must not screw up so fast, or the drill will be broken off in the hole.

With wood the strain is seldom sufficient to damage a drill, and therefore it does not require such careful management; but with metal the case is different. The strain must be carefully watched; and it will require some little practice and a breakage or two before the beginner will have learned to judge the strain that drills of certain size will bear with safety. Should the operator be so unfortunate as to break a drill in the

H

hole, unless it will fall out by shaking, the article must be put in the fire and annealed, so as to soften the steel drill, before the work can be proceeded with. Spiral drills clear their own hole from the shavings, the spirals being made for that purpose ; but with other drills, whether for wood or metal, it is advisable to frequently withdraw the work from the drill, and clear out the hole with a wire or otherwise.

Wrought iron and steel require lubrication ; and, therefore, either soda-water or oil must be poured into the hole so as to keep the point moistened.

Spiral drills have this disadvantage—besides withdrawing the shavings, they prevent the lubricant from reaching the drill's point; these drills are, therefore, better adapted to brass and cast iron than to wrought iron or steel; they are not used for drilling holes of large diameter, since in these there is plenty of room for the shavings, which do not consequently impede the action of the drill. For very small holes spiral drills are capital instruments, especially when the holes are rather long, as they very seldom become choked, but for drilling even the smallest hole through *sheet* metal the ordinary drill is quite as good as the spiral.

The amateur will probably consider it rather a feat to take an ordinary good-sized pin, and send a drill through it, leaving it a complete tube, without any external evidence of having done so except at the ends. Or to take a shilling, and drill a series of holes through it edgewise—each hole to be a diameter of the circle of the coin—until the whole of the interior metal is removed, and the two faces or films, with the figured impressions, are held together only at the extreme edge by the small pieces of metal left between the holes. This is, however, done, the silver shavings kept, and the interior filled up with some composition of lead, and the coin again passed into circulation ; and as this is done for gain, it is evident that the time thus spent cannot be very long, or it would not *pay*.

When a hole is to be tapped with a screw thread, the drill must be the size of the bottom of the thread of the male screw or *tap*, and therefore it is usual to keep two sizes of standard drills—one called the tap drill, to make holes the size for tapping, or for a male screw to be screwed into ; and the other, called the clearance drill, for making a hole the size of the outside of the screw, and to allow the screw or bolt to be passed through it without screwing into it.

Workmen keep sets of these drills of all the various standard screw sizes in general use ; the size should be marked on the square shank of each drill, and it should not be altered ; but when a drill wears small it should be re-drawn, and again ground to proper size, as this prevents confusion and mistakes.

It is usual to have a standard drill gauge, or a piece of flat steel, having a series of the proper sized holes through it, and to these holes the various drills are ground, and not to any measurements taken from an ordinary rule by the callipers, as measurements thus taken are both uncertain and unsatisfactory.

For long holes to be drilled in articles placed between the centres, it is usual to drill the hole half from each end, and if this be carefully done the two holes will generally meet pretty well in a line and form one hole, but this is not sufficiently exact if the hole be required to receive a spindle, and act as a bearing to it; in this case the hole should be drilled out from each side, but with a drill rather smaller than the intended hole, and then a sharp drill of the proper size passed through, all from one end.

Or, instead of the last drill, the rhymer, Fig. 118, should be passed through; the work being forced into cut very slowly, and kept well lubricated. This rhymer is lubricated for cast iron also, but not for brass, except in cases where it rubs a great deal, when a little oil may be put about the flats of the tool, but not at the cutting edges. Rhymers will generally make a smooth straight hole, but it is usually found that the hole is very slightly larger at the end where the rhymer is inserted, and therefore it is advisable to put it through the hole in the same direction as the spindle is to be worked.

For drilling articles where the drill is required to come through, it is a good plan to use a sort of chuck in the place of the centre of the moving headstock, as the drill's point is apt to get damaged in coming against the hard steel centre; this chuck is made with a deep recessed mouth, and with a shank to screw into the place of the centre. For long work it should not be used until the drill or rhymer is nearly through, as for such work it has not the same steady directing effect as the centre; but for thin work, this instrument should always be used, as for that it has *greater* steadying power.

The pin, or recess drill, Fig. 115, is used to cut recesses to receive the heads of screws, &c. A hole of the size of the pin must first be made with an ordinary drill, the pin-drill being then used, the recess is cut out concentric with the small hole.

The cutter drill, Fig. 116, is more of a turning tool than a drill; it is very useful for turning up the bosses of levers, or other articles which cannot be fastened in the lathe. The cutter itself can be moved in or out in the slot, and fastened by the wedge at its

FIG. 120.

back, to enable one cutter to turn bosses of different sizes. The cutter can also be removed, and one of any other shape put in its place.

The countersink drill, Fig. 117, is used for countersinking the mouth of a hole, to enable it to receive the head of an ordinary screw. All those drills are used in the drill chuck, and the work pressed against them precisely the same as the others.

Although these operations are of great utility, it is generally preferable to make the holes in articles when the work is in motion and the drill is stationary; as when the work is fastened to the lathe spindle, we are better able to drill the hole concentric with any given part of the material, and with greater certainty of having a true and straight hole. It is also easier in this method to watch the progress of the tool, and more convenient to remove the tool than the work from the lathe, to allow the hole to be cleared of shavings. At the same time it is more difficult to fasten the work than the drill to the lathe-spindle, but the other advantages much more than counterbalance this, as there are several contrivances for receiving and holding the work.

Amongst these the face-plate, Fig. 120, and the

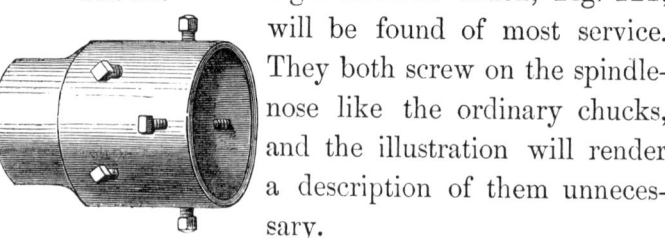

FIG. 121.

eight-screwed chuck, Fig. 121, will be found of most service. They both screw on the spindle-nose like the ordinary chucks, and the illustration will render a description of them unnecessary.

The tools used for work in motion are the same in cutting principle as those described; they are, however, shaped somewhat differently for convenience of holding. The smaller sizes are made like Fig. 122, which is the ordinary drill bit; these are kept of two sizes, for tap and clearance. The larger sizes are made like Fig. 123, which is the boring bit, these are also made in two sizes for roughing and finishing.

For long holes the cylinder, or D-bit, Fig. 124, is

well adapted, and its use is strongly recommended, especially for small or moderate sized holes.

There are a number of other instruments used for drilling and boring, but they are all modifications of the ones described, and made with moveable and expanding cutting parts, but they are not to be recommended. The moveable parts are always getting out of order or becoming detached from the rest of the tool and lost; besides which they are all more expensive.

Fᴵɢs.
122. 123. 124.

Some very good mechanics are partial to these contrivances, and amateurs especially are taken with their ingenuities; but for my own part, I prefer the simpler tools, and think it will save disappointment if the intending buyer allows them to remain in the shop-windows.

In addition to the drills, &c., there are several other instruments used which I will now describe. The boring-rest, Fig. 125, is made to fit the socket of the rest-holder, and when in place to have the centre line of the two slots shown, exactly level with the centres of the lathe.

Fɪɢ. 125.   Fɪɢ. 126.

The die-stay, Fig. 126, is a small cast-iron frame fastened to the lathe-bed when in use, and having grooves

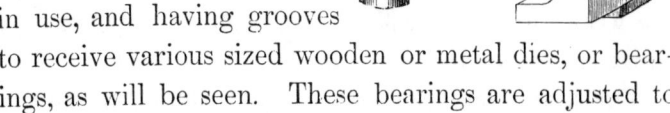

to receive various sized wooden or metal dies, or bearings, as will be seen. These bearings are adjusted to

the height of centres by moving the screw underneath.

Figs. 127. 128.   The boring wrench, Fig. 127, is merely
a piece of iron bent to the shape shown.

Laps, or lead grinders, Fig. 128, are
cylinders of lead or copper, cast on to a
square iron spindle or stem, they are carefully turned up parallel and very slightly
under the standard sizes.

Flat articles are most conveniently driven
by the face-plate, and long articles by the
screwed chuck. The manner of attaching
work to the former depends altogether
upon the shape of the article, and no
description will give an idea of all the
methods employed. The operator will
very frequently have to devise means for attaching his
work, but this is not at all difficult. Any means may
be employed that will not twist or strain the article,
or in revolving come in the way of the lathe-bed or
tools.

A set of bolts of various lengths and with T-heads
will be very useful, and a set of four of the clamps at

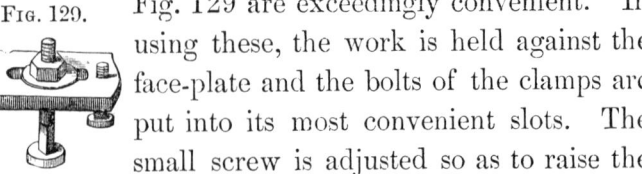

Fig. 129.   Fig. 129 are exceedingly convenient. In
using these, the work is held against the
face-plate and the bolts of the clamps are
put into its most convenient slots. The
small screw is adjusted so as to raise the
end of each clamp, rather more than the thickness of
the work off the face-plate, the large bolt being then
tightened in all the four clamps, the work is pinched
at four places between the face-plate and the ends of
the clamps. It is generally necessary to bore holes

as nearly as possible concentric with the rest of the work; for instance, when the article is a spur wheel or a pulley, it is necessary that the hole should be made concentric or true with the teeth of the wheel, or the face of the pulley; so that when the hole is made, on driving the article on a mandril the rim will run true, and will not require much to be turned off it, or more from one side than from another.

When certain parts of articles have to remain unturned, it is a good plan to chuck the work true with those portions, without regarding those parts which have to be turned; so that, when these points are rendered true by turning, the whole article is nearly concentric.

As the surface of the plate is quite true, it is evident that the surface of the article, or those points of the surface which are against the face-plate, will run true when the hole is bored and the work put on to the mandril. But there is no such guarantee that any part of the edge of the article will be true; it is therefore necessary, before tightening the bolts finally, to set the edge or rim true, in the same manner as when centering a piece of iron. That is, a piece of chalk is held against the work in motion, and, as those parts showing the chalk are the farthest from the centre, a tap with a hammer or mallet is given the article at those points, to drive them nearer the centre of the lathe. This is repeated until the chalk touches either all round, or at opposite points, when the clamp bolts may be tightened and the boring commenced.

When articles have to be true with their inside edges, it is evident that this operation must be reversed.   Wherever the chalk shows, those points must be hammered away from the centre.

It is a difficult matter for one pair of hands to hold work against the face-plate whilst putting in the bolts for fastening it on in place.   Workmen are in the habit of keeping it temporarily in place by forcing it against the face-plate by the boring bit or drill and the centre of the moving headstock.   This practice cannot altogether be recommended, as, besides a direct tendency to damage the points of the drill and of the centre, it is a very frequent occurrence for the whole —the work and drill—to come down with a run on to the lathe-bed or to the ground ; and this leads to serious damage to all things concerned, as the workman will readily admit if his toes happen to be between the work and the ground.

Other more careful workmen—if the work have a rough hole through it already—fasten the work temporarily to the face-plate by means of a bolt, screwing into the centre hole of the lathe-spindle, and a piece of straight iron with a hole through it, for a cross piece to span the hole.   This practice is certainly all that can be desired, so far as both safety and convenience go ; but it has one objection—the screwing and unscrewing of this bolt are apt to damage or wear the centre hole, and cause the centre to fit slackly.

Probably the best plan, when chucking heavy work, is, either to put a block of wood of the right height under the work, or to remove the face-plate from the lathe, and lay it horizontal, with its face upwards, when the work may be fastened to it with ease and convenience.

When the work is properly chucked, it is set in motion, and the place where the hole is to be commenced should be trued up. The boring-rest is then put in place, just in front of the work; care being taken not to put it near enough for the bolts in revolving to strike against it.

There are two holes in this boring-rest; one—the large one—is for the boring bits, the small one is for the drills. One of these holes is placed just opposite the centre of the work, and the proper drill or bit is put through it; the other end of the bits is furnished with a centre mark, into which the centre of the moving headstock must be placed, and the cutting edge of the drill forced into the revolving work, by moving the hand-wheel and forcing out the screw.

The rectangular hole in the boring-rest only prevents the bit from revolving; besides this, it has to be kept steady, especially at the commencement of the hole. If the hole be a small one, the boring-wrench is put on over the drill, and the other end of the lever forced down by the workman's left hand. When the hole is a large one, the pressure thus obtained is not enough; but a larger lever of the same sort is then used, and a good heavy weight hung on to its end, and kept there whilst the bit is cutting its way through the hole.

If the article be of wrought iron or steel, the cutting edge of the bit must be kept moist with soapsuds or soda water; but with brass and cast-iron this is not required.

In cutting large holes out of the solid, all the material cannot be removed by one instrument. A small drill must first be sent through, to be followed by a

series of others, each taking an increasing cut, until the
required size of the hole is nearly obtained, when the
last bit should be carefully sent through; but it must
not be made to take so heavy a cut as the bits preceding it.

In taking a series of heavy cuts at the hole, the
metal composing the article—especially if cast-iron or
brass—will be rendered rather hot by the friction;
it is, therefore, a good plan to allow the article to cool
before passing through the finishing or last bit. If this
be not done, and the hole is finished whilst the surrounding metal is hot, it will be found that, when the
metal has cooled, the finishing bit is unable to enter
again, owing to the contraction of the metal.

It may, however, happen that the spindle to work
into the hole has been made rather under the standard
size. In this case it will be advisable *to take advantage
of this expansion and contraction* of the metal, and
make it subservient to our purpose, by boring the last
cut but one with a dull bit, and taking a heavy cut.
The metal will then be made very hot, and the hole
will expand; so that if the finishing bit be then quickly
passed through, the result will be that when the metal
cools the hole will again contract, and form a closer
fit with the spindle previously turned too small. These
little facts are small in themselves; but, by bearing
them in mind, they may frequently be turned to useful
account.

It is scarcely necessary to observe that, in all cases,
care must be taken not to exceed a certain heat, or to
allow the work to get hot enough to lower the temper
of the tool.

Long cylindrical or other shaped articles, through which a hole is required, cannot be conveniently attached to the face-plate; and therefore, for these articles, the screwed or bell-chuck, Fig. 121, is used. The chuck being put on the lathe-spindle, the article is inserted between the screws, which are then screwed down to encompass and tightly hold it. The beginner will, probably, have some little difficulty in adjusting these screws so as to hold the work true; but the matter is much simplified by trueing the inside set of screws first, and afterwards adjusting the outside ones.

These screws should be set down tight enough to prevent the article slipping or moving about; but if when the hole is made the material will be thin, care should be taken not to set the screws down tighter than necessary, as otherwise the metal will be compressed, and the hole rendered out of shape in their neighbourhood. When the articles to be drilled are too long for this chuck alone, the ends are turned up true for an inch or two; and one end is then chucked true, and held between the outside set only of the screws of the chuck, whilst the other end is supported by being run in the die-stay. This is fastened to the lathe-bed, at the proper place, and a wooden or metal bearing, having a hole the same size as the end of the work, is put into the V's, and adjusted so as to bring the centre of the work in the line of lathe-centres. The lathe is then set in motion, and the hole drilled in the usual manner.

For these long articles the best tool I know of is the D-bit, shown at Fig. 124. This tool is not half so much used as it ought to be, and, when used, it is in conjunction with several other drills, and in such a roundabout manner that very few have patience to use it at all. These other drills are, however, quite unnecessary after the D-bit is once started. The best manner of proceeding is as follows: First, place the boring-rest in position, and with an ordinary drill, of the same size as the D-bit, drill out a recess about $\frac{1}{8}$ or $\frac{1}{4}$ of an inch in depth; remove the boring-rest, place the centre-mark at the end of the D-bit, against the centre of the headstock, and screw up carefully until the drill is in-to cut; the hole may then be bored through with ease and the certainty of its being true. The drill must be kept well lubricated with soda-water and oil, and occasionally removed, and the hole cleared of shavings. If the hole be more than a foot long, it will be better to drill it half from each end; and, if great truth be required, two of these drills should be used as in the other cases. As in long holes it is rather difficult to keep drills well moistened, the workman will find it a good plan to have a small syringe, and inject or squirt the lubricant into the hole with force; by so doing, not only will the drill be kept wet, but the shavings will, in a great measure, be washed out and the hole cleared.

On comparing the D form of drill with others, it will be found that the cutting edge is only equal to half the diameter of the hole; at the same time the drill stem is strong and well able to stand torsional strain, to which drills are mostly subject. In the ordinary drill, the cutting edge is equal to about one and a half diameters of the hole, whilst the stem is not nearly so well calculated to bear the strain. It therefore appears reasonable to conclude that the D-bit is better adapted than the others to cut a long hole out of the solid, or indeed to cut a long hole out at all; and this is found to be the case.

I have had considerable practice with this drill, and have so much confidence in its powers that I would undertake, with it alone, to drill a one-inch hole through a shaft thirty or forty feet long.

Holes required to be very smooth and straight, or which require to be very slightly enlarged, are ground out on a lead or copper lap, Fig. 128. Also in the case of articles which have been hardened or case-hardened, the action of the fire is sure to have had a slight effect upon the hole. In some cases the hole is slightly bent; in others, the surface is rather blistered; and in all cases it is rendered somewhat rough. All these imperfections are removed by grinding the hole out on a lap.

The method of using these laps is very simple : they are put between the lathe-centres, and driven by a lathe-carrier in the ordinary way. The laps' surface is covered with a coat of fine emery powder and oil; the former may be caused to stick to the lead by being slightly forced into it by a few taps with a hammer. The hole is then put on the lap, which is set in rapid rotation, and the article moved up and down ; and, being prevented from moving around with the lap, the inside of the hole is ground by the adhering emery. The emery and oil must be continually replenished, and the surface of the lap kept moist with it, as, if allowed to get dry, the two surfaces will bind or cling to each other, and abrasion will result.

If the article be heavy, precaution should be taken

of turning it over, so as to grind every portion of the hole alike; otherwise the weight of the article, pressing all on one side of the hole, will cause it to be ground more on that side than the others, and the hole will be rendered non-circular.

Care must also be taken to keep the middle of the lap well supplied with emery, and not to grind one end or the two ends of the hole larger than the middle. This, however, is a very common occurrence, and requires some little address to get over. Where practicable, it is also advisable to reverse the direction of the lathe occasionally, as sometimes, in lapping out a hole, the hole will draw itself onwards, and the workman's whole force will be insufficient to prevent its tightening itself on and *binding*. In this case, the best way is to either let the work go around with the lap, and to immediately stop the lathe and drive the work back with a mallet before it gets cool and contracts firmly on to the lap; or to reverse the direction of the lathe, when the hole will generally run back of its own accord, unless it is gone on too far and become very tight. It is sometimes a very difficult matter to get work off a lap when the grinding surfaces have been allowed to get dry and to abrade themselves.

MISCELLANEOUS OPERATIONS.

Circular saws applied to the lathe will enable one to do a great deal of work. The saw is mounted on a spindle placed in the lathe-centres. This spindle has a collar, between which and a washer and nut the saw is fastened; the spindle ends are hardened in the same manner as ordinary mandrils. The saw table is made with a shank to fit into the rest-holder, and it has a fence or flange for regulating the thickness of the wood to be cut. These circular saws should not be very large ; nor must the user imagine that he can cut up thick or heavy work—the power required to drive being such as to render the work of treading exceedingly laborious ; but for cutting up veneers, or slices of ivory and hard wood, and any light work of that nature, these little saws are admirably adapted.

Thin pieces of wood or ivory can also be readily planed by having a cylindrical cutter revolving rapidly between the lathe-centres, the wood being meanwhile pushed underneath it, and supported on a wooden or other frame, arranged so that it can be easily adjusted to receive various thicknesses of boards.

In a similar manner, but with properly-shaped fly-cutters, any length of wood may be cut to any required moulding, or it may be grooved. The wooden dies of the stay-bearing, Fig. 126, may also by this means be very readily cut at the sides with the necessary V-groove, by which they are fitted into the casting. To do this, of course, the cutter must be the exact shape of the V-sides of the casting.

A reciprocating saw is frequently applied to lathes, and arranged to be driven by the lathe treadle. These saws are very convenient for fret-work, for pattern making, and many other purposes ; as, by their means, all sorts of curved and angular work are easily accomplished.

Very small serrated discs are also used in the lathe for cutting iron, such as nicking, or cutting the grooves in the heads of screws, cutting off lengths of small pieces of iron, &c. Such saws should be well lubricated, or they will not work satisfactorily.

Plain milling tools are made by pressing small round blank pieces of steel against a fine-threaded tap revolving in the lathe; the screw, in revolving, causes the blank milling tool to revolve slowly also, and its edge to become cut with a concave screw thread. When the milling tool so cut is properly hardened, it may be used to produce other milling tools, but these will be convex; the convex tools may again be used to reproduce concave tools similar to the first. In these cases the tools are reproduced by simple pressure and rotation, a little oil being placed against the surfaces in contact.

Chasing tools are made from the master-taps, by the tap being driven in the lathe, whilst the blank chasing tool is pushed against it and supported on the chasing-rest, exactly as in the operation of chasing a screw, except that the blank chaser is generally held with its face downwards. Lubrication should be plentiful, the pressure nearly uniform, and the blank tool held as straight as possible.

The various tools can, when very dull, be sharpened by means of a grindstone rotated in the lathe. The stone must be kept moist, and great care must be taken not to lower the temper of the steel tool by the excessive friction. The tools should be held firm and steady on any convenient support, otherwise the stone will soon get out of truth by wearing faster one place than at another. The tools should also be traversed slowly along the stone's surface to prevent its grooving.

Small stones, driven at a greater speed, are also useful for grinding the surface of iron work which has to be polished, but which is not required absolutely true. After grinding, these and other surfaces are polished more highly, by being held against revolving glazers and buff wheels. These polishing wheels are mounted on a spindle, and are covered with thick leather, to which is glued a coat of emery powder. It is usual to have several of these wheels on one spindle, each wheel being covered with a coat of different sized emery, from coarse to fine. The coarsest is first used, and then finer and finer, the last or buff wheel being covered with soft chamois leather, and no emery used with it.

PART III.

THE SELF-ACTING LATHE.

VARIOUS self-acting and screw-cutting lathes have been already noticed, but I shall here describe another, which is designed as a multi-purpose lathe; inasmuch as many operations can be performed by its aid, which are usually performed in two or more separate lathes, or are not done in the lathe at all. This lathe is also of great service both to the amateur and to the engineer for private amusement and use. I have myself made one, in all essential particulars as shown in these drawings, and have found it answer extremely well.

As there are many peculiar operations to be described in connection with this lathe, it will be necessary that the reader should thoroughly understand its construction. To aid this perception, I have given several drawings to scale, and these I will now proceed to explain.

The bed is of cast iron, and is shown in section at Fig. 130; it is carried upon two standards in the usual way. The cone-headstock is cast solid with the bed, which is much neater than having them separate, and is quite as convenient an arrangement. The boring out of the bearings for the spindle requires perhaps rather more care, but on the whole there is

Fig. 130

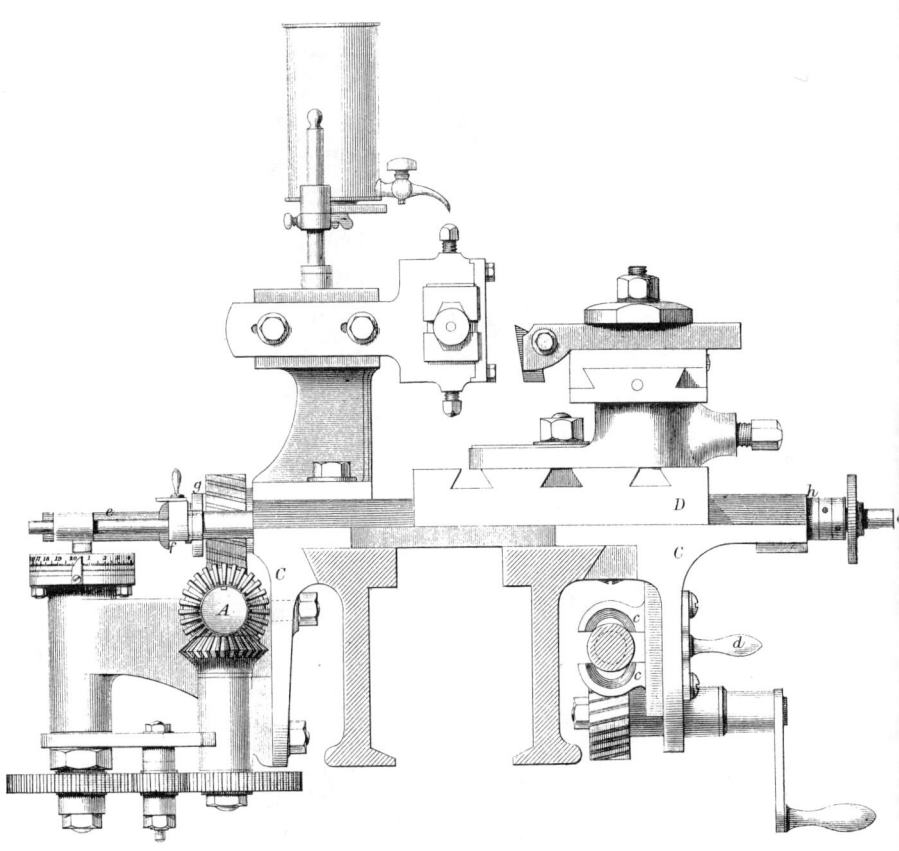

H. Adlard Sc.

End elevation of slide rest
showing Northcott's mechanism
for turning irregular shapes.

Front elevation of Multi purpose Lathe.

H Adlard Sc

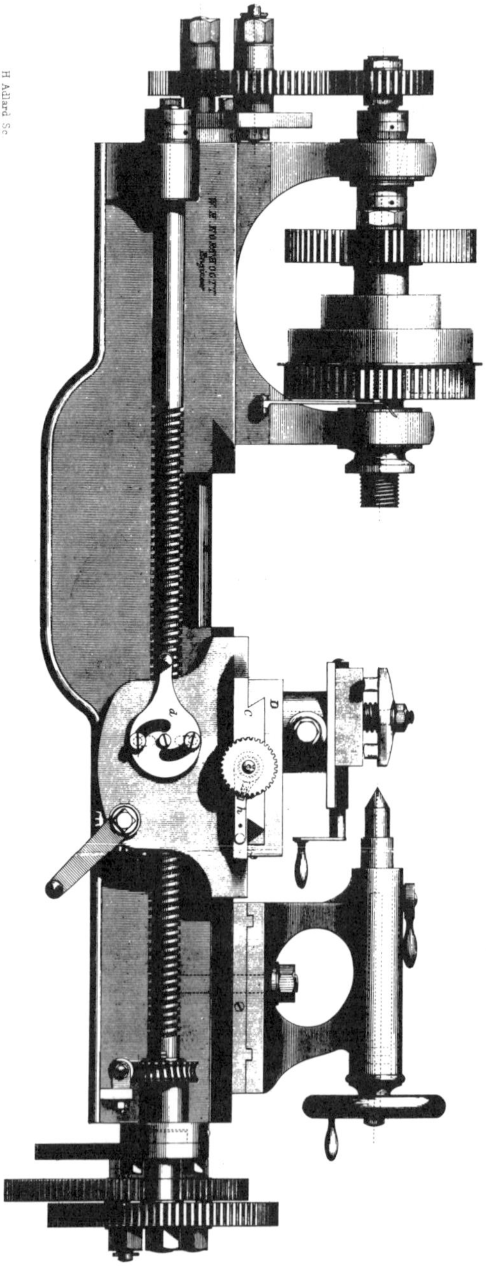

Fig 131

a saving of labour. The spindle has conical necks, which can either run direct in conical holes in the metal of the headstock, or hardened steel or wrought-iron bushes can be inserted as shown, which is the better, although rather the more expensive plan. The front neck of the spindle is solid with the spindle, but the other neck slides on a feather, and is set up by two nuts behind it.

The thrust is taken inside the headstock by two adjustable nuts, with antifriction washers, as shown ; of these washers there should be at least two, and one of them should be brass, the other of hard steel. The spindle is bored throughout with a half-inch hole. The change-wheels are carried direct upon the spindle end without any socket, the nut shown inside being only used as an abutment or shoulder for the boss of the wheel.

The large gear-wheel is keyed to the spindle, and bears against a slight shoulder on the key, which again is prevented from moving towards the neck by the shoulder of the key groove. The small gear-wheel is made of wrought iron, and has a long continuation or boss, which nicely fits upon the spindle, and upon which is the cone-pulley.

There is another nut on the spindle just behind the small gear pinion, the use of which is to connect the cone-pulley to the spindle, when the single speed only is required. In this case the nut is screwed fast against the pinion, so as to hold the cone firmly between the nut and the large gear-wheel—this latter wheel being prevented from receding by the arrangement of shoulders just mentioned. When the back gearing is

required for slow speeds, the nut is screwed the other
way, and slightly jammed against the lock nuts. The
cone-pulley and pinion are then free to move around
upon the spindle without moving the large wheel.
By then moving the eccentric handle, the back wheels
are thrown forward to gear with the wheels on the
cone and spindle. The eccentric handle cannot be
seen, but the motion will be understood by referring
to Fig. 132.

For light lathes, this nut-locking motion is to be
preferred to the usual arrangement ; first, because it is
more accessible, and secondly, because the usual lock
nut, unless balanced, causes a great deal of oscillation
of the lathe, when running at high speeds. The front
of the large wheel on the spindle is turned plane and
divided, so that by the addition of a simple index
pointed as shown, it may be used as a division plate.
This pointer must be turned down, or removed when
not in use.

The outside of the spindle-nose has a coarse screw
thread to receive the various chucks and driving-plates,
the inside has a fine thread for taking the centres, &c.

The screw-headstock is of the usual internal screw
pattern. It has a transverse slide moved by a screw for
setting the centre out of line, and a handle, by moving
which the spindle is held firmly in its place without
shake or vibration. The spindle is graduated, which
is useful as a guide when drilling and boring ; and it
is fitted at the nose with a screw of the same size and
thread as the cone-spindle, to receive all the centres in
common.

The lathe-spindle, instead of directly driving the

Fig. 132

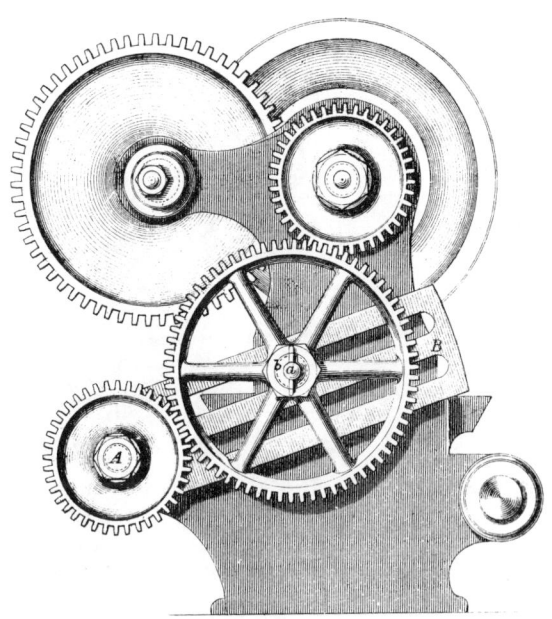

H. Adlard Sc.

End elevation (left)

Fig. 133

End elevation (right.)

leading-screw, drives a shaft (A) at the back of the lathe-bed. This shaft can be driven by change-wheels at any speed within the range of the wheels; usually, how-ever, it will be driven at the same speed and in the same direction as the lathe-spindle itself, by means of a 40-tooth wheel on both the spindle end and the back shaft, through an intermediate wheel of seventy or other con-venient number of teeth. The intermediate wheels are carried on a radial arm in the usual manner; but the amateur may need a word of explanation to enable him to understand the arrangement.

The lug or bracket carrying the shaft has a circular flange, to which is bolted the radial arm (B) by means of two small bolts passing through curved slots cut in the arm, and screwing into the metal of the bracket. These curved slots allow the arm to be shifted some distance radially around the centre of the shaft (A), and thus to accommodate change-wheels of different sizes. This arm has also two straight parallel slots, as seen; one of these is used to fasten a spindle (a) to the arm by means of a nut on the other side, and the other slot is occasionally used to carry another spindle or stud when double intermediate wheels are necessary. This second stud is usually made of the full size of the holes in the change-wheels, which revolve directly upon it, but the stud (a) is made much smaller, and the wheels do not revolve upon it, but are fastened upon a socket (b) which fits the stud (a). The socket is made wide enough to receive two wheels, the wheels being held upon it and prevented from revolving by a key and nut.

It will be seen, therefore, that the radial arm can be

shifted around the shaft to bring the slots nearer to
or farther from the end of the lathe-spindle, and the
stud carrying the wheel-socket can be shifted anywhere
along the slots in the arm. The uses of these powers
of adjustment will be more especially obvious when
screw-cutting is treated of.

The shaft (A) is supported at the other end by another
bracket springing from the lathe-bed, and at the extreme end of the shaft there is provision for taking
change-wheels for driving the leading-screw. By referring to Fig. 133, which is the end elevation of the
lathe, this arrangement of wheel gearing will be
understood. The intermediate wheels are carried by a
radial arm in the same manner as at the end already
described. The wheels shown in place are those used
for ordinary traversing. A 20-tooth pinion on the
shaft (A) drives a wheel of 95 teeth on the socket (b),
and a 21-tooth pinion on that socket drives a wheel of
100 teeth on the end of the leading screw.

There being an equal-sized wheel on both the lathe-
spindle and the shaft (A) it is clear that this shaft must
make the same number of revolutions as the spindle.
The intermediate socket (b) being driven from the shaft
(A) by a pinion of 20-teeth gearing into a wheel of 95
teeth, it is equally clear that for every revolution of
the shaft, the socket (b) will only make $\frac{20}{95}$ of a revolution; and the socket driving the leading-screw by a
pinion of 21-teeth gearing into a wheel of 100 teeth,
it will be seen that for every revolution of the socket,
the leading-screw will only make $\frac{21}{100}$ of a revolution,
and for every revolution of the shaft (A), the leading-
screw will make but $\frac{21}{100}$ of $\frac{20}{95}$ of a revolution. The

shaft must therefore revolve $22\frac{13}{21}$ times to cause the leading-screw to revolve once. The leading-screw has four threads to the inch, so that for one revolution of the screw, the slide-rest carrying the tool is moved along the lathe-bed one-fourth of an inch; it will therefore require four revolutions of the leading-screw to traverse the tool one inch, and to cause the four revolutions, the lathe-spindle must rotate $22\frac{13}{21} \times 4 = 90\frac{10}{21}$ times. Work turned with these wheels would consequently have $90\frac{1}{2}$ cuts to the inch; and by altering these wheels, almost any required speed of traverse may be obtained, as will be hereafter explained.

The slide-rest is perhaps the most important part of a screw-cutting lathe, and it is in this that there is the greatest extent of variation in design. In the lathe now under notice, the saddle (c) of the rest is in one casting; its shape will be best seen at Fig. 130, which is a side elevation of the slide-rest and a section of the bed.

The front part of the saddle carries the mechanism for gearing with the leading-screw. This consists of two half nuts (c), which are brought together to clasp the leading-screw, or are separated, by a curved slot-plate (d), the action of which is better seen in the front elevation. The half nuts are so shaped as to work in slides attached to the saddle; the two screws—the heads only of which are seen—go through the slot holes and screw into the metal of these half nuts. The screw at the centre is merely for the purpose of keeping the slot-plate in proper position.

On the other side of this plate, there is a horizontal spindle passing through the front flange of the rest, and having on its inside end a worm-pinion gearing with the leading-screw, and on its outside end a handle. This pinion and spindle is for traversing the saddle along the bed by hand. This, of course, can only be done when the half nuts are withdrawn from the screw. To traverse the saddle in this manner, the handle is quickly turned around by hand, when the threads of the leading-screw act as the teeth of a rack. Besides this, it is convenient in other ways ; as when the screw is in motion, this spindle is necessarily also in slow rotation, so that if it be required to move the rest a very short distance at the usual speed of traverse, it is much more convenient to place the hand or knee against the handle and prevent it rotating, than to throw the half nuts into contact with the leading-screw.

By preventing the handle rotating, the rest may be started at any point; but when the leading-screw is used, either the rest must be moved by hand until the threads of the half nuts coincide with the spaces of the leading-screw, or the operator must wait, with the rest stationary, until the spaces of the screw come round to coincide with the nut threads.

The saddle-slide (D) is made to have a long movement, exactly at right angles to the bed. It has three dovetail grooves made in it, to receive similar shape bolt-heads for fastening the other mechanism or work to the slide.

The movement of the slide (D) is obtained from a screw passing through the top part of the saddle. This screw (e) has 10 threads to the inch. In front it is fitted to receive a handle for hand rotation, and at the back it has a worm-wheel of 21 teeth, driven by a three-threaded worm on the shaft (A).

For every revolution of the back-shaft the worm-wheel will make one-seventh of a revolution, and during one-tenth of a revolution of the screw (e) the slide (D) will traverse one-tenth of an inch. For every revolution of the back-shaft, it is plain that the slide (D) will move the one-seventieth of an inch. When, therefore, the speeds of the lathe-spindle and shaft (A) are alike, the surface traverse will have 70 cuts to the inch.

The worm-wheel is not directly connected to the screw (e), but is free to revolve upon it without communicating its motion to the screw, so that the slide may be traversed by hand or not moved at all. The worm-wheel is kept in place by the tail-plate (g); but when it is wished to traverse the slide (D) automatically, the sliding clutch (f) is pushed forwards to gear with a corresponding clutch on the boss of the worm-wheel. The clutch (f) is only capable of a sliding motion on the screw, but *it* cannot be revolved without the screw revolving also. When not gearing with the clutch on the worm-wheel, the clutch (f) partakes of the motion of the screw, but when in gear with the worm-wheel, the motion of that wheel, derived from the worm of the back-shaft, is communicated to the sliding clutch, and necessarily also to the screw itself, and the slide (D) is consequently caused to traverse.

There is other mechanism attached to the back of the saddle, but that will be described when treating of its uses.

The thread of the screw (e) is square. It begins just behind the worm-wheel, and continues the whole length of the spindle. The bearing for the screw (*e*) in the front part of the saddle is not in the metal of the saddle itself, but the screw goes through a smooth hole in the larger screw (*h*), which is made with a much coarser pitch, and is screwed into the saddle.

This coarse screw is about half an inch longer than the nut formed for it by the saddle. It has a double thread, and its pitch is equal to one turn in three-quarters of an inch. As just mentioned, this screw is hollow, and its hole serves as a bearing for the traverse screw (*e*), which latter screw has upon it two lock nuts on each side of the bearing. These nuts serve as shoulders to the screw (*e*), and give means of taking up its end play and preventing 'loss of time.' Outside the saddle the screw (*h*) terminates in a lever handle as seen in the front elevation. The end of the screw (*e*) is fitted to receive a handle, and also the division plate shown in place, and into which takes a spring attached to the handle of the screw (*h*). The compound slide has a Professor Willis's tool-holder, permitting the tool to be fastened down on the tool-plate in any position by merely tightening the top nut. The holding-plate can be shifted around the pin in the centre, to any convenient place.

The tool-slide is moved along by hand only, by turning the small handle attached to the end of the traverse-screw. The traverse-screw is held in place by two small lock nuts inside, so that by adjusting these, all end play may be prevented.

If found more convenient for any peculiar position of the rest, the traverse-screw may be removed and changed end for end, so as to have the handle on the

other side. The bottom part of the slide has a stout
pin, which fits into the rest-socket. By means of this,
the slide may be placed at any angle with the socket,
and raised or lowered in the hole, being firmly held in
any desired position by the screw at the side of the
socket. The socket also has a slot hole, where the bolt
for holding down is inserted, which allows it to be
fastened down in any convenient position on the top
of the slide (D). The bolt may be placed in either of
the three dovetail grooves in the top of the slide (D),
slid anywhere along these grooves, and the socket may
be moved lengthwise the distance of its slot, and turned
around the holding-down bolt to any extent. By loos-
ing the tightening screw of the socket, the compound
slide may be removed, and either of the hand-tool rests
substituted. Or the compound slide and socket may
be removed altogether from the slide (D) and any other
apparatus or article put on in its place.

These powers of adjustment and alteration are often
exceedingly convenient, and make all the difference
between a good and a bad slide-rest.

The leading-screw is usually driven through the
change-wheels of the lathe-spindle, but in some cases
it is more convenient to drive it by hand. For that
purpose it has a worm-wheel, geared into by a tangent-
worm, upon the spindle of which a winch handle may
be placed. The tangent-screw must only be in gear
with the wheel when that method of driving is in use.
When the screw is to be driven otherwise, the tangent-
screw must be lowered out of gear by slacking the nut
at the side.

It will be seen that the lathe-bed has a gap or

well, which allows a lathe of given height of centre to occasionally admit a piece of work either for turning or boring, of larger size than the real height of centre. This gap, when not in use, is filled up level with the rest of the lathe-bed by a properly shaped casting.

The lathe is arranged to be driven from overhead by a countershaft, carrying a suitable cone-pulley. One of the arrangements for stopping and reversing the motion of the lathe which have been described is also introduced.

The drawings are taken from a five-inch lathe, with bed long enough to admit articles three feet long. In the drawing, however, the bed is shown shorter, to save space.

SELF-ACTING TRAVERSE AND SURFACE TURNING.

I now come to those operations in which the hand of the operator plays, as it were, but a secondary part, the tools being held by hands far steadier and more certain in their movements than in the previous cases. The workman now has to select the proper cutting instrument, to place it in the most convenient position for cutting, and to set the lathe, or such parts of the lathe in motion, as will move the tool in the required direction. He has then to keep a watchful eye on the lathe and tool until the work, or a certain part of the work, is completed.

Some writers—probably not practically acquainted with self-acting mechanism—have asserted that to work these machines requires neither skill nor previous knowledge of the work, all the motions being automatically performed. Such assertions are absurd and untrue, as, although an inexperienced hand may soon be instructed to attend to these machines, the work produced is of very inferior quality, and of small quantity. By comparing such work with that produced by a similar lathe worked by a good hand, a remarkable difference will be perceived. Not only so, but as these lathes are valuable and require to be kept in good order, it is manifestly bad policy to entrust such machines to the hands of ignorant and inexperienced workmen. For a man to be a thorough good workman at the self-acting lathe, he must have experience, intelligence, carefulness, and patience.

Success in these operations depends but little upon the imagination or taste, and not much upon education; indeed, nothing but experience will enable a man to be a thorough good hand at the self-acting lathe. I can scarcely tell how it is, but a workman looking at a piece of work can usually tell at a glance whether it was done by an amateur or a professional mechanic. This distinction does not rest altogether with the quality of the work, since, although work done by the amateur may apparently be as true as the other, there is nevertheless a different look about it which distinguishes it from that done by a workman.

It is not intended by the foregoing to dissuade amateurs from attempting to practise this branch of turning. Quite the contrary; as by the exercise of greater care and intelligence, amateurs will have no difficulty in producing work which will be quite good enough for their purpose, and, leaving the question of time altogether out of the account, amateurs can become as good turners as professional mechanics.

I will first describe the chucks and tools, and afterwards their uses.

The square centre, Fig. 134, is a steel centre fitting

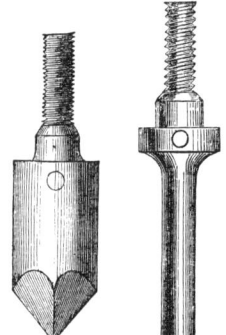

Fig. 134.   Fig. 135. the centre hole of the lathe-spindle and the screw-spindle; it is turned to the same angle as the ordinary centre, but is cut down with four flats, leaving four edges which convert the centre into a cutting instrument.

The long centre, Fig. 135, will be found convenient when turning long small work; it is the same as the others, except in being only smaller and longer.

The standard plug and ring, Fig. 136, are cylin-

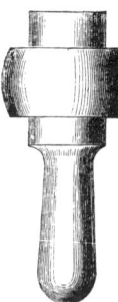

Fig. 136.   drical instruments used in gauging the sizes of turned work. They are used in exact fitting instead of callipers, than which they are much more exact and more certain to ensure uniformity. Good mechanics use them in all standard sizes.

The travelling steady bearing, or stay, is an instrument which is attached to the slide-rest to hold and support long slender metal rods, whilst being turned. The standard is screwed to the slide-rest, the die-holder is firmly fastened to the standard, and has power of adjustment horizontally. The dies are of steel, and have power of vertical adjustment by means of screws.

The travelling bearing is shown in place, properly arranged for use, at Fig. 130. Three or four sets of dies will be found to answer every purpose. This is the best form of stay I know of, but some workmen, instead of the die and holder, use a piece of plain iron shaped like an inverted **L**, and attached to the standard on the slide-rest, in the same manner as the die-holder is in this instrument.

A socket bearing is merely a hollow cylinder of iron, fitted with six or eight screws, and sometimes used when turning portions of long shafts. It is slipped on to an unturned or rough shaft, and by moving the set screws is adjusted so that its surface runs true. The socket is then used as a bearing for the shaft, by being caused to run in the dies of the die stay shown at Fig. 126.

Another modification of this bearing is sometimes necessary, as, when the shaft to be turned has large collars on it, the socket cannot be slipped on to the shaft. In these cases, a bearing such as the last is used, but made in halves, which are put together, when on in place.

The four-jawed chuck, Fig. 137, is a very useful contrivance for chucking and holding work whilst being turned or bored; it is very like an ordinary face-plate, but has four jaws on its face, which are moved in and out, towards or from the centre, according to the size of the work, by turning the screws at the edge of the plate. These jaws being turned out in steps, articles varying greatly in diameter can be chucked without much movement of the jaws. Articles such as rings may be chucked or held by their inside surface by putting them on the *outside* of the jaws and screwing *from* the centre.

There are various modifications of this chuck in use,
in which the jaws are simultaneously moved towards
or from the centre, without having to move each by a
separate screw. But these self-centreing jaw-chucks,
as they are termed, are useful only for circular work,
whereas the one described will chuck work of almost

Fig. 137.

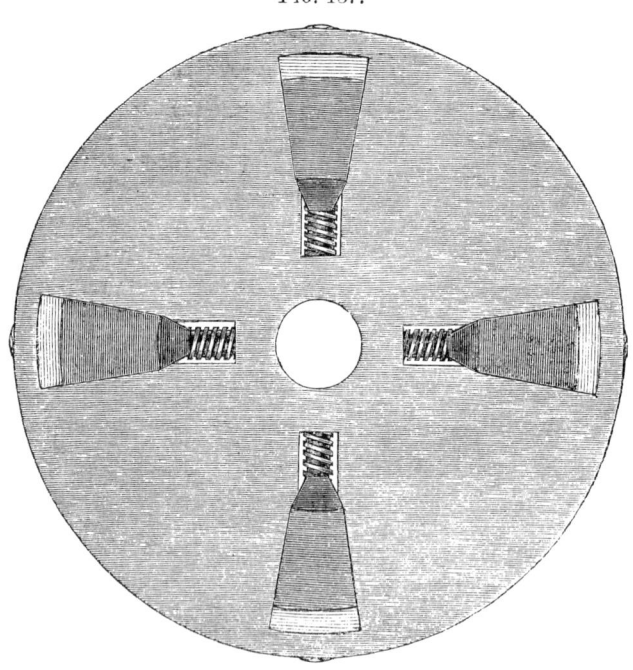

any shape. The self-centreing chucks are, however,
much liked by amateur mechanics, but are not used to
any great extent by practical men, as, although occasionally convenient, most varieties are too clumsy and
complicated to give continued satisfaction.

The tools used in the slide-rest for self-acting turning are various. The ones described have been found
effective, and they are as simple as any. Most work-

ing men have some slight difference in their tools, but the difference is usually obtained without impairing the cutting power of the tool, and also in most cases without increasing its efficiency.

Amateurs are fond of universal tools: mechanics seldom or never use such, and although they are very pretty to look at, their use cannot be recommended.

Fig. 138 is the ordinary hook-tool. Fig. 139 is the

Fig. 138.   Fig. 139.   Fig. 140.   Fig. 141.   Fig. 142.   Fig. 143.

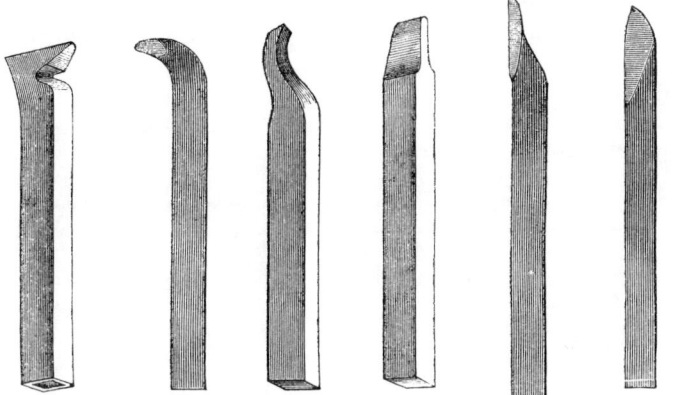

side-hook tool ; these are made for cutting both to the right and left hand. Fig. 140 is the square-nose, Fig. 141 is the round-nose tool. Fig. 142 is the knife-tool, made both right and left hand. Fig. 143 is a simple roughing tool. Figs. 140, 144, 145, are the spring-tools. Fig. 146 is a simple tool and holder, sometimes made with a triangular instead of a round tool. This tool is merely a piece of round steel, ground off as shown. Fig. 147 is something like the last, but adapted to light work ; the tool is made of a flat piece of steel, ground and held in a holder as shown. The cutting

part of this may also be made with a round edge, with
a square edge, or with an angular edge. Such tools
all work very well, and are both easily made and
readily ground when dull. Upon the whole, the
amateur will find these tools and holder to be as useful
as any he can get. Fig. 148 is the ordinary holeing
tool. Fig. 149 is the compound holeing or internal
turning tool.

The metals turned by these operations being those
already mentioned, no further remarks on them will be
necessary; but work to be turned by self-acting tools
requires different treatment, in some respects, from that

Fig. 144.   Fig. 145.   Fig. 146.   Fig. 147.   Fig. 148.   Fig. 149.

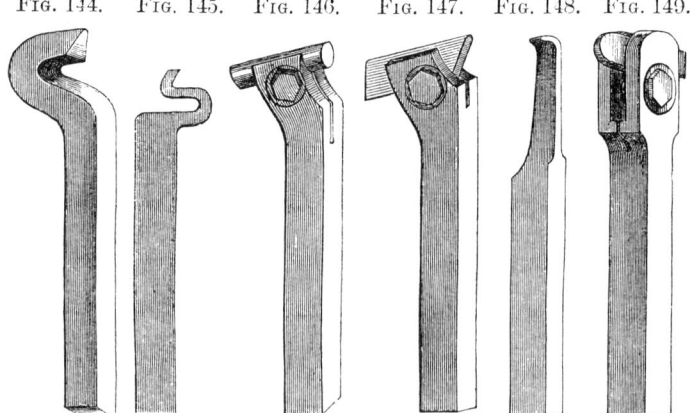

of the same material turned by hand-tools. I will now
endeavour to make this difference understood.

The tools described are all held in the tool-holder of
the slide-rest, and the screw or screws holding them
should be screwed down reasonably tight, but care
should be taken not to strain the screws or damage
the screw-thread. Many workmen fancy they cannot
use too much force in screwing down their tools; they

pull with all their power at the end of a long lever in the shape of a wrench, and the result is, that their screws are frequently either breaking or having their threads sheared off. The tool should not project too far outside the rest or support, as the nearer the cutting edge of the tool is to the support, the better the tool will work; but it is not necessary, if the tool be of the proper size, to work it close to the rest, nor is it convenient to do so.

Slide-rest tools should not be double ended, or made with a cutting edge at each end, as, when this is done, the end not in use seems to be always in the operator's way, and inflicting serious cuts on his unfortunate fingers. The steel for all the tools should be of the best quality. It seems bad policy to use soft or cheap steel for these purposes. Some use Bessemer steel; but, admirable as that metal is for constructive use, it can scarcely be recommended for tools, and, however costly the best steel may be, it is the cheapest in use.

The cutting edge of the tools should be just level with the centres, but the slide-rest tools, for internal turning or boring, may be placed above the centres with advantage. The practice in the matter of speeds varies somewhat in different workshops, and with different workmen; but no exact rule can ever be given, owing to difference of materials. The speeds are somewhat under those for hand-turning, because, in hand-turning, the tools are frequently withdrawn from cut, and so have time to partially cool, whereas, in self-acting turning, the tool is continually cutting, and without any time to cool.

The speed cannot be ascertained with certainty by calculating the speed at which a certain workman drives his lathe, nor even by taking the average of a good number of workmen. It will puzzle many to account for this; but I will mention a still more remarkable peculiarity.

The average speed in large workshops will generally be under the average speed in small establishments, or, in other words, the average speed in establishments overlooked by the master will usually be found above that of establishments overlooked by a foreman. Another more remarkable fact is, that the speed in hot weather will often be less than the speed in cold weather. I will mention that these results are not owing to any peculiarity in the metals, and will now leave the reader to account for them according to his fancy.

There are many little dodges practised by workmen, especially in warm weather, to render the work easier. Amongst these I may mention running the lathe at too slow a speed, taking a number of light cuts, keeping the lathe in motion seemingly with a heavy cut, but *forgetting* (?) to throw the traverse mechanism into gear. I have seen many of these little tricks, and have practised most of them myself.

The power required to drive a lathe when cutting is, in reality, a point worth serious consideration, but very little attention is usually given to it. Nothing causes one to form better ideas of this than having to drive the lathe by foot. Most workmen would profit by a few months at a foot lathe, as with the best of tools the work is rather tiring; but, with a badly shaped tool, the work is still more laborious, and the difference is readily perceivable, so there is a weighty reason for altering the tool to a good cutting shape. It has always been my impression that, with the same power, a larger quantity of metal can be cut off with hand-tools than with self-acting tools; I cannot, however, assert positively that this is the case.

Cast iron and brass are both turned dry; but iron and steel should be sufficiently lubricated. Lubrication makes a great difference in the power required to drive the lathe against a certain cut, reducing it considerably; and also, the cut is much smoother, and the work and tool being kept cool, a much faster circumferential speed is feasible without injury to the tool.

The heating of the tool and work, besides doing the former an injury, is a positive waste or loss of power, as, for every unit of heat produced, 772 foot-pounds of power are lost.

The lubricating liquids are various. Oil is good, but expensive; soapsuds are also much used; but perhaps a solution of common soda in water is as good and cheap as anything. A little dirty oil, or oil that has run through bearings, may be advantageously mixed with the soda-water. Water, if used alone, would cause the work and lathe to be covered with rust half an hour after using; the addition of soda not only softens the water, but to a great extent prevents its rusting the metallic surfaces. Soda-water very seldom rusts wrought iron or steel; but, dropping on the cast iron surfaces of the lathe, and allowed to stay some time, it will frequently result in spots of rust. As, however, the soda-water is not used in turning cast iron, and the bright cast-iron parts of the lathe are generally oily and subject to rubbing, this is not found very detrimental.

Except in the cases mentioned, hand-turners in metal do not often use lubricants; this is chiefly owing to the difficulty of making them fall on the right spot. In self-acting turning this difficulty does not exist, as the spout of the soda-water pipe is attached to the slide-rest, and travels with the tool; it is either carried by a can mounted on the saddle of the rest, or, what is a much better plan, it is supplied through small flexible piping, from a tank or reservoir placed overhead, so as to give it some slight pressure. It should be caused to drop just on the cutting point of the tool, or where the tool engages with its cut. It should not be niggardly supplied, not only because it is inexpensive, but because it can be partly collected in a tray placed under the tool, and returned again to the reservoir. At the same time, it is both useless and inconvenient to be too profuse in lubrication.

When filing iron, it can be driven at about double the cutting speed, no lubrication being necessary, except a few drops of oil on the file.

The number of cuts to the inch, proper for metals, varies from about 100 fine traverse to about 40 rather coarse. In exceptional cases, these figures are very much within the mark. By the expressions, 100 and 40 cuts to the inch is meant, that the work must rotate 100 or 40 times whilst the tool's point travels along the work one inch.

Straight cylindrical pieces of metal are placed between the centres and driven by a carrier, Fig. 70, as in hand-turning. Articles with smooth cylindrical holes are forced upon a round mandril, Fig. 77. Articles with screwed holes are put upon the screw mandril, Fig. 79. Cylindrical articles having screw-threads on them are driven by the screw-carrier, Fig. 72. Large articles are generally fastened to the face-plate, Fig. 120, or to the four-jawed chuck, Fig. 137.

An example or two, showing how articles in metal should be turned, will now, probably, convey more general information than any other mode of explanation.

In turning a cylindrical rod of wrought iron or steel, say twelve inches long and one inch diameter, the *modus operandi* would be generally as follows:— The piece of rough iron should be about $12\frac{1}{8}$ long and $1\frac{1}{8}$ diameter. Knock in a centre mark at each end, as near the centre as can be judged; put a carrier on the bar, and place it between the centres; firmly fasten the moving headstock down in place, taking care that the spindle of the headstock is not screwed out too far, and that it is locked by the locking lever. Now, without further trial as to centrality, put the left-hand knife-tool, Fig. 142, in the rest, bring it up to cut, and just true up the end of the rod. Remove it from the centres, change ends with the carrier, and reverse the position of the rod in the lathe. With the same tool turn this end off until the rod is nearly the proper length, remove the work from the lathe, take off any small projecting piece of metal that may be left at the centres, and knock in small new centres. Take out the ordinary centre from the spindle of the moving headstock, replace it by the square centre,

Fig. 134, put the work again between the centres, and place a tool in the rest, with its *blank* end against the work, raising the rest in its socket until the middle of the blank end of the tool comes about level with the centres. Put some oil about the square centre, and a drop on the blank end of the tool. Set the lathe in motion, and simultaneously move the tool carefully towards the work, until the blank end presses against it, and carefully screw up the hand-wheel, so as to force the square centre into cut. This must be done until the work, in revolving, touches all around against the tool, which may then be withdrawn, and slight pressure given to the square centre alone for a few rotations. The work is then removed from the lathe, reversed, and the other end centred truly in the same manner, after which it is taken from the lathe, and the square centre is removed, and replaced by the ordinary centre. With a small drill in the spiral or other drillstock, drill a hole into each end of the rod, at the centres, about $\frac{3}{16}$ or $\frac{1}{4}$ inch deep. Wipe the centres clear of grit or shavings, and put the work again in the lathe; also put a drop of oil on the centre. Now, with a sharp knife-tool, touch over the ends, and bring the bar to the exact length required. Take out the knife-tool, and substitute one of the tools at Figs. 138, 143, 144, 146, 147. Set the callipers at $1\frac{1}{32}$ inch, and adjust the tool to cut the bar to that size. Push down the handle of the slot-plate so as to throw the traverse mechanism into gear, and reduce throughout to this size. With a sharp tool, carefully turn down about $\frac{1}{20}$ of an inch at the end, to let the standard cylindrical ring, Fig. 136, fit on tightly. Withdraw the tool *very*

slightly, and take a cut over the whole length, to reduce it *very nearly* to the size of the small portion at
the end. Some turners would now finish the rod by
filing it with a smooth file; others would take a very
slight cut off it with a sharp spring-tool, Fig. 145.
The peculiarity of these tools is, that they cannot
' catch in,' they being so made that any extra resistance will cause the cutting edge to spring away from
cut, instead of going deeper into cut. If the rod be
required very exact in size and parallelism, it is not
fitted into the ring entirely by tools, but is left very
slightly too large, and is then ground to size, either
by the emery clamps, Fig. 105, or by forcing a piece
of copper or lead against those parts requiring to be
reduced—meanwhile plentifully supplying the surfaces
in contact with emery and oil—or by slowly revolving
the work in one direction and applying a rapidly revolving copper glazing wheel, held in the slide-rest, to
the surface of the work, and causing the glazer to
traverse along the places requiring to be reduced. This
cylinder or rod must be cooled each time before trying
it into the gauge ring, as otherwise, even if fitted exactly when hot, it will contract and become a very bad
fit when cold.

With pieces of iron very long compared with their
diameter, great difficulty will be found in turning them
in the usual manner, owing to the shaft springing or
receding from the tool. This springing also increases
as the tool gets to the middle of the shaft; and, as
the ends are supported in the centres and prevented
from swerving, the shaft is turned larger in the middle
than at the ends. Long bars are first centred in the

usual manner, and then straightened; after the bar is roughly turned, it will frequently require to be again straightened before the finishing cut is taken off it. Bars and shafts are prevented from swerving in several ways, the most convenient is by a steady bearing or stay, travelling along the bar with the tool, but in some cases it is more convenient to use a fixed bearing for the purpose. In the latter case, if the shaft be not too weak, a small place is carefully trued up at the middle of the bar, and that place is caused to run in the die-stay fastened to the bed. Sometimes, however, the shaft is too weak to allow the place to be turned up true, owing to the great vibration; then the socket or collar bearing previously described is put on in place, and a true bearing obtained by adjusting the set screws. The socket itself is then run in the die-stay. When the inverted **L**-travelling stay is used it must be very firmly fixed, and a plentiful supply of soda-water allowed to fall on the work just behind the tool, not only for lubrication but to wash off the shavings. It is also a good plan to loosely tie a piece of string or leather around the shaft between the tool and stay, and to the stay to keep shavings from getting into the bearing. When the shavings are allowed to remain on the shaft they are very apt to get between the bearing surfaces of the stay and shaft, the latter is therefore forced outwards towards the tool, a distance depending on the thickness of the shaving. At the moment the shaft is thus forced outwards the tool goes deeper into cut, and so long as the shaving remains between the bearing surfaces, the tool cuts a groove equal in depth to the thickness of the shaving. I have seen long shafts completely disfigured by being covered with grooves caused in this way.

The L-stay is much used, but in some respects its action is not at all satisfactory, and this is especially the case with bad iron and small shafts. The ends of the shafts being supported by the centres do not swerve, it is usual to first turn down the end of the shaft nearly to its proper size for an inch or two according to the diameter of the shaft; then to adjust the stay to the size of the first cut, and to take that cut along the shaft.

If there be too much to be taken off by one rough and a finishing cut, then the second cut must be taken a short distance up the shaft and the stay adjusted to that diameter as at first. Great care must be taken with the finishing cut to have a sharp tool, and also to have the stay properly adjusted, as if the L-stay be carelessly adjusted, the work instead of being parallel will be all sizes. If at starting it be adjusted rather too tight on the shaft, or to a smaller diameter, then the shaft, when the stay reaches the larger part, will be forced towards the tool, and as the tool and stay are *relatively* immoveable, and are travelling parallel, the shaft will be turned smaller until the stay has passed over the large diameter and reached the small place. On reaching this, the shaft will not be forced so much against the tool, and consequently it will be again turned larger. These alternate large and small places will continue the whole length of the shaft.

A similar result is also produced when the tool's point breaks off and is left unchanged—the distance between the point and the stay being thus slightly increased, the tool cuts a larger diameter. When the stay reaches this place, having the larger diameter, the shaft is forced deeper into cut, and is turned smaller until the stay reaches the small part, when it is again turned larger, and so on.

Should there be a flat upon the shaft of greater length than the stay, this flat will cause the tool to cut a corresponding projection on the shaft, and when the stay in travelling reaches this projection a flat will be cut by the tool in a similar manner. When turning long shafts made of bad iron, the ribs of vitrified oxide or veins of dirt in the iron will not allow a sharp point to remain on the tool; consequently, the tool, being blunt, will not cut these hard places, and the shaft is turned of an oval or irregular section, instead of being truly circular. I have found it thus; and, in spite of every precaution, this irregularity has been continued nearly the whole length of a shaft, the various irregularities shifting their position as in the former cases.

Notwithstanding these defects and difficulties the L-stay is a useful tool, and with good iron and proper care, the work may be depended upon as being practically true and circular. Its simplicity and ready application to its work are its chief recommendation, and cause it to be more used than most others. But the stay illustrated at Fig. 130 is on the whole preferable, for though it is somewhat more complicated, it has advantages in use not possessed by any other. In this instrument the dies may be adjusted to take the differences in size caused by the successive cuts without altering the position of the instrument. Any variation in the size of the shaft does not therefore affect its central position, nor do the above conditions alter its size throughout the length.

Metal dies are used in the stay, and a set of three or four pairs of them will answer for all the different sizes of work which need such support. The dies are readily removed and others replaced, and are easily adjusted to nicely fit the shaft, without having any tendency to displace it. It is generally more advantageous to let the dies clasp the shaft just behind the tool, as in this position they may be slid along past the end of the bar whilst the extreme end of the bar is being turned; then, as the tool traverses, the dies follow it up and come to the place just turned, when they can easily be adjusted to fit it without even stopping the lathe. The top of the standard also carries the water-can, which is arranged so that it can be raised or lowered and swung around on the upright spindle, and it can also be moved on its supporting arm, which has precisely the same action as the radial arms carrying the change-wheels. The whole of this apparatus can be removed if in the way of any large work.

For turning surfaces the work is either put upon a mandril or fastened to one of the chucks, whichever is most convenient. When the ordinary face-plate is used, the work is fastened to it, just the same as for boring; care being taken that the bolts fastening it on do not come in the way of the tool. The jawed chuck, Fig. 137, will, however, generally be found the most convenient, as with this there are no bolts required to hold the work, and almost any shaped work can be chucked in any position without much trouble. In turning large surfaces it must be borne in mind that the speed of the work passing the tool increases as the tool goes from the centre, the angular velocity of the work must therefore be reduced as the tool recedes in order to keep the cutting velocity as nearly constant as possible.

For traverse-turning the cut is almost always taken right-handed, that is from the right to the left, or from the moving headstock to the cone-headstock. For surface-turning the cut is generally taken in the same relative direction, that is, from the centre to the circumference. The same tools will therefore generally answer equally well for both cases, the straight tools having only to be placed at about right angles to the surface to be cut.

Sometimes, however, it will be more convenient to use the cranked tools for surfacing, and this is more especially the case when the work is on a mandril. In turning up the edges of articles of large diameter these cranked tools are also much more convenient than the straight tools—indeed, unless these tools be used, the work cannot be turned, as the rest cannot always be shifted to a convenient position for using the other straight tools.

The spring-tools, Figs. 143, 144, and 145, are equally useful for surfaces as for cylinders, and they are used for all materials. They are made of shapes other than straight, so as to finish out curved corners and places which would otherwise require the application of hand-tools. These spring-tools for ordinary turning are made from $\frac{3}{8}$ to 1 inch wide on the cutting edge. For curved work they are sometimes used four or six inches wide, and even at that width answer well.

When surfacing, especial care must be taken that the spindle and consequently the work has no end play. This may be prevented by adjusting the lock nuts of the lathe-spindle. When the work is supported by both centres, the spindle is kept from moving endways by the pressure of the forcing screw; any looseness of the spindle in its necks is not of much moment, but when, as in surfacing on the face-plate, the pressure is removed, any movement of that sort in the spindle causes irregular and untrue work. For very delicate work the spindle will sometimes require re-adjusting with the changes in the temperature of the room in which the lathe is placed. Such cases are very exceptional, and as a rule the fewer times the adjusting nuts are meddled with, the better the lathe will work. For turning the insides of articles or making large holes, the left cranked tool will be found useful, but the ordinary tools of this sort are too large for any but the largest work. The tools at Fig. 148 will therefore be found the most convenient; these are precisely the same in shape and in use, but they are made more slender, to allow them to go into deep recesses or holes, without rubbing against the side of the hole.

The auxiliary tool-holder, Fig. 149, is also useful for turning in positions requiring long reach. A tool such as used in it is shown in its place. When turning out holes the tool is frequently raised rather higher than for other work; the traverse motion is used in just the same manner as for turning cylinders. Care should always be taken not to let the tool go too far through, otherwise it will come against either the face-plate or the spindle-nose, and these will be seriously damaged.

If the hole be required of a certain standard size, it should be gauged by turning it large enough to let the standard plug fit nicely in. When the hole is to be used rough or without 'lapping out,' the plug must be fitted into the work when the latter is cold. But if the hole is to be lapped out, the better plan is to let the plug fit the hole nicely, when the metal surrounding the hole is warm with turning, as it will then contract slightly, and when cold will be a little too small; but after it is ground out on the lap, it will be just the right size.

The workman must be careful in trying the standard plug into a hole that it is put in fairly and not on one side, and also, if the hole be warm, the standard must be removed immediately from the hole, as if allowed to remain it will be found that the hole will contract on the plug, and there will be great difficulty in getting it out again. Should the workman at any time neglect this precaution and get the gauge shrunk in, he should not use force in removing it unless gentler methods fail. The best way to get it out is to hold the outside of the article to the fire so as to cause it to again expand, cold water being dropped upon the projecting parts of the plug to prevent it from expanding also. If this be carefully done, the gauge will generally drop out without force being necessary. No workman should, however, allow himself to be thus caught more than once.

Besides being able to turn either cylinders or surfaces in this lathe, cones and angles of any degree can just as easily be produced.

It will be seen that the motion of the rest along the bed is always parallel to the bed, so that with the line of lathe-centres parallel also with the bed, cylinders of uniform size will be produced by that motion.

The motion of the slide (D) along the saddle of the lathe described is always at right angles to the bed, so that under the same conditions as the last the surface produced by this motion will be a plane surface.

By putting both these slides in motion at the same time, it will be seen that as the tool travels along the bed it will also recede from the centre, and a cone will be cut instead of a cylinder. The angle of this cone will depend upon the relative speed of these two motions. If the cone so produced be cut into two along the centre line, the section will be an isosceles triangle with the perpendicular equal to the distance the tool travelled along the bed, and a base equal to double the distance the tool receded from the centre, or the figure each side of the centre will be a right-angled triangle with a perpendicular equal to the longitudinal motion of the tool and a base equal to its transverse motion.

The actual distance travelled by the tool will be equal to the square root of the sum of the squares of the base and perpendicular. Now we see the relation each motion bears to the figure produced, it becomes an easy matter so to speed the two slides as to produce any required cone or taper, by means of the change-wheels at each end of the lathe-bed.

Short angles can be produced in a simple manner, by moving the small compound rest to the required angle, and traversing the tool by hand.

Taper shafts of very slight angle can be turned with the ordinary traverse of the saddle along the bed, but the lathe-centres must first be shifted out of parallelism with the lathe-bed. This is readily done, by turning the screw, the head of which is seen in front of the headstock, and so moving the centre of the screw-headstock out of its position. If the rod has to be larger at that end than at the other, the headstock must be moved from the operator, or from the tool; but if it is to be smaller at that end, then the centre must be shifted towards the workman. One end of the shaft will be larger than the other by double the distance the centre is moved out of line. These sizes will be altogether irrespective of the length of the rod, but the tool is supposed to travel the whole distance between the centres.

The headstock being set, the work is proceeded with in the usual manner.

Some lathes are constructed with a moveable cone-headstock, for turning out taper holes; but these are very troublesome to adjust and re adjust. The lathe-spindle being set at an angle causes the change-wheels to gear badly, and altogether the plan cannot be recommended.

Taper holes can easily be turned by setting the small rest at an angle, and by the method first spoken of—speeding both the slide movements.

SELF-ACTING SCREW-CUTTING.

I have already explained the manner of cutting or chasing screw-threads with hand-tools, and everyone's knowledge of what a screw is is sufficient to enable him to cut a screw in that manner. But before explaining the operation of screw-cutting in the screw-cutting lathe, it will be necessary for me to explain what a screw geometrically is.

The following is taken from Gregory's 'Mathematics': —' The screw is a spiral thread or groove cut round a cylinder, and everywhere making the same angle with the length of it; so that, if the surface of this cylinder with this spiral thread on it were unfolded or *developed* into a plane, the spiral thread would form a straight inclined plane, whose length would be to its height as the circumference of the cylinder is to the distance between two threads of the screw; as is evident by considering that, in making one round, the spiral rises along the cylinder the distance between the two threads.'

The distance between two threads is termed the pitch, or, rather, the horizontal distance travelled by the spiral in one round is termed the pitch; and it will be useful to bear in mind that a screw may have almost any number of separate spirals or threads, but the pitch of all must be the same.

When this spiral is developed, as mentioned above, the circumference of the cylinder, the pitch of the spiral, and the spiral line, form a right-angled triangle, of which the perpendicular is the circumference of the cylinder, the base is the pitch, and the hypothenuse is the spiral line.

Now, the old mechanics, before the screw-cutting lathe was invented, used to take advantage of this property of the cylindrical spiral to enable them to describe a screw-thread. The sides of the triangle, as above, were laid down on a piece of stiff paper, or on a piece of thin sheet metal, and this triangle being wrapped around the cylinder upon which the screw was required, the course of the thread was scratched on the cylinder, the groove cut out with hammer and chisel, and smoothed over with a file. This operation was sometimes modified, but the principle was always the same.

It may appear surprising, but, rude as the method is, screws were cut much faster and much better than one would imagine; and many men clung to the old method long after the screw-cutting lathe was invented and in general use.

The amateur reader may not have thought so, but, in the preceding operations of self-acting turning, screws have been cut. In turning up a shaft, as described, the tool has cut a screw the whole length of its cut. If the traverse has been sixty cuts to the inch, a spiral was described which, if developed, would be a triangle, with a base of one-sixtieth of an inch; and that this is a screw may easily be practically proved. When drilling a hole through a long piece of iron, both ends of which were turned up true, one being gripped in the four-jaw chuck, and the other running in wooden bearings in the die-stay, I have frequently found the wooden bearings act as a nut, and the screw formed by the traverse marks to have sufficient power to *pull the article out of the chuck.* It will, therefore, be easily seen that, in ordinary traversing, a very fine screw is described, and that to cut what is usually known as a screw we only require a coarse traverse cut.

It is evident that the depth and shape and pitch of a screw-thread should bear some relation to the use of the screw and the diameter of the cylinder upon which it is cut. For instance, it would be absurd, where great strength is required, to cut a very large thread on a small shaft, but the two should be so proportioned that both are equally strong.

After a large series of experiments and comparisons of screws in use, Mr. Joseph Whitworth, the well-known engineer, laid down certain proportions for screws, which are known as the Whitworth Standard Threads. This standard is now in almost universal use, much to the advantage of engineers and machinists. It will be useless to detail these experiments, but I will merely state the general conclusions arrived at and the proportions laid down. These are best expressed in a table :—

WHITWORTH STANDARD SCREW THREADS.

Diameters	$\frac{1}{4}$	$\frac{5}{16}$	$\frac{3}{8}$	$\frac{7}{16}$	$\frac{1}{2}$	$\frac{5}{8}$	$\frac{3}{4}$	$\frac{7}{8}$	1	$1\frac{1}{8}$	$1\frac{1}{4}$	
No. of threads per in.	20	18	16	14	12	11	10	9	8	7	7	
Diameters	$1\frac{3}{8}$	$1\frac{1}{2}$	$1\frac{5}{8}$	$1\frac{3}{4}$	$1\frac{7}{8}$	2	$2\frac{1}{4}$	$2\frac{1}{2}$	$2\frac{3}{4}$	3	$3\frac{1}{4}$	
No. of threads per in.	6	6	5	5	$4\frac{1}{2}$	$4\frac{1}{2}$	4	4	$3\frac{1}{2}$	$3\frac{1}{2}$	$3\frac{1}{4}$	
Diameters	$3\frac{1}{2}$	$3\frac{3}{4}$	4	$4\frac{1}{4}$	$4\frac{1}{2}$	$4\frac{3}{4}$	5	$5\frac{1}{4}$	$5\frac{1}{2}$	$5\frac{3}{4}$	6
No. of threads per in.	$3\frac{1}{4}$	3	3	$2\frac{7}{8}$	$2\frac{7}{8}$	$2\frac{3}{4}$	5	$2\frac{5}{8}$	$2\frac{5}{8}$	$2\frac{1}{2}$	$2\frac{1}{2}$

Square threads are usually made double of the angular thread pitches, for the same diameter of shaft.

The Whitworth threads are all made of a common angle of 55°, and are slightly rounded, both top and bottom.

The angular thread is the most easy and convenient to make, but it is frequently advisable to use threads of other shapes, the most usual of which are shown at Fig. 150.

The rounded angular thread (a) is almost always used for general engineering purposes, bolts, and screws. The square thread (b) is used for the largest and most powerful screws; frequently the thread for these purposes is made of the shape of (c) and sometimes of (g). The deep rounded angular thread (d) is mostly used for small slide-screws. The round thread (e) is mostly used for large tangent worms, which are also frequently made similar in shape to the teeth of spur-wheels. Small tangent screws are usually made with an angular thread. The acute thread (f) is used for wood screws.

Fig. 150.

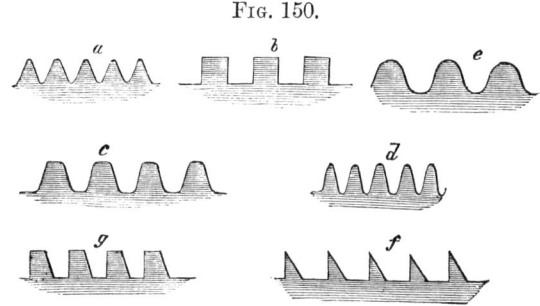

It will not be supposed that because a table is laid down it must in every case be adhered to; but for ordinary engineering practice, where the threads have to stand the same strain as the bolt, and it is necessary to divide this strain equally, the above table will be found useful. It will very seldom be necessary to use a coarser thread than that given for a shaft of a given diameter, but very frequently large cylinders will have to be fitted with threads of fine pitch.

The pitch of a screw is not at all dependant upon the diameter of the cylinder upon which it is cut.

Thus, if a screw be cut upon a cylinder of one inch or one foot diameter, if the movement of the slide-rest be the same, the pitch or number of threads to the inch in length will be the same in both cases. Also in both cases the lathe-spindle will revolve the same number of times whilst the tool traverses one inch. If, therefore, we want a screw of certain pitch, we have to calculate the wheels required to obtain the requisite number of turns, whilst the tool traverses one inch or a foot, the diameter of the shaft need not be thought of at all.

In the lathe here described, the changes, when possible, should always be made at the right-hand end of the bed where the shaft (A) drives the screw, because then the motion of the other mechanism is unchanged.

For all the ordinary traversing and screw-cutting, there will be no necessity for altering the relative speed of the lathe-spindle and back-shaft, there being room for the required alterations at the other end, but for finer pitches than $90\frac{1}{2}$ to the inch or coarser than about 1 in $5\frac{1}{2}$ inches, the change-wheels must be applied at both ends, which enables us to get a traverse as fine as over 1,300 turns to the inch, and as coarse as one turn in 6 or 7 feet.

I will here give a table of the wheels required for the pitches in most general use. It is convenient to have an extended list prepared and engraved or stamped on brass, as it saves much time otherwise spent in calculating the required wheels.

In the table given on the next page, it will be seen that all the changes are arranged for the right hand only of the bed. If, however, the workman requires a

pitch of 100, 200, or 500 turns to the inch, he can easily
arrange this and without much trouble, by putting on
larger wheels at the other end to make the shaft (A) run
$\frac{1}{2}$, $\frac{1}{4}$, or $\frac{1}{10}$ the speed of the lathe-spindle. So also when
coarser pitches are required, he can use any of the
wheels given in the table for a coarse pitch, and
render it much coarser by change-wheels, arranged on
the other end of the lathe-bed, to cause the shaft (A)
to rotate much faster than the lathe-spindle.

Cuts per inch.	(A.)	Driven intermediate.	Driving intermediate.	Leading screw.
$90\frac{1}{2}$	20	95	21	100
60	20	100	20	60
50	20	100	20	50
40	20	100	35	70
30	20	100	50	75
20	20	50	35	70
18	20	—	100 { or other in-	90
16	20	- -	100 { termediates.	80
15	20	100	—	75
14	20	100	—	70
12	20	100	—	60
10	20	90	—	50
9	20	100	—	45
8	20	100	—	40
7	20	100	—	35
6	60	50	—	90
5	60	50	—	75
4	20	100	—	20
3	60	100	—	45
2	60	100	—	30
1	80	100	—	20
$\frac{3}{4}$	80	20	60	30
$\frac{1}{3}$	80	20	75	25
$\frac{1}{4}$	80	20	100	25
$\frac{1}{5}$	100	20	80	20

These wheels will all produce right-hand threads, or
the tool will traverse from right to left. To produce
left-hand threads the same wheels will do, or wheels
having the same ratio ; but another intermediate wheel

must be placed upon its stud, and attached to one of the slots of either of the radial arms.

The operator will not have much difficulty in arranging this wheel; as it matters little whereabouts it is placed, so that it gears with the other wheels. It only has the effect of altering the direction of motion, the relative velocities remaining precisely the same.

The pitches given, although those mostly in use, are not by any means the only ones required, the workman should therefore be able to calculate for himself the wheels required for any given pitch. I have known men in workshops make rather a mystery of their method of calculating change-wheels; but the method is extremely simple, and the knowledge of arithmetic required not very profound. By bearing in mind the following, the workman will have no difficulty in calculating his changes, or the pitch to be obtained from any given wheels.

The pitch of the required screw divided by the pitch of the leading-screw will give the number of revolutions of the leading-screw to the number of revolutions of the lathe-spindle.

Thus, supposing a pitch of seven to the inch to be required, the number of revolutions of the lathe-spindle will be seven, to four of the leading-screw, the lathe having to revolve the number of threads in the inch of the required screw whilst the leading-screw revolves the number of times necessary to move the tool one inch. Knowing the ratio the speed of the lathe bears to the work, it is an easy matter to calculate the wheels which will give these speeds.

Many workmen can calculate the changes required

for any whole number of threads to the inch, but cannot do so for any broken or fractional pitches. In reality, fractional pitches are almost as easy to calculate as whole numbers. We have only to multiply the fractional pitch by any number that will eliminate the fraction, and then to multiply also the number of threads of the leading-screw by the same number, the two numbers thus obtained will be the number of the revolutions as before. For example:—Suppose we require to cut a screw having a pitch of $1\frac{3}{10}$ inches:

Then $1\frac{3}{10}$ multiplied by 10 is equal to 13, which is the number of revolutions for the lathe-spindle:

Also, 4 multiplied by 10 is equal to 40, the number of revolutions of the leading screw.

Again, if we want a thread of $\frac{3}{22}$ of an inch:

$\frac{3}{22} \times 22 = 3$, number of revolutions of lathe-spindle,

$4 \times 22 = 88$, number of revolutions of leading-screw.

When the changes are properly arranged, the work in the centres, and the required shaped tool in its place, the handle (d) can be pushed down so as to connect the slide-rest with the leading-screw, and the lathe set in motion precisely the same as for ordinary traverse turning. When, however, very coarse pitches are required, say anything over a 2 or 3-inch pitch, the motion of the saddle and leading-screw is so fast compared with the cone-pulley that very great power is required to drive the lathe; and the belt will generally slip, being insufficient to drive it, or, if the belt be wide and tolerably tight, some of the changes will either slip out of gear or the teeth will break off. Such screws or spirals, or spirals of one turn in any number of feet, can easily be cut in the lathe by a method hereafter

to be described, the arrangement of the change-wheels
remaining the same.

The tools for cutting screws on wood Fɪɢ. 151. Fɪɢ. 152.
are shown at Figs. 151, 152, the for-
mer being used for external, the latter
for internal threads. These tools answer
tolerably well for both hard and soft
woods.

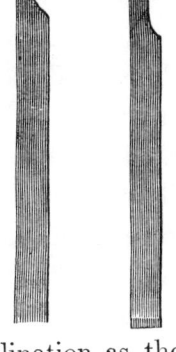

The external screwing tools for metal
are generally made similar to Fig. 141,
the cutting edge of course being made
to correspond with the shape of the
screw-thread, and the front of the tool
ground oblique sideways, the same inclination as the
pitch of the screw.

It will be seen that even with the same shape of
thread fresh tools are required for every change in
the pitch, as, otherwise, the side of the tool rubs
against the side of the groove it is em-   Fɪɢ. 153.
ployed in cutting. For very fine pitches
and fine threads, however, any slight
change of pitch does not necessitate another tool. And although in workshops
where a great number of all the pitches
are in constant requisition, it is not so
great an inconvenience to keep a separate
tool for each pitch; still to the amateur
this is exceedingly inconvenient, as his use
for each tool of any pitch is very limited.
Many plans have been proposed, and are
in use, for making one small slip or blade of steel do
for any pitch, by placing it in a holder so contrived as

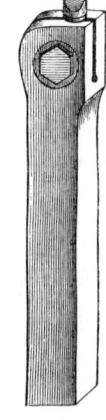

to swivel, and to place the cutter at any required angle. Most of those I have seen are much too clumsy and expensive to be recommended; that shown at Fig. 153, and devised for my own use, works well, and its simplicity can be seen by the sketch. A small piece of round steel, fitting a hole in the tool-holder, is ground at one end the shape of the thread. This being properly hardened and tempered, is placed in the hole of the holder and held firmly at any required angle by tightening the screw at the side, the holder being slit to allow of contraction. Any angle of the tool is of course obtained by moving round the circular piece of steel in its hole.

The angle or inclination of the thread can very readily be ascertained by calculation; but the simpler plan is to place the tool as near the angle as can be guessed, then to set the lathe in motion and cut a small portion of the thread, after which the tool can be properly adjusted by comparison with the part of the thread already cut.

For internal threads tools similar to Fig. 148 are used, but with their cutting edges ground to the shape of the groove they are intended to cut. For larger holes requiring screw-threads the tool-holder at Fig. 149 may be used, carrying a tool blade of the right shape. Or, if the workman wish to be very economical in his tools, a tool-holder may be used carrying the same tools as and in a similar manner to Fig. 153, previously described. One disadvantage, however, attends the use of this tool and holder—it will not cut a thread the entire depth of a recess, as the end of the holder projects into the hole farther than the point of the tool it carries.

These holders are placed in the slide-rest in the same manner as the ordinary tools, and the holders may all be used to carry tools shaped to cut either wood or metals or other materials.

The ordinary working threads are usually cut almost to size with a single point tool, and finished with a chasing-tool or tool of many points, held either in the hand or slide-rest. If held in the rest, this tool should be constructed on the spring plan, as such tools produce better work.

Other comparative exceptional threads are begun and finished by single-point tools : the first cut being taken by a tool rather smaller than the required groove, and the screw finished by a sharp well-ground tool of the right size.

For ordinary threads of fine pitch, whether internal or external, it is a good plan—unless the thread go the entire length of the shaft, or quite through the hole —to turn a groove around the cylinder or in hole where the thread is to terminate. This groove acts as a 'landing-place' for the point of the tool, and prevents the point being broken off in withdrawing it from cut. The same object is effected for square or any shaped threads of coarse pitch by drilling a small hole in the shaft at the spot where the screw groove is to end. If the screw is to have several threads, a hole must be drilled for each. It is also a good plan to turn down a very small portion of the metal at the commencement of the thread, whether internal or external, to the size of the bottom of the threads; this acts as a guide to the workman, as, when the screw-cutting tool reaches this place, the thread is cut to the proper depth.

There are one or two features in the slide-rest which are used mostly for screw-cutting and work of the like nature, to explain the uses of which it will be better to take an example in screw-cutting, and go through the operation with the reader.

Suppose it to be required to make a screw of, say, 10 threads to the inch on a steel cylinder, the screw when cut to be used as a 'hob' or 'master-tap.' By referring to the table, we see that the pitch corresponds with a diameter of $\frac{3}{4}$ of an inch, and if we were making an ordinary tap, that is the size we should turn our steel, but for a master-tap the diameter must be larger by double the depth of thread. The steel should be turned down to this size and to the usual shape for a master-tap. The smaller part to be made the size of the bottom of the thread on the larger.

The turned steel being placed between the centres, take either of the external screw tools, ground to the required angle and shape, and place it in the tool-holder of the slide-rest, taking care to have it as nearly as possible at right angles to the line of centres. The requisite change-wheels being put on in place, throw the nut of the leading-screw into gear, and slowly move the lathe around by the left hand, whilst screwing the surfacing slide towards the work with the right, until the point of the tool just touches the surface. Unscrew the small screw which fastens the handle (h) to the slide-rest, let the index-spring rest in one of the divisions of the division-plate on the slide-rest screw, and move the handle (h) upwards towards the left hand. This will have the effect of withdrawing the tool from against the work. The lathe is then set in motion the reversed way until the motion of the leading screw brings the tool's point at the right-hand end of the work. Now move the slide screw one or two divisions of the plate, bring the handle (*b*) back to its usual position, which will throw the tool again inward, and start the lathe in the forward direction. The tool will then traverse along the surface, and cut a spiral line. At the end of its cut withdraw the tool by moving up the handle (*b*), reverse the lathe, and, whilst the slide-rest is running back, move in the tool one or more divisions of the index-plate. When the tool gets to the end, again reverse the lathe and throw the tool into cut. Proceed in the same manner until the required depth is attained.

To cut a good screw, the tool must be sharp and of the right shape, and especial care be taken that it has plenty of clearance and does not rub at the sides. The lubrication must be plentiful, and the finishing cuts slight.

The tool should always be withdrawn *before* the lathe is stopped or reversed, and its point must not be allowed to come against the right-hand lathe-centre.

It will generally be expedient to tie the carriers to the driving arm, and when a tool is changed, care must be taken to re-adjust it so that it will enter the groove already cut.

The amateur will probably imagine that if he were to cut a groove in a cylinder on reversing his lathe the tool would run back in the groove; but this is not the case. He will find on reversing, that the lathe-spindle will run back some distance before the tool will commence moving; this, as previously explained, is owing to the clearance between the teeth of the wheels, and play of the leading screw, &c., and is termed 'loss of time.'

SELF-ACTING DRILLING, BORING, ETC.

The operations described hitherto under the above head can all be performed with ease in the self-acting lathe; the various motions of the slide-rest, however, afford the means of doing some classes of work which cannot be managed in the hand-lathe. The work in most of these cases is fastened to the saddle of the slide-rest, and does not rotate; the boring tool, however, rotates between the lathe-centres. The required

FIG. 154.

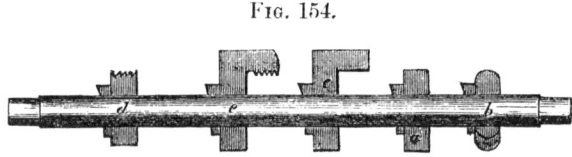

traverse is obtained by moving the slide-rest along the bed, and not by any movement of the cutting tool.

The boring bar, Fig. 154, is the instrument in most general use, and very useful and efficient it is. It is placed between the lathe-centres, and is usually driven by a carrier. A glance at the figure will show the reader that it is simply a straight bar of metal—generally steel. It is centred at the ends like a mandril, and has two or three slot holes cut through it to receive various shaped cutters; these cutters are fastened in place by a small wedge driven in the slot at the back of the cutter precisely the same as at Fig. 116. Several cutters are shown in the bar, to give the reader an idea of the manner in which each sort is fastened in proper place for use.

The cutters used in this bar have only two cutting points—frequently only one—but for large holes a stouter bar is used, and the cutters are more numerous, being 4, 6, 8, or any higher number according to the size of the hole. They are arranged around a boss which can be keyed to the bar in any convenient part of its length; the cutters are fastened to this boss by being wedged in a dovetailed groove. This instrument is driven in the lathe in the same manner as the last. Frequently, every alternate groove of the cutter boss is fitted with a piece of hard wood, which, bearing against the side of the hole, steadies the bar, and, by preventing vibration, causes a better hole to be made than when all the grooves are fitted with cutters.

When either of these instruments is used, the work through which the hole is to be bored is fastened to the receiving plate of the slide-rest by bolts, or by any other convenient means, and so that the axis of the required hole shall coincide with the line of lathe-centres. The work must of course have a rough hole through it to allow the boring bar to be put in place. The cutter is then set to take the proper depth of cut, and the lathe being set in motion and the handle (*b*) depressed, the leading screw will carry the work forward against the rotating cutters, and the hole will be bored.

All large holes should be bored at one operation— that is, when the finishing cut is taken, the hole should be gone through without stopping the lathe, as otherwise if the hole be bored partly through and the lathe then stopped long enough to allow the metal to get cool, the hole will neither be smooth nor parallel.

For boring with the small bar, one of the cutters (a) or (b) is used. The cutter (a) is also used for facing up the end of the hole, or recessing, the same as the drill at Fig. 115. For facing up the boss or sides of a hole, the cutter (c) is used, and for cutting a screw inside or outside a hole in an article which cannot be conveniently attached to the face-plate of the lathe, the cutters (d) or (e) are used.

These two last cutters are, however, but seldom required, and their use is very inconvenient owing to the difficulty of reversing the lathe and running the work back. Nevertheless, with care and patience, these tools will enable the operator to cut a very good thread in the cases mentioned without the expensive apparatus otherwise required. When cutting a screw by this means, the proper change-wheels for the pitch must of course be used to obtain the traverse of the work.

In some cases where the strain on the cutter is such as to cause the bar to swerve from its work or vibrate, it will be found expedient to steady the bar by running it in the bearing at Fig. 126, as near the cutter as it can conveniently be placed.

TURNING IRREGULAR SHAPES.

If the reader will refer to the side elevation of the slide-rest, Fig. 130, he will there see some mechanism which has not yet been explained. This mechanism I have contrived for the purpose of turning articles of irregular shape in the screw-cutting lathe. It differs both from the Blanchard or copying lathe and the Rose engine lathe, and is of more extensive application than either.

A stationary point held against a rotating surface will describe a circle, but if that point have also a varying reciprocating motion, towards and from the centre of rotation, it is evident the point will no longer describe a circle, but a figure whose shape will depend upon the relative motions of the rotating surface and reciprocating point.

The mechanism attached to the back of the slide-rest is for the purpose of giving the tool's point the varying reciprocating motion necessary to produce the required irregular shape.

The shaft (A) at the back of the lathe-bed carries a small wrought-iron mitre-wheel; this wheel is, by means of a sliding key, allowed to slide anywhere along the shaft, following the motion of the saddle, but cannot rotate except when the shaft rotates. This mitre-wheel gears into a similar wheel below it, and which is attached to a short vertical stud or shaft, having its bearing in the casting bolted to the slide-rest saddle. At the other end of the vertical shaft is a spur-wheel, one of a series of changes, any of which may be placed on the shaft as occasion requires. The frame casting also carries another vertical shaft, longer than the former, and which revolves in a long boss forming part of the frame. At its lower end the shaft is fitted to receive a change-wheel, driven either directly by a wheel on the other shaft, or, through double or single intermediates, placed on a socket which revolves on a spindle attached to the radial arm.

This arm radiates from the centre of the longer vertical shaft, and is fastened at any required angle by tightening the nut on the boss of the frame casting. This nut, I may here mention, should have a left-handed thread. The arm has a slot for receiving the intermediate spindle.

The top of the vertical shaft has a large collar or disc, and to this is fastened another disc or iron plate, and these are so fitted as to be quite free from shake, or in fact to be like one piece.

The fastening is made by two bolts with T-heads fitted into a circular under-cut groove in the top plate, and passing through the collar on the vertical spindle. The edge of one disc is graduated, and the other has a pointer attached to it; the top plate may therefore be moved round any number of divisions, and there fastened by tightening the nuts below. This movement is easily made by hand, but, if preferred, the edge of one of the discs can be made into a tangent wheel, and a tangent screw attached to the other. The movement may then be made with greater ease and exactness by moving the tangent screw one or more turns.

The top surface of the upper disc is fitted with a number of holes tapped to receive screws of the same size, and also a large hole in the centre, which is also tapped. The tapped holes serve for fastening a shaper-plate, or cam-plate, to the upper disc, and the central hole serves to keep the shaper-plates in position, by means of a pin fitting into it, and also fitting a hole in the shaper-plates.

The screw of the surfacing-slide is continued outwards

past the worm-wheel and clutch behind, and is there fitted with a bearing on which the sliding-guide is placed, and fastened there by a nut, on the extreme end of the surfacing-screw. The sliding-guide has three holes through it, the central one is the bearing for the screw, and the outside ones are made to fit the guide-bars, and slide upon them. The sliding-guide has also several other holes underneath for attaching various rubbers. The shape of the rubber will vary with the shape of the copy-plate. In some cases the rubber is a flat bar, in others a roller on a small spindle, and again in others an angular point.

On the lathe being set in motion, the bevel-wheel on the shaft (A) will drive the first vertical spindle, and the motion will be communicated to the other vertical spindle, and consequently to the discs and the shaper-plate fastened to the disc. The shaper-plate, in revolving, presses against the rubber attached to the sliding-guide, and this guide will be moved on the slide-bars, and will cause the surface-screw also to reciprocate or move endways in its bearings. The reciprocating motion of the screw will of course be partaken of by the surface-slide, and tool attached to that slide.

When using this apparatus, before starting the lathe, care must always be taken to move the nuts which act as collars in front to the surface-screw, a sufficient distance on the screw to allow of its so reciprocating; should this not be done, some part of the mechanism will be strained or broken.

The velocity of the reciprocating motion of the screw will vary according to the shape of the copy-plate, and its shape therefore will govern the shape of the work produced. The rubber is kept up against the copy-plate by a weight attached by a cord to the surface-slide. The cord is passed over a pulley at back, so that the surface-slide may be moved anywhere on the saddle without influencing the pressure against the shaper-plates, the only difference being that the farther the surface-slide is moved from the centres, the higher will the weight be raised off the ground.

The rubbers should be of steel, nicely polished and hardened, the copy-plates are also best made of steel, but I frequently use both cast and wrought iron.

The surface-slide should be kept well oiled, so as to slide freely, as then the weight required to keep the rubber in contact with the shaper-plate is not so great. No more weight should be employed than is absolutely necessary.

The shape of the copy-plate is not as a rule very difficult to ascertain, but the shape of that plate is not always the shape of the figure to be produced; although for most required shapes, a copy-plate of the same shape, having equal angular velocity with the figure turning, can be made to produce its counterpart.

If we use a circular copy-plate, placed eccentric with the copy-plate disc, the figure produced by a point-tool on a surface attached to the face-plate will be determined by the position of the point of the tool, its distance from the lathe-centres, and whether above or below the centres.

1. It is, therefore, essential in most cases that the tool's point should be level with the centres.

2. With equal revolutions of copy and work, and

when the tool's point describes a figure much smaller than the eccentric plate, the figure produced is cardiod, or shaped like a heart, and this shape will gradually become more decided, and finally become looped, as the figure becomes very small.

3. When the figure is of the same size as the copy-plate, its shape will also be the same, namely, an eccentric circle, and this rule applies to other shaped copy-plates.

4. When the figure is made much larger than the copy-plate, its shape is still the same as the copy, but the eccentricity will not be increased, the motion of the tool's point being the same in every case.

The tool's point describing an eccentric circle on a surface, if this point be traversed by the leading screw in the usual manner, an eccentric cylinder is produced, and this cylinder may be turned the entire length of the distance between the lathe-centres, as in ordinary traverse turning.

For producing an ellipse, the copy-plate must be an ellipse having equal rotations with the lathe-spindle, or it may be an eccentric circle rotating twice whilst the work revolves once. In either case the shape of the ellipse produced will be determined also to a great extent by the position of the tool's point. By altering its position, ellipses of almost any proportion may be made from one copy-plate.

Parallel eccentric circular, and parallel elliptic, and other shaped shafts, are thus produced by traversing the tool in the usual manner.

Taper eccentric circular, taper elliptic, and other shaped articles, are turned also just as for plain con-

centric circular turning, namely, by moving the headstock out of line, or speeding the surfacing slide-
screw.

Spiral eccentric circular, spiral elliptic, and other
shaped articles, are turned by giving the shaper-plate
a slightly faster or slower speed than the work. In
the case of the former, the line passing through the
concentric and eccentric centres, and in the other case
the long diameter continually alters its position at
every revolution of the work. Thus, when turning a
spiral elliptic shaft, if the difference between the speeds
of the work and copy-plate be the one-hundredth of a
rotation, then at every rotation of the work, the long
diameter of the ellipse will be $\frac{1}{100}$ of a revolution behind or in advance of the same diameter of the ellipse
which was cut at the last rotation. At the end of
twenty-five rotations of the work, the long diameter
will have shifted just quarter round, at fifty rotations
just half round, and at one hundred rotations the
spiral will have made one complete turn. This work
is very singular in appearance; when cutting, it looks
like and really is a double-threaded screw or spiral,
and is cut with a slow traverse of the tool. If the
copy-plate rotate faster than the work, the spiral will
be left-hand; if slower, it will be right-hand.

The pitch of the spiral depends upon the relative
speeds of work, copy-plate, and screw. The figure
makes one complete turn in every one hundred or other
number of rotations : the pitch of the spiral will consequently be the distance traversed by the tool whilst
the work has rotated one hundred times. The article
may be made of a tapering spiral-elliptic, or other shape

by shifting the headstock, or speeding the surface-slide.

When the leading screw is driven in the usual manner by the change-wheels, the spiral is formed of one continuous line, but it may be formed of a series of separate circles, by disconnecting the leading screw and back-shaft, and by moving the leading screw a certain portion of a rotation by hand after turning each circle.

A secondary spiral or screw may be cut upon these shapes in almost any position, and either with rotating drills, revolving cutters, or ordinary tools, as is most convenient.

Some of these shapes, both wood and metal, can be cut with the same tools that are used for ordinary cylindrical turning, but in most cases the work is better performed by revolving cutters in the wheel-cutting apparatus, or other frame made to carry a cutter, but without the slides.

The shapes to be produced are almost unlimited, and I purpose giving more information on this point when treating of ornamental turning. The foregoing examples are given mostly to show how all the various motions may be combined, each being capable of independent alteration and arrangement.

The shaper-plate, &c., will not admit of very rapid using, and in most cases it is advisable to keep its speed as slow as possible. When the work is such that revolving cutting tools are used, the lathe is only required to move very slowly; in these cases, therefore, the lathe must not be driven by the belt in the ordinary way, but by the worm and wheel on the leading screw. This manner of driving I find convenient for most work when the copy-plate runs at the same speed or faster than the lathe-spindle.

The irregular shape mechanism is very useful when applied to turning cams, the cutting tool being either the ordinary slide-rest tool or a revolving cutter, according to the shape and size of the cam. They are thus turned far better and cheaper than by the old process of chipping and filing to a template.

Another useful application is to the cutting of curved slots and grooves; this is done by a rotating drill in a frame, guided automatically by a properly-shaped copy-plate.

It will be understood that when articles are to be turned of irregular transverse section only, the work and copy-plate must make equal rotations; when the position of the shape is required to vary, there must be a slight difference between the number of rotations.

By giving the copy-plate a very slow motion compared with the work, instead of the article being turned of irregular transverse section, it is turned circular, but of irregular longitudinal section. For instance, by means of this mechanism, we can produce taper shafts and angular work. The shaper-plate for this work must be a portion of a true spiral, and the rise of this spiral will determine the difference between the small and large diameters of the shaft, and the relative speeds of leading screw and copy-plate will determine the length of the base of the taper-shaft or angle. Thus if the spiral have a rise of a quarter of an inch, the large diameter of the shaft will be half an inch larger than the small diameter, and the base of the angle will be equal to the distance travelled by the tool whilst the shaper-plate has made its rotation.

With an eccentric circle, as the shaper-plate, and with it rotating slowly compared with the work, the work produced is of circular section, but is longitudinally formed of a series of alternating internal and external curves. The difference in diameter of the small and large places is equal to double the eccentricity of the copy-plate, and the length of the curve is equal to the distance travelled by the tool during one rotation of the copy-plate. This irregular shape can be continued for any length, or can be varied by making it tapering in the same manner as for ordinary turning.

A screw or spiral of fine or coarse pitch can also be cut upon these shapes just as easily as upon a plain cylinder.

In these applications of the mechanism, the copy-plate runs *much slower* than the work, so therefore the work, even if of wood, may be run at about its usual speed; and the ordinary slide-rest tools I find to act efficiently.

Eccentric circular plates of different degrees of eccentricity are very useful, but it is not necessary to have a separate plate for each purpose, as one plate may be made with a slot, or long hole through it, and fastened to the disc-plate either by one or two screws. The slot-hole allows the eccentricity of the plate to be varied, which is very convenient, and this is the plan I adopt in my own practice. Many sorts of work for which the eccentric circle copy-plate is applicable will present themselves to the reader's mind, but I will enumerate one or two. The connecting-rods of steam-engines, &c., require to be turned larger towards the middle, and the boundary lines of their longitudinal section form portions of curves of very high radii. These shapes are very readily obtained by an eccentric circle for the copy-plate, speeded to get the right length of chord. The faces of pulleys for belts again require to be curved, and this curve can be given to any extent, and either to one pulley or to any number on the same shaft, by the repeated rotations of an eccentric circle for the copy or guide-plate.

By using guide-plates, of other shapes, moulded shafts are produced. The drawing-rollers of spinning machinery, ships' bolts with countersunk heads, &c., can be turned with as little attention on the part of the attendant as plain cylindrical shafts, the shapes being produced automatically. Care must, however, be taken on changing tools to put the cutting point of the fresh tool in the same place as the point of the tool removed. This precaution is essential.

A shaper-plate can also be arranged to automatically throw the tool out of cut when screw-cutting, and to do a great deal of other useful work, and the same apparatus will do a great variety of ornamental work, but its uses in this respect will be explained here-after.

WHEEL-CUTTING.

To be able to cut wheels is a great desideratum, and wheel-cutting engines being rather expensive, not only the amateur, but the professional mechanic, will find it very convenient to have a small apparatus attached to the lathe to answer that purpose; and as that apparatus is useful for other work, its cost will be but small in comparison with its uses.

The contrivance shown at Fig. 155 answers its purpose well, and is a very valuable addition to the lathe.

FIG. 155.

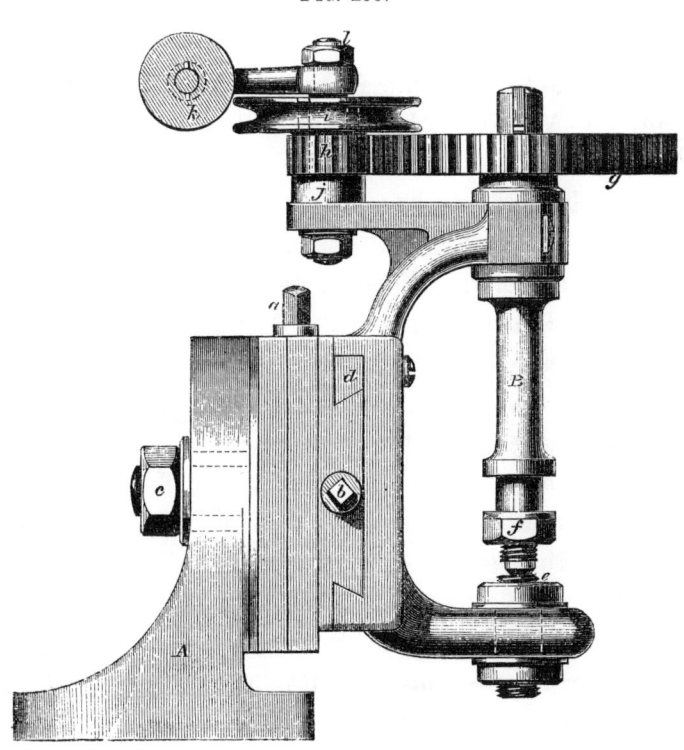

It consists of an upright (A) with its bottom planed, and a slot-hole through it, and two slides at right angles to each other traversed by the screws (*a* and *b*). The position of these slides, with regard to each other, is immovably at right angles, but the slides can be placed at any angle with the surface of the lathe-bed, by slacking the nut (*c*), and moving around the slides; the back surface of the slide (*a*), and the front surface of the upright (A) being fitted to each other, so as to allow of the former being swivelled and fixed in any required position by tightening the nut (*c*).

The bottom of the upright is arranged to be bolted to the receiving slide of the slide-rest, and this can be done in any position, and the traverse of the slides made to have any required angle with the line of lathe-centres. All these adjustments are useful, as will be seen.

Both slides should have means of taking up wear or slackness, by being fitted with a loose strip (*d*). The moving part of the slide (*b*) carries projecting arms fitted with bearings for receiving the cutter spindle (B). The top bearing is an ordinary parallel neck bearing, with a moveable cap, the bottom is a centre point bearing, the end of the cutter spindle is turned to a centre, and rotates in a corresponding female centre in the footstep (*e*). This footstep passes

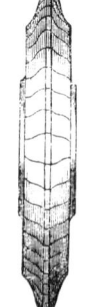

Fig. 156.

through the arm of the slide and is screwed each side, and fitted with adjusting nuts for taking up any wear of the cutter spindle, and preventing end play and *shake*. The cutter spindle shown in place is for carrying a cutter for wheel-cutting in metals. One of these instruments is shown at Fig. 156; it is placed on the spindle and held between the collar and the nut (*f*), a small key on the spindle, and a key groove in the cutter, more effectually preventing the latter slipping around on the former. All the cutters should be made with the same sized hole and key groove, so that they may all be used alike on the spindle by removing one and substituting any other. The top end of the cutter spindle has a spur-wheel (*g*) keyed on it, and this wheel is geared into by a small pinion (*h*) attached to the pulley (*i*). Both the pulley and the pinion revolve freely on the spindle (*l*). (*k, k*) are a pair of guide pulleys carried by an arm attached to the spindle (*l*) in the manner shown; these pulleys may be shifted around and placed in any convenient position.

FIG. 157.

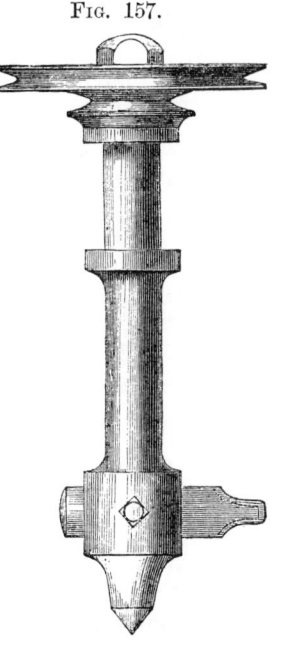

The spindle at Fig. 157 is for carrying cutters for wood; one of these cutters is shown in place, it is merely a flat piece of steel, filed at one end to the shape required, and nicely sharpened on the oilstone.

The spindle carries a small pulley on its other end, and is driven without the intervention of gearing, as a greater speed is required for cutting wood than for metals. This spindle is made to fit into the bearings of the instrument in the same manner as the one shown in place at Fig. 155.

The wheels used in mechanism are termed spurwheels, bevel-wheels, spiral-wheels, worm-wheels, oblique-wheels, and racks.

Spur-wheels are those whose teeth are cut on a cylinder. The wheels (*g* and *h*) are spur-wheels, they are used to transmit motion when the axes are parallel to each other.

Bevel-wheels have their teeth cut on frustra of cones, and are used to convey motion when the axes are at an angle to each other, but in the same plane.

Skew bevel-wheels are very similar to the last, but are used to communicate motion when the axes are at an angle with each other, but not in the same plane.

Worm-wheels are those driven by an endless screw or worm, and are used to obtain very slow motion when the axes are in different planes, and at an angle to each other.

Spiral wheels are portions of multi-threaded screws, each tooth being a portion of a thread of a screw of coarse pitch; they are used when the axes are in different planes, and at an angle to each other, and when the motion is not required to be reduced so much as with an ordinary worm and worm-wheel.

Hooke's oblique wheels are the same as the last. One wheel is a portion of a right-handed screw of many threads; and the other a portion of a left-handed screw. They are used to communicate motion under the same conditions as spur-gearing, but when the motion is required to be absolutely uniform, and without jerk. These wheels are much more used on the continent than in this country. Many very excellent specimens were exhibited in the Paris Exposition, applied to various purposes.

Racks may be considered as spur-wheels of infinite radii; in these the teeth are cut on flat rods of metal, and they are geared into by spur-wheels.

Worm-racks are those geared into by a worm or worm-wheel.

The methods of striking out the various shaped teeth, the relative values of the involute, epicycloidal, Willis', and other shaped teeth, &c., form no part of the present work.

Most small gearing is now constructed according to the approximate epicycloidal method of Professor Willis. Almost all the old millwrights had a method of their own for striking out their gear teeth, and of course each method was considered by its user better than all the rest. There is still a number of different sorts of teeth in use, but whatever shape of tooth be used, the method of cutting it is the same.

The pitch line, or pitch circle of a wheel, is the circle which has a common boundary with the wheel with which it is geared. The inverse ratio of the diameter of the pitch circles of any two wheels, as well as the inverse ratio of the number of teeth in the wheels, will give the velocity ratio.

The pitch of a wheel is the distance between the centres of two adjoining teeth, measured on the pitch line.

For small gearing the pitch is now generally expressed by the number of teeth to an inch of diameter. By ten pitch is understood that for every inch of its diameter a wheel contains ten teeth; if the wheel were five inches in diameter, it must have fifty teeth. The simplicity of this mode of calculating the pitches renders it very convenient, and causes it to be extensively used.

Small wheels, whether of wood or metal, are almost

invariably cut out of the solid material. The wheel is first bored with its required hole, then turned to the size of the outsides of the teeth, and then the teeth are formed by cutting out the spaces between the teeth. Generally the cutting out is performed at one operation, that is, the whole cut is taken at once; sometimes the bulk of the metal is taken out with a plain cutter, and the teeth are finished by a cutter of the proper shape.

Whatever the shape of tooth, it is obvious that the cutter must be made with a cutting edge the shape and size of the required space. And these vary for every diameter, as the reader may see by striking out, with dividers, on paper or tin, a pinion of say twenty teeth and a wheel of 100 teeth. The larger the wheel, the smaller the space. It is certain that a difference of one tooth in the size of two wheels must make a difference in the size and shape of the spaces. This difference is so very small, however, that it can scarcely be detected, and, practically, one cutter will answer for wheels of considerable difference in diameter. The cutters are rather expensive articles, but it is bad policy to use a cutter for wheels to which it is not adapted, for the sake of saving an extra one. They can be bought of any size and shape, and instructions for making these instruments and others of like nature will be given hereafter.

The wheels to be cut are placed in the lathe, just as for turning; if driven by a carrier, its arm is firmly tied to the arm of the driving plate. The lathe-belt is thrown off, as the lathe-spindle is not required to revolve. The division index-pointer is raised to the position shown in the front elevation of the lathe.

The divisions on the front of the lathe-cone will enable one to divide wheels into almost any number of teeth, and other divisions may be obtained by means of change-wheels so arranged that one or more revolutions of the leading screw, moved by hand, will cause the lathe-spindle to move any fractional part of its revolution. But for numbers unobtainable by the ordinary dividing plate, it is a better plan to have another plate divided as required, and placed on the end of the lathe-spindle, the pinion being removed for that purpose. The wheel-cutting apparatus is then placed on the slide-rest, at a convenient distance from and parallel to the pitch surface of the wheel to be cut; and the cutter is adjusted by moving the screw (a) so that the centre of its cutting edge is precisely the same height as the lathe-centre. A gut is then passed around a large grooved driving pulley, on the overhead shaft, under the guide-pulleys (k), and around the pulley (i). On the overhead shaft being put in motion, it is clear that the cutter spindle and cutter will be driven by the gut as shown. The speeds at which the cutters are driven are greater than those at which the same materials are driven when being turned. Lubrication is required for the same materials as for turning.

For spur-wheel cutting the traverse can be got either by the movement of the slide-rest by hand, or by moving the handle (b), either of which will cause the revolving cutter to be carried past the work, cutting on its way a groove, which is the space between two teeth. The slide being then moved back, and the division-plate moved as many divisions as will give the pitch of the wheel, another space is cut in the same manner.

Bevel wheels having teeth which are smaller as they near the apices of the cones, of which the pitch surfaces are frustra, it is impossible to use a cutter which will cut the space between two teeth at one operation. For a bevel-wheel the cutter is of the size and shape of the smallest place of the space between the teeth. The slide of the apparatus is placed parallel to the pitch surface of the wheel, and inclined slightly downwards, so as to cut one side of the tooth first, the division-plate is then moved until all the spaces are cut in this manner, after which the instrument is adjusted to finish the other side of the tooth in the same way.

Skew bevels are cut similarly, the slide being placed parallel to the pitch surface, but inclined up or down according to the amount of 'skew,' or inclination of the teeth.

Worm-wheels are cut with the slide (b) parallel to the lathe-centres, and inclined up or down according to the direction and pitch of the tangent screw by which the wheel is to be driven; the traverse of the cutter being obtained by moving the screw (b). Very frequently, however—especially for those purposes for which the fit between the wheel and its tangent screw is required to be very nice—worm-wheels are cut by a worm-cutter, that is a cutter the facsimile of the one to work into the wheel, but made of steel, and serrated. The spaces are first roughly cut by means of any other cutter, rather smaller than the finished groove, but no traverse is given it, the slide of the rest being merely moved in and out, so as to cut a curved recess, instead of a straight groove. This being done all around, the worm-cutter is substituted for the other, the carrier is taken off the mandril, and both centres are oiled, so that the wheel and its mandril may rotate freely. The cutter is then adjusted to the right height, and to the middle of the wheel's thickness, it is put in rather slow motion, and set into the grooves already cut. By its rotation it causes the wheel itself to rotate, and being forced into cut by turning the slide rest-screw, the grooves are accurately cut, and a good fit between the wheel and its worm is ensured.

Spiral and oblique wheels are the same, and they are manufactured in the same manner. I have cut them in the lathe with single point tools, in the same manner as worms, which in fact they are. They can, however, be more satisfactorily manufactured by circular cutters.

The ordinary spur-wheel cutters are used, and the apparatus arranged precisely as for worm-wheel cutting. The traverse is obtained by change-wheels connecting the cone to the leading screw, and moving the slide-rest along the bed, the leading screw being rotated by a handle on the end of the tangent screw, and by its rotation driving the lathe-spindle through the change-wheels. The cutter is drawn out of cut on its return traverse by the handle (h), as in ordinary screw-cutting. The wheel is divided, not by the division-plate in the usual manner, but by placing a wheel of the same or double the number of the teeth of the required wheel on the lathe-spindle end, and moving it forward one or two teeth in gear with the wheel it drives, for every cut taken.

For rack-cutting the piece of metal to be cut is attached to the face-plate of the lathe in a horizontal position, the cutter slide placed exactly vertical ; the spindle is then horizontal. Motion is given to the cutter in the same manner as before, except that the gut need not pass over the two guide pulleys, but direct on to the pulley (i). The traverse for the cut is of course obtained by moving the screw (b), and the pitch is divided by moving the screw of the slide-rest.

With regard to spur-wheels, they are generally circular, but elliptical and other shaped spur-wheels are frequently required to transmit variable motion. Wheels of irregular shape can be turned by the apparatus, and, in the manner described under the last heading ; they can also as readily be cut by using the wheel-cutting apparatus, combined with the shaper-plates. Dividing the teeth must, in these cases, be done by hand, the division-plate not being applicable.

The diameter of the wheels to be cut in the lathe-centres is of course limited ; but those who wish to cut larger wheels can do so with the same cutting appa-ratus, but by having another spindle fastened to the lathe-bed at right angles to it. One end of this spindle can carry a division plate, and the other end be screwed to receive various sized studs for carrying the wheels to be cut. The wheels must project and come just outside the edge of the lathe-bed, the cutting appa-ratus is placed in the same relative position with the work as before, and the whole operation is conducted in the same manner.

By this means wheels of any required diameter can be cut, up to 6 or 8 feet, but the pitch must not be very coarse.

MILLING OR CIRCULAR CUTTER MAKING.

The very small cutters used for cutting watch wheels are small pieces of steel turned to shape, and portions of the metal filed away to convert the circle into a cutting instrument.   This method is also occasionally used for larger wheels, and for cutters for other purposes, but only in the absence of the proper instrument. The larger cutters, whether for wheel-cutting or any other purpose, are, according to the best practice, carefully milled or serrated in a machine for the purpose. The cutters made by the machine are much better than the ordinary cutters in every respect.   Their cutting principle is almost perfect, they are far more durable, and are hardened with greater certainty of not flying or warping.   Of course, the work produced by them is also of a superior quality.

FIG. 158.

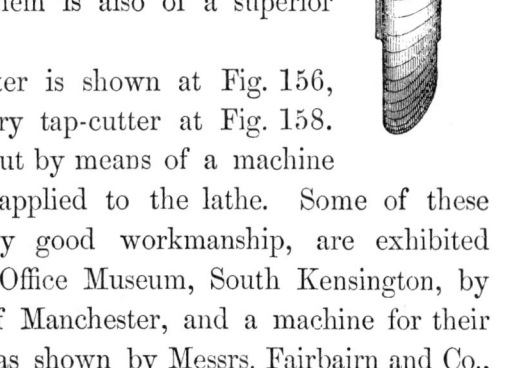

A wheel-cutter is shown at Fig. 156, and an ordinary tap-cutter at Fig. 158. All these are cut by means of a machine or instrument applied to the lathe.   Some of these cutters, of very good workmanship, are exhibited at the Patent Office Museum, South Kensington, by Mr. Bodmer, of Manchester, and a machine for their manufacture was shown by Messrs. Fairbairn and Co., of Leeds, in the Exhibition of 1862.

The contrivance described at Figs. 159 and 160 is different from, and I believe somewhat simpler than, those in ordinary use.   It consists of a base plate (*a*), which is fastened to the receiving plate of the slide-rest by two dovetail bolts (*b*), in the same manner as the rest of the apparatus. The nuts of these bolts are, however, fitted into recesses to be out of the way of the slide. The bottom of the plate (*a*) is cast with a rib, which is planned to fit lengthwise in the groove of the receiving plate of the slide-rest. This rib answers the double purpose of strengthening the plate (*a*), and keeping the apparatus in proper position, with one of its slides parallel to, and the other at right angles with, the line of the lathe-centres.

The top face of the plate (*a*) has two cheeks, forming the sides of a short slide, and into which fits the lower part of the slide (*c*). This slide is at right angles to the lathe-centres, and is traversed by the handle (*d*) at the back of the instrument, the link (*e*) forming a connection between the handle (*d*) and moveable part of the slide (*c*). The top of the slide (*e*) also has cheeks forming the sides of another slide (*f*) at right angles to the under slide.

The slide (*f*) is a casting of the shape shown, and forming a frame or standard for the cutter spindle (*g*). This spindle is of hardened steel, and runs in the neck of the frame, and also in a hole in the lower part of the slide (*f*), as will be understood from the dotted lines.

The cutters are small serrated pieces of steel, forming frustra of cones. One is shown in place, its lower edge is just level with the lathe-centres. The cutters do not screw directly on to the spindle, but on to a receiving piece which is screwed to the spindle, and forms a part of it. The receiving pieces vary in shape, according to the cutter to be used. Some of the cutters are very small,

Fig. 159.

Fig. 160.

and therefore will not admit of a hole through them ; they are therefore made solid, with a small projecting screw, which is screwed into a receiving piece made for the purpose. The pulley for driving the spindle and cutters is placed between the two bearings of the spindle, and being screwed against a slight shoulder on the spindle, acts as a collar to keep the latter in place.

The two small pulleys at the side are merely used as guides for the driving gut, which is brought from a large pulley on the shaft overhead, under the guide-pulleys and around the pulley on the spindle.

If we had to cut teeth longitudinally on and around a cylinder, a simple revolving cutter carried by the slide-rest, and moved along the cylinder by the leading screw would answer our purpose, and we could dis-pense with the slides of the instrument just described ; but the reader will see, by referring to the figures of circular cutters, that the teeth have to be cut on curves of different and peculiar shape. The slides of the mil-ling instrument are devised to enable us to pass around these curves, and their action is very simple.

Whatever shape cutter we wish to serrate, we place a shaper-plate (h) on the raised sides of the base plate, of such a shape that, on the handle (d) being pulled out, the bottom slide shall be traversed from the lathe-centres—a distance equal to the height of the curve of the cutter from its base, whilst the shaper-plate, by pressing against the guides (i), shall cause the top slide of the instrument to move a distance equal to the base of the curve, and in such a manner that the relative speeds of traverse of the two slides shall cause the cutter to describe the required curve.

The shaper-plates are fastened to the plate (*a*) by screws and washers as shown; the holes in the shaper-plates are slightly slotted or elongated, to allow them to be arranged the proper distance apart. They are made of steel, and carefully hardened, the curved edges being also nicely polished, and made as smooth as possible. They should be numbered, and a list kept with corresponding numbers, mentioning the date of make, pitch of wheels (if for a wheel-cutter), or the use of the cutter for which the shaper-plates are required. The guides (*i*) are the rounded and hardened ends of a straight piece of steel fastened to the bottom of the slide (*f*).

In using the milling instrument, the cutter to be serrated is first turned to its proper shape upon a mandril; great care should be taken to have the steel properly annealed. After the blank cutter is turned, it need not be taken from the lathe, but the milling instrument fastened to the receiving plate of the slide-rest in place of the ordinary rest and tool.

The cutter of the instrument alone is set in motion, and the division-plate and index of the lathe are used to obtain the required pitch or spacing of the teeth. The instrument is brought up to its work by means of the traverse of the rest along the bed, and the motion of the surface slide. When once adjusted, the position of the instrument should not be altered until the serrations have been made all around one side, after which the shaper-plates should be transposed, and the other side of the blank cutter serrated in the same manner. The rotating cutter should be kept well moistened, and the whole operation conducted in much the same manner as wheel-cutting.

There are one or two peculiarities with respect to the size of the small cutters for the instruments, and the shape of the shaper-plate which should be understood. The cutters for serrating the blanks for wheel-cutting must not have a greater diameter than that of the curves forming the sides of the wheel teeth, plus double the depth of the serrations or teeth.

The guides (i) may either be round or pointed—if pointed, the curve of the shaper-plates will not be the same as the curve the cutting wheel has to describe. When these curves differ in shape, there is some difficulty in finding the shape of the plate necessary to produce the required curved movement of the cutter ; and a special apparatus will be required to facilitate the finding of the curves of the shaper-plates. It is therefore more convenient to have shaper-plates the same curve as the blank to be milled, but in this case the ends (i) of the guides must be made semi-circular, and with a diameter equal to the diameter of the wheel-cutter, minus double the depth of the serrations.

The speed of the cutters should be from 25 to 60 feet per minute, according to the quality of the steel composing the blank cutter.

Worm-cutters are milled in much the same manner as the ordinary cutters, it being only necessary to connect the leading screw to the lathe-spindle by a train of wheels which will produce the required pitch of worm—the same wheels, in fact, as were used in cutting the worm. The serrations are spaced by the division-plate, as before ; but in this case every movement of a division of the plate not only moves the blank cutter round the distance between the serrations, but moves the slide-rest and rotating cutter along the bed—a distance corresponding to the traverse of the screw for that portion of its revolution.

Fly-cutters can also be cut by the milling instrument with greater precision than they can be filed up. The cutter is fastened in the cutter-spindle, the spindle itself is then placed between the lathe-centres, with the cutter blade lying horizontal. The milling instrument is used in the same manner, and with the same shaper-plates and same diameter of cutter as for a circular blank intended to cut wheel teeth of equal pitch. The division-plate in this case is not necessary, but care must be taken to hold the blank fly cutter immoveable in the horizontal position.

FLUTING OR GROOVING, FACING AND SLOT DRILLING.

Wheel-cutting is not the only use of the wheel-cutting apparatus; it is obviously of use in many other operations of analogous nature.

Many classes of machinery require long fluted rollers, long pinions, &c., and these fluted rollers and long pinions being merely spur-wheels of small diameter but wide face, are cut in precisely the same manner as spur-wheels, and with revolving cutters the same shape as the groove to be cut.

The drawing rollers of spinning machinery also are fluted with a series of shallow angular grooves, and these are easily done in the lathe by a circular revolving cutter.

Key grooving in shafts, grooving taps and rhymers,

cutting square, hexagonal, and polygonal shapes, either parallel or taper, are also easy of accomplishment with circular cutters, the motion being attained by shifting the slide-rest very slowly along the bed. The number of grooves is obtained by moving the division-plate the required distance, and the taper is obtained by shifting the screw headstock out of line, as for taper turning.

Spiral grooves of coarse pitch, spiral rhymers, spiral drills, spiral squares, and polygons, are cut by revolving cutters, the lathe-spindle and leading screw being con-

FIG. 161.

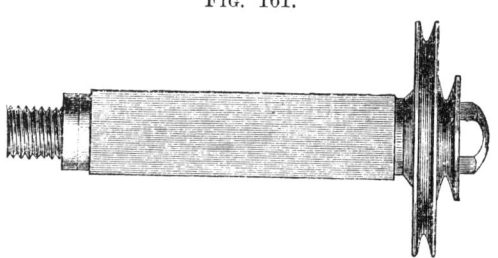

nected with a train of wheels of such a ratio as will produce the required pitch. The number of grooves being obtained by moving the wheel on the lathe-spindle or leading screw, and putting it in gear at a place one third, one fourth of a turn from the former place.

For all spiral fluting the revolving cutter must be placed at the same angle as the inclination of the thread, and for coarse pitched spirals the lathe-spindle must not drive the leading screw, but the leading screw must drive the lathe-spindle and work, the motion of the lathe being much slower than that of the screw. The leading screw is itself actuated by hand by means of the worm and wheel at its end; its motion must be very slow, and as regular as possible. The tangent screw is hinged, to allow its being withdrawn from gear with the wheel when the leading screw has to revolve separately.

FIG. 162.

By using the circular cutter in conjunction with the vibrating slide-rest, squares or polygons, either straight or spiral, can be cut of very irregular longitudinal sections.

The drilling instrument, Fig. 161, affords a ready and effective means for doing much useful work. This instrument is merely a steel spindle, rotating in a long steel bearing, which is made square on the outside for holding in the ordinary toolholder. The steel spindle in front is fitted with a male screw, and also a hole for receiving the various drills and cutters, and at back it carries a grooved pulley, by which the drills are driven by a gut from a pulley on the shaft overhead.

The drills for using in this instrument are shown at Figs. 162 and 163.

FIG. 163.

The flat-faced drills are much used for cutting key grooves. The shaft in which the groove is to be cut being placed between the lathe-centres and held without moving; the drilling instrument is placed in the tool-holder, with its centre just level with the lathe-centres. The drill should be at right angles to the surface to be cut, and therefore of course quite horizontal. In using the drill it is put into rotation, its point kept

lubricated, and a cut being taken by moving the surface slide farther in, the slide-rest is moved along
until the drill has taken a cut of the required length;
it is then set farther in to take another cut, and is
again traversed along the groove. This is continued
until the key-groove is made the depth required.
Slot-holes and mortices are cut in connecting-rods and
boring-bars, &c., by continuing the depth of the slot
until the drill—which should be rather smaller than
the finished slot—has cut rather more than half
through the shaft. It is then turned half round, and
the drill worked the other side until the hole is
through; after which a proper-sized drill is worked
quite through from one side to finish the slot.

Key-grooves and mortices are made in this manner
much faster and better than by the old method of
chipping, drilling, and filing.

Flat grooves and slots may be drilled spirally by
giving the required relative speeds to the lathe-spindle
and leading screw. The same methods are applicable
to woods and all the metals.

By turning the drilling instrument a quarter round,
so as to be at right angles to the face-plate, grooves and
slots may be cut in work on the face-plate—radially,
by having the work stationary, and moving the surface-
slide of the rest; concentric and circular, or portions
of circles, by having the drill stationary, and moving
around the work. Involute spiral grooves or slots
may be cut, by having both the work in rotation and
the drill travelling, the lathe-spindle and surface-screw
of the rest being connected by changes; and eccentric-
circular, elliptic, cardoid, and cam grooves, by using

the revolving drill with the irregular-shape turning apparatus in the manner described.

PLANING AND SLOTTING.

Amateurs who wish to make their own apparatus will find a planing head very useful. There are many varieties of this contrivance, all derived from the planing machines of the engineers. It is, of course, far better to have a small plane apart from the lathe,—a separate or special machine in fact; but this, of course, is much more expensive.

In those instruments applied to the lathe, the slide of the rest is generally used as the plane slide, and to this is attached the work, the tool being carried by a frame with a slide for obtaining its side traverse. All the tool frames I have seen are much too heavy and clumsy—so much so as to make it almost necessary to use a block and tackle to take them on and off the bed. Another variety of planing apparatus has revolving cutters instead of the ordinary tool. This instrument cannot, however, be recommended.

One of the uses to which a planing apparatus is often applied is to plane the V-slides of the various chucks and cutting instruments, and in order that these may be so planed, the tool must be carried by a swivelling head, or a head which will enable the tool-slide to be placed at any required angle.

The contrivance shown at Fig. 164 is designed for use with the lathe shown at Figs. 130, &c.

It consists of a hollow cast-iron frame, or tool head, which is planed to fit on the lathe-bed, where it is firmly bolted; it is, of course, removable at pleasure. The box frame terminates in front in a circular flange, to which is bolted the slide-head, this also is circular; the bolts fastening the two together have dovetail heads, and fit into a circular dovetail groove cut in the back part of the slide head. The bolts come through the flange, and are then fitted with nuts,

FIG. 164.

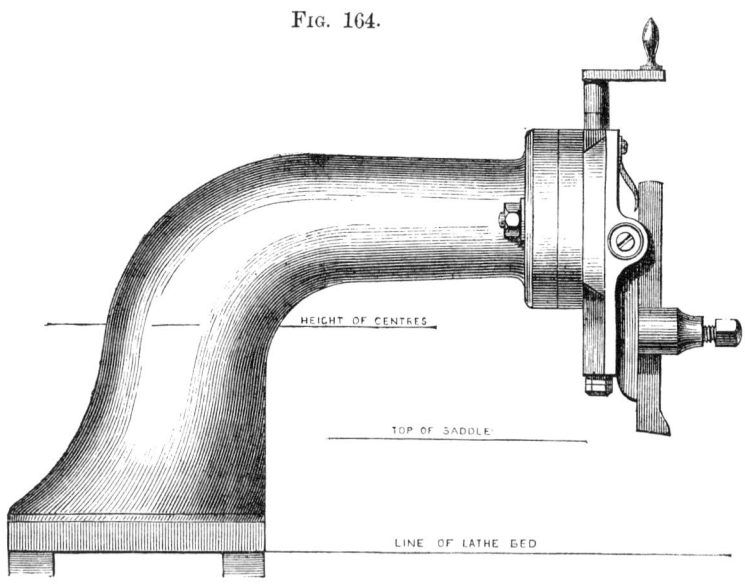

HEIGHT OF CENTRES

TOP OF SADDLE

LINE OF LATHE BED

as will be seen. It will easily be understood that the slide-head can be turned around in either direction, and to any extent without difficulty, as the dovetail heads of the bolts will slide in the circular groove, and are not at all affected by the rotation of the slide-head. The tool is held by a swivelling slot tool-holder, moving on hinges or centres, which allows the tool to rise on the return stroke, and prevents damage to the point of the tool. The holder is attached to the tool slide, and the slide can be traversed by moving the screw-handle seen on the top.

Small work can be conveniently attached to the slide plate of the rest by being held in a planing machine vice bolted to the receiving plate, instead of the compound slide-rest. Larger articles are fastened to the plate by bolts in a manner depending upon the shape of the article.

The ordinary slide-rest tools are used with the apparatus, some few special ones being occasionally necessary for particular work. The article to be planed having been fastened to the receiving plate of the slide-rest, the rest is moved backwards and forwards under the tool, the depth of cut and vertical traverse being given by turning the handle of the tool slide, and the horizontal traverse obtained by moving the handle of the surfacing slide of the rest. When cutting V-slides and angles, the tool slide must be placed at the required angle by moving around the slide-head. The depth of cut is then given sideways by moving the slide-rest screw, the traverse being obtained by moving the handle of the plane slide.

All movement into cut must be given between the termination of the return stroke of the work, and the commencement of the cutting stroke, and not before, as the tool would have to rub back against its cut, which is to be avoided. The various traverses can easily be made self-acting if necessary, but that I leave to the ingenuity of the amateur. The speed for cutting should be rather less than when turning. Wrought iron and steel require the same lubrication as for turning.

So far as the plane-head is concerned, a cheaper apparatus can be used, inasmuch as the head-slide and tool-holder can be dispensed with, and the small compound slide-rest and its holder attached to the flange of the frame. This is not quite so complete; nevertheless, I can vouch for its answering. It also can be adjusted to cut at any angle, and it has the additional advantage of allowing of the adjustment of the slide for position and height.

Hitherto I have only spoken of the plane-head and the slide, and mentioned that the work must be traversed backwards and forwards under the tool; this traverse, of course, can be obtained from the screw, but to do so is inconvenient and inadvisable. It should be obtained from a crank arm with adjustable throw, and forming part of a large wheel of about 12 inches diameter, fastened horizontally on the bed, and geared into by a small pinion of about twenty teeth, on a spindle, having a small pulley for receiving motion from the overhead shaft, by means of a leather belt or a gut line. The crank arm is connected to the saddle by means of a strong connecting-rod.

The most convenient manner for using the apparatus is to place the plane-head near the cone-headstock with the slide projecting towards the right hand, the crank-wheel is placed between the slide-rest and the screw headstock. The travel of the work is of course forwards and backwards, a distance equal to double the eccentricity of the crank arm. The throw of the crank should always be adjusted to give the saddle a traverse equal only to the length of the work to be cut.

It is easy to combine the plane-head and the traverse

mechanism in one, but this is not so convenient as having them separate, because the traverse mechanism is useful for other purposes. For instance, with the traverse apparatus and one of the tools, such as Fig. 165, placed in the slide-rest, slotting or paring may be

Fig. 165.

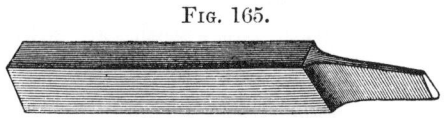

efficiently accomplished on work fastened to the face-plate of the lathe. The circular motion of the lathe, and the straight line motion of the saddle-slide, allow a variety of useful work to be done which would otherwise require the laborious use of the chipping chisel and file. Amongst such work, I may mention cutting key-way in the holes of wheels, and other articles, paring the curved parts of the bosses of levers, that will not admit of being turned, shaping the edges of work that cannot conveniently be fastened to the slide-rest and planed.

The traverse mechanism is also useful in conjunction with the drilling frame for slot-drilling, &c.

ATTENTION TO LATHE AND REPAIRING TOOLS, etc.

Lathes and tools, being subjected to usage and wear, need care and attention to prevent unnecessary damage, and occasional renovation to repair the deterioration resulting from ordinary wear.

The wearing surfaces of the slides should be kept lubricated with good clean oil, and dust or grit of any sort prevented getting about them. However much care be taken, it is not possible to keep off all dust ; it is, therefore, advisable to occasionally take apart the wearing surfaces, and clean off all the oil and dust adhering to them, taking care to well lubricate them before again setting to work.

Proper holes should be made to allow of easy application of the oil, and these holes should always be kept open and free from dirt, as otherwise they are worse than useless.

It is especially difficult to prevent grit getting between the surfaces of the slide-rest and bed ; but this must be done as much as possible, or the surface will soon become scratched with deep lines, and also ' untrue.'

Soda-water does not rust wrought iron, but if allowed to remain on un-oiled cast iron for any length of time, rust will be formed ; this, if not allowed to get very deep, may be rubbed off with a piece of oily waste, without leaving any disfiguration.

The various slides of the lathe and rest should be tightened up as soon as they wear slack and begin to vibrate, all well-made lathes having their slides provided with loose cheeks and side screws for the purpose of taking up the wear.

The necks of the lathe-spindle must also be screwed together whenever the spindle begins to vibrate, or give endways against the cut.

As a rule, all meddling with the adjustable parts of the lathe is to be avoided, and no change made unless required, which, with proper usage, will in every part be very seldom.

The lathe-centres must occasionally be looked to, and a spare set kept on hand. With use the stationary centre will get blunt, and they both, even with care, will sometimes get broken off; they will then need re-turning, and to that end must be first annealed, and then screwed into the lathe-spindle and turned to a gauge. The proper angle must always be retained; they must not, therefore, be turned at random, but turned carefully until they fit a thin sheet steel gauge made to the right angle. They must then be hardened and tempered, after which, placed again in the centre hole of the spindle, to see whether they run true.

It will sometimes happen that they were not screwed up quite tight when being turned, or that a bit of dirt was between the surfaces that should have been in close contact, and sometimes the centre will warp in the hardening. In either of these cases, on the centres being returned to the lathe-spindle, and set in motion, it will be found that their points will not run true, but will be eccentric or erratic. An untrue centre in the lathe-spindle would cause the work turned on it to be eccentric to the centre mark, so that when changed end for end, the turned part will run eccentric, and the shaft will be untrue.

An untrue centre in the screw-spindle may or may not make any difference; this depends on the position of the point when in its place. If the point of the untrue centre and the point of the proper centre be in a vertical line, the work will be either very slightly raised or lowered, and very little, if any, difference be made to it; but if that line be horizontal, the work turned between the centres will be either rather larger or rather smaller at that end than at the other.

Should a tool or drill break off, and become much damaged, it must be annealed, and brought to shape roughly again by forging or filing, after which it is hardened and tempered, and ground again to the right shape for use.

Most of the ordinary tools are hardened and tempered at one heating, the tool being made red-hot for some distance, and the cutting part only quenched in water, the heat in the remaining part being generally quite sufficient to reduce the steel until the proper coloured oxide is formed. When the end of the tool is quenched, it is usual, on drawing it out of the water, to rub the hardened part quickly on a piece of brick, as this brightens it somewhat, and allows the colours to be better observed. When the required colour appears the whole tool is quenched in the cooling trough. Other more delicate tools are first hardened altogether, and then tempered by being held on a lump of hot iron until the colour appears, when they are again immediately immersed.

Circular cutters require that the water of the cooling trough should be still, and not oscillating or in waves ; the hot cutters must also be immersed flatly and moved quickly but steadily up and down under the water. They are best held by a three-branched spring made of wire, and passed through the hole ; the wire does not interfere with the cooling, as it allows the water free access to the hole, which is a great desideratum, as otherwise the contraction is unequal, and the cutter frequently either warps out of truth or flies—that is, cracks. These cutters require to be carefully tempered, but, so far as my experience goes, it makes no difference whether they are tempered by being placed on a hot lump of iron, or immersed in oil and 'blazed off.'

Emery glazing-wheels, when worn smooth, are renovated by first washing off all the remaining emery, then coating with good glue, and rolling in emery of the required degree of fineness. When the glue is dry the wheel is again ready for use.

PART IV.

THE ORNAMENTAL LATHE.

As mentioned before, the ornamental lathe is very similar to a hand-tool lathe with slide-rest, its chief difference being in the addition of certain appliances, to facilitate and make more convenient the application

FIG. 166.

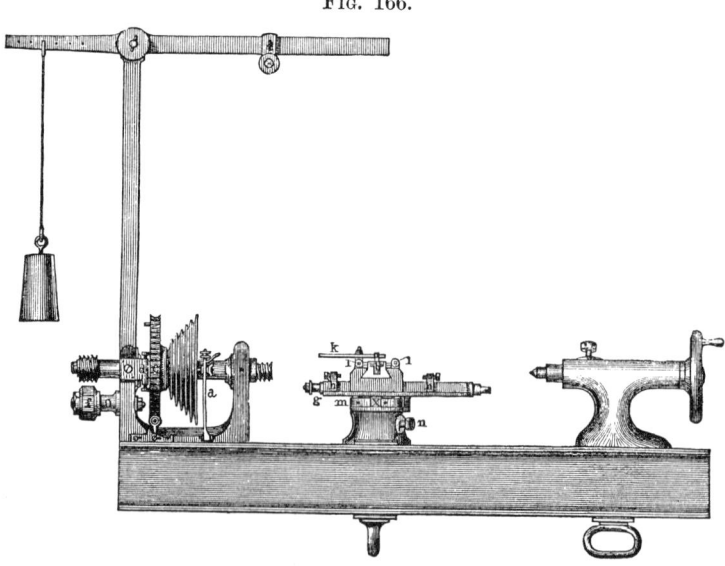

of the various ornamental apparatus. The bed of the lathe, Fig. 166, is of metal, and supported on two cast-iron standards, which it is unnecessary to show in the illustration. These standards carry the cranked shaft with driving cone, and also the treadle.

Sometimes these lathes are fitted with chains for communicating the motion of the treadle to the crank, and sometimes with the ordinary connecting-rod. They are seldom driven by other than foot power; and as the power required is as a rule very slight, the working parts are made no stronger than is necessary to resist vibration. The driving pulleys are usually two, both placed on the crank-shaft; these pulleys are always grooved, and the gut required to drive them seldom exceeds three-sixteenths in diameter, and one-eighth inch gut is sufficient for the over-head motion. These guts are either nicely spliced or jointed by hooks made specially for the purpose. The former plan is considered the neatest, but the latter is most convenient, as it can be unhooked so readily; also, as the guts require to be of different lengths for the overhead apparatus, a short length can be hooked on or taken off as required.

The large cone-pulley is used to drive the lathe-spindle; the smaller cone is generally employed to drive the various cutting instruments through the over-head motion. Sometimes the lathe only requires to be driven, sometimes the cutting instruments only, and occasionally both are set in motion at the same time.

The screw headstock is very similar to the one already described, only of a much lighter construction; it is sometimes fitted with a hand-wheel, and sometimes with a hole and pin. It can be moved along the bed and fastened at any place required by turning the hand-screw underneath the bed.

The cone-headstock is of somewhat peculiar construction. The spindle has on it the usual cone, and this cone has its front edge divided into several lines of divisions; at each of these divisions there is a small hole drilled, and the pointer (a) has a small pin on its top to fit into these holes. The index-pointer is so made that it may, when not in use, be shifted out of the way without the trouble of removing it altogether; and it also has the power of adjustment by means of a screw and nut. By moving this screw around, the point of the instrument is either raised or lowered, and this power of adjustment is very useful in ornamental operations.

These lathes are seldom fitted with double gearing, as the nature of the work is not such as to require great power. Slowness of motion is, however, frequently necessary; but that is obtained by means of the tangent screw (b) working into corresponding teeth cut on the edge of the wheel (c). This wheel is termed the segment divider, and has another use assigned to it. It is perforated with seventy-two holes at the side, and into these holes is sometimes fitted one or two pins in such position that the lathe in rotating will cause them to come in contact with the segment stop (d), and so prevent the lathe-spindle making more than a certain portion of a revolution.

The segment stop (d) also has a power of adjustment by means of the screws shown, so that should a movement be required to commence or end at a point on the work represented by a space on the segment wheel between two divisions, these screws can be so moved up or down as to meet the segment pin and terminate or commence the motion at the required point.

The segment stop and this power of adjustment are both very useful, and are frequently required. It is a distinct apparatus to the division plate of the lathe, and is used for a different purpose.

The lathe-spindle has also another appliance, which gives it a very useful motion, usually called a traversing or pumping motion ; and lathe-spindles so constructed are termed traversing mandrils. The spindle itself is made of hard steel, and is for some length, in addition to the part that runs in the bearings, turned perfectly cylindrical and parallel. Any part of this parallel portion will therefore pass into the hardened steel bearings of the spindle, and will fit the bearings equally well. At the back of the spindle, a little distance after it has passed through the second bearing, it is turned down rather smaller to receive certain sockets, which sockets have on their outside surface spiral grooves, or grooves of wavy curves. Just below the spindle is a small arbor or stud for carrying a piece of steel peculiarly shaped. Its edge is formed of the concave halves of circles, and each of these curved parts is fitted with a screw-thread of an inclination corresponding to the spiral cut on the various sockets fitting on the end of the lathe-spindle. The arbor carrying this set of nuts or half-circles of screw-threads is made to have a certain amount of vertical motion to bring the corresponding threads of the socket and half nuts either into contact or out of reach of each other.

These two screwed parts being brought into contact it will be readily seen that they will act precisely as an ordinary screw and nut. The nut being held stationary, any rotation of the lathe-spindle causing the screw socket to rotate, will cause the spindle to move or traverse forwards or backwards longitudinally in its bearings, according to the direction of rotation and inclination of the thread. Thus, supposing the screw-thread to be right-handed, a forward rotary motion of the spindle will cause the spindle to traverse outwards towards the other headstock.

It is of course necessary, when the lathe is working in this manner, that the motion should be slow ; indeed, it is generally pulled round by hand, and when the spindle has traversed, either as far as required or so far as the length of the screw-threads will allow, it is caused to move backwards by reversing the direction of rotation, and moving it around by hand in the contrary direction.

It is also necessary, when the spindle has this motion, that all obstructions to its motion should be removed. The index-pointer must be turned downwards, and the tangent screw must be lowered out of gear with the worm-wheel. When this motion is not in use it is evidently necessary to have some means of holding the spindle steady, and prevent longitudinal motion of any sort. This is effected by removing the screw guide from the lathe-spindle and substituting a plain socket larger than the hole of the spindle bearing, which therefore acts as a collar, and prevents the spindle moving endways.

The slide-rest can be moved from the bed and the hand-rest put in its place. The hand-tool rest and holder is very much the same as the ones already described. They do not, therefore, require further illustration or description.

The slide-rest, in its essential particulars and move-

ments, is also the same as those already described ;
but as it possesses many little points which the others
have not, it will be necessary to give some explanation
of it.

In the first place, it fits into a separate slide, which
is fitted to slide along the bed lengthways between
the longitudinal bars forming the bed. This slide allows
the corresponding part of the slide-rest to be placed
into it and the whole rest moved as near to or far from
the line of centres as the nature of the work makes
convenient. And, however placed, it always retains its
parallelism with the face-plate of the lathe. The rest
is fastened down to the bed by a hand-screw underneath the bed, the same as the shifting headstock.

The two slides of the rest are permanently fixed
at right angles to each other, and cannot be altered.
The bottom slide, it will be seen, is by far the longer,
and this is fitted with a screw for causing the top
slide to traverse along it. This screw has a pitch of ten
threads to the inch, so that one turn of it will cause
the slide to be moved exactly one-tenth of an inch, it
also has a small division-index at one end for smaller
or more convenient measurements. The index-plate is
divided into twenty divisions, but marked at every
other division, so there are only ten marked divisions.
The screw being moved the distance shown by one
marked division, the slide will be moved only the one-
tenth of the space which it would have been moved
by a complete turn or $\frac{1}{100}$ of an inch, and if moved
only one division the slide will only traverse the $\frac{1}{200}$
of an inch. The screw may be also fitted with tangent
screw and pulley for driving from overhead.

P

At the other end the screw is prolonged through the metal of the slide, and is turned to receive various spur-wheels, which are required in some of the ornamental operations. There are also on the slide two move-able stops (*h*), each having screw adjustment, as will be seen. These stops are required to determine the travel of the slide, or to allow the tool to traverse only within certain required limits.

The top slide is a short one, and is not traversed by a screw in the usual manner, but it has two screws (*i i*); the left-hand one being shorter than the other, this determines the depth of the penetration of the tool ; the other side screw is used to govern the movement of the slide, which is usually forced into and withdrawn from cut by means of the lever (*k*).

The tools are held in the groove cut in the internal slide, and are fastened down by two screws (*l*), as will be seen by the illustration. This tool-slide can be readily removed by sliding it out endways and any other slide put in its place.

The two side screws are also made with a pitch of ten threads to the inch, and the heads of the screws are used as indices, being divided around their edges. There is also means of adjusting the tools to the exact height of centre, by shifting round the nut (*m*) at the bottom of the slides.

This long slide may be placed either parallel to the line of centres for cylinder turning, or at right angles to it for surface turning, and there are stops placed below, so that when the rest is shifted around to touch one of these stops, it is perfectly parallel, and when in contact with the other stop it is exactly at right angles. Any intermediate angle can be obtained according to the divisions marked on the socket, and the whole slide is fastened firmly at its required angular position by tightening the screw (*n*).

The groove in the tool-slide is made large enough to receive the socket of the various ornamental instruments to be used with the slide-rest; but as the tools are most of them much smaller than these, there are grooved receivers, fitting the groove of the tool-rest slide, but having grooves in them to take the various smaller tools.

At the back of the lathe, there is generally a shelf or board about level with the bed, and this is very convenient for resting the various tools and instruments upon, whilst not in use but only temporarily laid aside. There is also in some lathes a set of drawers for keeping the various tools and chucks, &c. And in this arrangement the whole is contained in one, which is an advantage in some cases; but it is more convenient, as a rule, to have the instruments kept in drawers or cases apart from the lathe. Some of these lathes are also made with a casing which turns on hinges, and which, when the lathe is not in use, can be brought over, and the lathe covered up, so as to represent a bureau or other similar article of furniture. So far as this serves to keep the mechanism of the lathe from dirt, it is certainly an advantage; but I do not think any amateur turner need be at all ashamed of having a good lathe seen in any room of his house.

The overhead apparatus is merely a lever hung on an upright standard; this lever has at one end a hook, to which is fastened various weights, and there are also several small guide-pulleys over which the gut passes on its way from the driving pulley to the cutting instruments. Some of these guide-pulleys are fixed—those just over the driving pulley—others may be moved along the lever until just over the pulleys of the cutting instruments.

The further these pulleys are from the fulcrum of the lever, the more weight must be put on to the short end of the lever to keep the gut strained. Any small deviation of position of the pulleys, caused by the traverse of the slide, does not necessitate any shifting of the guide-pulleys, the weights on the lever end keeping the gut taut by allowing the lever to move up or down, to accommodate itself to the varying length of gut; but a change of position of the slide-rest on the bed will usually necessitate a corresponding shifting of the guide-pulleys on the lever.

PLAIN USES OF THE ORNAMENTAL LATHE.

Although this lathe is constructed for ornamental purposes, it is equally adapted to the production of plain work; and any of the ordinary operations in hand-turning which have been previously described can be conveniently and successfully conducted in the ornamental lathe. The same tools and the same rests are used, and in the same manner as has been already explained. When any of these simple hand-turning operations are to be conducted, it is only necessary to remove the slide-rest, and substitute the hand-tool rest, the instruction given will then apply in every essential particular. It will, of course, be seen, that owing to the lightness of the lathe, heavy metal work must not be attempted.

The ornamental operations are therefore additional, and will not fail to be very interesting to the amateur, and productive of great pleasure and gratification to all who choose to try their skill at the work.

The slide-rest is of great service for plain-turning, as well as for ornamental work ; its use is much the same as in the self-acting lathe previously described. It will be necessary, however, to give some further explanation of its uses, and mode of using for light work, as the work itself differs somewhat from that to which I have before adverted.

The various chucks used with this lathe, to hold and give motion to the work, are the same as those used when the work has to be done with hand-tools; the work is also chucked in the same manner. In this division of the work it will not be necessary to give detailed instructions for chucking, or to describe the primary steps to be taken in preparing and fixing work, as the reader is already acquainted with the main particulars. With regard also to the speeds for turning in the lathe with slide-rest tools, they are the same as have been given elsewhere. The number of cuts to the inch is, however, usually much greater. For very fine work two or three hundred to the inch is about the usual thing, but it is not conducive to good work to have too fine a traverse. About a hundred to the inch will usually make very good work, and when the tool has to travel far, this cannot be exceeded with advantage, as the edge gets blunted before the whole surface is gone

over, and all fine work should, where possible, be
finished by one tool, and without alteration or shifting,
as it is rather a difficult matter, when such great delicacy of surface is required, to shift the tool and replace
it without leaving some sign of this having been done.
For short lengths, or where the tool has not got to
travel far over the work, the speed of traverse first
mentioned may be advantageously used, and a good
and uniform surface be obtained by it. The tool
should always be made sharp, and with a keen smooth
edge before putting into the rest, and the cutting angle
should be retained as near as possible.

For soft woods, the tool shown at Fig. 146 is used;
it is merely a piece of steel tube ground off as shown.

FIG. 167.

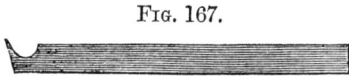

It is held in the holder, and the holder itself fits into
the groove of the slide-rest. This tool is used for
roughing only. The tool for smoothing soft wood is
shown at Fig. 167; this being smaller than the other
tools, fits into a holder, and the holder again into the
groove of the slide-rest.

Both these holders are common to all the tools of
those particular shapes.

The tools for turning hard woods are of the shapes
shown at Figs. 168 to 177. The round tool is used for
roughing down the work nearly to size; the angular
or point tool, for turning vees or angular grooves and
other work; and the flat tool for smoothing or finishing. The cranked tools are of the same shape in the

cutting edge, but are cranked or bent sideways to adapt them to inside turning.

For deep inside and other work of large diameter, the straight tools are used, but are held in the holder shown at Fig. 149 ; this allows the straight tools to be held at any required or convenient angle. The tools are put between the sides of the groove at the required inclination, and are held firmly there by tightening the screw, as will be readily understood by a glance at the illustration.

There are a great number of other tools required for various work, such as beading tools and tools of certain

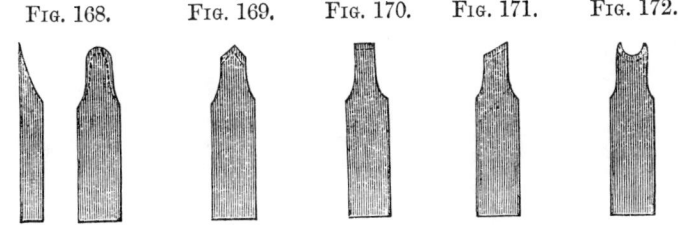

FIG. 168.　　FIG. 169.　　FIG. 170.　　FIG. 171.　　FIG. 172.

curves ; but all these are made to fit the same toolholder, and are used in the same manner as those illustrated. All these tools, of whatever shape, are to be bought ready made, and of standard or uniform sizes of shanks, so as to fit the holder indiscriminately. Almost any good lathe or tool maker will have them in great variety, both as to size and shape ; the amateur can therefore choose those he wants from a large selection.

The roughing-tools are not particularly delicate, and the operator may generally safely take as heavy a cut as his work will bear, or as heavy a cut as he cares to drive, and the traverse may be tolerably rapid.

The last roughing cut, however, should be a light one, and made with a tolerably sharp tool, so as to leave the surface quite true, and to leave very little for the finishing tool. This tool should be very sharp and smooth, and properly adjusted to the right height in the lathe by means of the screw and nut adjustment underneath the slides.

To leave a good surface on ivory or hard wood, the finishing cut must be the *merest scrape* that the tool will take, and the traverse should be fine. It will then be generally found that no glass-clothing, &c., will be required, but that the surface may be polished

FIG. 173.   FIG. 174.   FIG. 175.   FIG. 176.   FIG. 177.

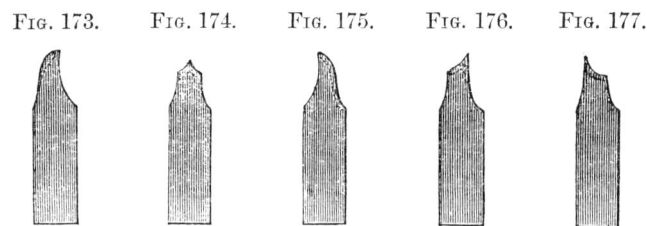

or ornamented without further labour being bestowed upon it.

Work which it is intended to ornament much, should never be touched with glass cloth or other polishing material of that nature, as the particles of glass or cutting substance get embedded in the fibre of the wood, and very injuriously affect the delicate cutting edge of the ornamenting instrument. When any polishing is required on work which is also to be ornamented, it should always be done before the ornamenting, and, by whatever method the surface is polished, as little rubbing as possible should be given it. Much rubbing is apt to render the surface untrue, and the appearance of some sorts of ornament would be much impaired.

Should the tool not leave the surface sufficiently smooth, the best way to render it smoother is to hold a little of the finest shavings against the surface when it is in motion ; but they should be applied equally over the surface, and kept in motion sideways, so as not to rub the work into grooves or to scratch any lines on it.

When polishing with any material, the work should first be rotated in the contrary direction to that in which it was while being turned, as the polishing stuff or rubber on being then applied will remove some of the loose fibres. The lathe can afterwards be run in the usual direction, and the polishing completed. As before mentioned, these lathes are not adapted to turn large pieces of metal either with hand or slide-rest tools, but more especially the former ; as with tools held in the slide-rest, the strain is certain and uniform, but with hand-tools the strain is sometimes sudden and is not under such complete control. All great strain should be most carefully avoided, as it would probably either break some of the slight mechanism, or injure its truth and power of exact measurement. Small pieces of metal can, however, be turned safely either by hand or slide-rest tools, if care and light cuts be taken. I may here also mention that it is a very bad plan to use heavy chucks on such lathes ; some of the self-centering and other chucks are much too heavy to be used with safety.

The tools for metal-turning are the same as those already described ; they are all made to fit into the toolholder of the slide-rest.

The work to be turned, whether of wood or metal, being properly fixed in the lathe, and the right tool placed in the slide-rest, the long slide of the rest is turned around and fixed parallel to the line of the finished surface. For parallel cylindrical work it is fixed parallel to the line of centres against that stop; for plane surfacing it is fixed at right angles to the line of centres, and for angular work it is fixed at the required angle.

The operations of bringing the work to shape are precisely the same as those described under self-acting turning. If the slide-rest have a tangent-wheel and screw motion, for long work it will be worth while to make the traverse motion of the tool self-acting; to do this it is only necessary to bring up the worm or tangent screw into gear with its worm-wheel, and pass the gut of the overhead motion around the pulley on the end of the tangent-screw. A very fast motion of the tangent screw-pulley will then cause the slide to slowly traverse and carry the tool along the work. It is seldom necessary to make the slide cut both ways, but the direction of traverse can be easily altered by merely crossing the gut, which will reverse the direction of rotation of the tangent-screw. The traverse can be immediately stopped when necessary without stopping the motion of the lathe, by shifting the gut off the fast pulley on to the loose pulley. The former is fastened to the tangent-screw, the latter runs loose on it; consequently, when the gut is on the former, it drives the pulley and the screw; but when on the latter, the pulley only is driven around on the screw. The rapidity or speed of traverse can be regulated by shifting the gut driving the rest, on to a smaller speed of the cone if for slower traverse, or to larger speed, if faster traverse be required. Or if a greater variation be necessary, by also treading faster or slower, and shifting the gut driving the lathe-spindle on to a smaller or larger speed to keep the circumferential speed of the work constant. It is, of course, evident that the mere treading faster or slower will not affect the *relative* speed of traverse; this can only be done by shifting one of the driving guts on to a different-sized speed or groove.

Screw-cutting in the ornamental lathe can also be managed with the chasing-tools already shown at Figs. 108 and 109, and in the same manner as there described; but the traversing mandril offers a convenient and reliable means of cutting a good screw-thread. This motion is especially useful for cutting short threads, such as the screws used occasionally to hold round fancy boxes together, and for fastening together in convenient pieces the various component parts of complicated work in ornamental turning. The work requiring the screw-thread being turned down to the right size—the size of the outside of the thread—the tool at Fig. 151 is put in the rest, if for a male screw, and the tool at Fig. 152, if a female screw be required, and the slide-rest is conveniently adjusted to allow these tools to come into cut. It must be understood that in cutting screws in this manner the thread is traced, not by the movement of the tool along the work, but by the work moving past the point of a stationary tool. The slide-rest now is only used as a holder for the tool, and to regulate the depth to which the thread is cut.

If the screw be required to have ten threads to the

inch, a screw socket (e) of that pitch is placed on the lathe-spindle at the back end, and is there fastened by the nut for that purpose. The segment nut (f) of a corresponding pitch of thread is then raised to gear with the thread of the socket, and a little oil being dropped on the surfaces working in contact, the segment tangent-screw (b), if in gear, is released, and the division-index of the lathe is moved clear of the lathe cone. The whole is then ready for action.

If the screw be tolerably long, the spindle may be moved around by the foot motion, the gut being on the slowest speed of the driving cone. For very short screws it is more convenient to rotate the lathe-spindle by hand. The tool is put into cut as in ordinary turning, and when it has cut as far as required, it must be withdrawn, and the lathe turned round in the opposite direction. This will cause the work to recede from the tool. The tool is now put deeper into cut, and the lathe moved around as before, and the operation is continued thus until the thread of the screw is cut of the depth and size necessary for its purpose.

For every separate pitch of screw there must be a socket-screw or guide-screw, and its corresponding half nut; also, there must be a separate guide-screw and nut for left-handed threads, but with one guide-screw we may cut a thread on any size cylinder of any shape, either round, angular, or square. The threads may be shallow or deep, or the screw may have one, two, or three separate threads, but the pitch must be constant, that is, with a screw guide of say ten pitch, or ten complete turns of the thread in one inch, we may cut screws having one, two, three, four, or more separate threads, but each of these threads will be a screw of ten pitch.

The method of dividing these threads is somewhat difficult with these apparatuses alone, and when a single point tool is used; but I shall have to describe an instrument for the purpose when treating of spiral fluting, &c., and that will apply equally well to the present operation. The reader will have no difficulty in understanding its application in this case after reading its use in the other.

By discarding the simple point tool, however, and using a chasing-tool of the proper number of teeth to the inch, the screw may be cut with ease and truth. The tool should be fastened in the slide-rest just as the other single-point tool, and at the same height of centre; it will then strike four threads at a time, but each thread will be a spiral of one-tenth inch size. This, however, has already been fully explained, and the reader who does not thoroughly understand the meaning of pitch, and the number of separate threads, is referred back to the chapters on screw-cutting.

Internal screws are cut in a precisely similar manner, but with the inside single point or screw-tools. As the operation is one not requiring much power, screws of fine pitch may be cut on metal work of considerable diameter without fear of damaging the lathe. The tool should be kept sharp, and very light cuts taken, the work meanwhile—if of iron or steel—being kept well lubricated with oil or oil and soda-water.

If the cylinder upon which the screw has to be cut, whether of wood or iron, be more than three or four inches long, it will require further support than at one part. It is evident that in this case as the lathe-spindle traverses, the end of the work cannot be supported in the usual manner by the centre of the moving head-stock ; it must therefore be supported by a stay or bearing, through which the work may slide in the same manner and to the same extent, as the lathe-spindle itself slides endways in its bearings. The bearing should fit well, but must not be too tightly screwed down ; such a stay bearing has been illustrated at Fig. 126 ; the dies may be either of metal or hard wood, and they must be arranged exactly central, or otherwise the screw-thread will be deeper on one side than on the other. The method of adjusting this bearing with the centre of the hole in the line of centres has been already explained.

Owing to the sliding motion of the spindle and the work, the latter must be driven by a chuck, which will not only drive it but hold it fast to the lathe-spindle. The ordinary method of driving by carrier, or by the prong or cross-driver, is for obvious reasons not applicable to drive work when the spindle has this traversing motion.

It may be that the work upon which the screw has to be cut is not parallel, or is not of uniform shape for sufficient distance, or in such part of the length as to allow the support to be applied with convenience. In such cases either the work must be turned to its right size only where the thread is to be cut, and the required length of the remaining part turned parallel, and of such a size as the largest part of the required shape, and this part used as the bearing, to be, after the screw is cut, turned to any irregular shape; or, if the work be already turned to shape, a socket of right size can be put on and adjusted true whilst the work is supported by both centres. This socket will then answer for a sliding bearing to support and steady the work whilst the screw is being cut.

Should the workman have no socket of convenient size, a piece of hard wood may be cut out to fit on to the work, and held there by glue, screws, or even with a piece of small twine. The piece of wood so fastened on should then be turned parallel, whilst the work is supported by both centres, which will ensure its being true with the work, and then *this* is used as the bearing part of the work. After the thread is cut the piece of wood can be taken off and the work itself is left uninjured.

REMARKS ON ORNAMENTAL ENGRAVING.

One of the most beautiful as well as scientific uses to which this lathe is applied is to the production, by means of the suitable instruments, of various highly ornamental and interesting figures or curves, generated by one or more circular movements, by right line and other movements, alone or combined.

These figures may be made of every conceivable shape, and in unlimited number and variety. Skilful operators having good taste can produce patterns which are really marvellous in their graceful and well arranged curves ; others, again, are produced of shapes so curious and so irregular that one can scarcely imagine them to be the result of circular movement. Irrespective of the use of these figures as ornaments, they are interesting to the scientific mechanic as demonstrating the various laws of kinematics, or results of various motion. The instruments used for conveniently producing the various motions are some of them rather complicated, and they are somewhat expensive. They all require the most accurate workmanship, and should be as light as possible, consistent with the necessary strength to resist bending or yielding under the strain to which they are subjected. Nevertheless, as a practical mechanic I must remark, that accuracy of workmanship and lightness combined with strength is to be obtained without very great expense, and that these instruments should be sold much cheaper than they now are. Probably the demand is too small to allow of the profitable introduction into the manufacture of special machinery; but then the high price to some extent is the cause of the smallness of the demand. One would fancy that but few would be without the instruments for producing such beautiful work, if their price were at all reasonable, and therefore that a reduction of price would lead to such an increased demand that the manufacturer would have good reason to congratulate himself on his liberal but true business policy.

The effect of so high a price is to keep some of the most beautiful instruments entirely in the hands of those who neither know the value of money nor the value of the instruments they buy, although we occasionally see serviceable and well-made, but not highly finished instruments, in the hands of those who are fortunate in being sufficiently practical workmen to be able to construct the apparatus for themselves. Many of the instruments can be applied to other work than ornamental line engraving ; but beginning at the most simple instrument, I shall explain the uses of each in this respect first, and devote a separate description to their other uses.

The woods best suited to this work are boxwood and African blackwood ; they must be dry, and perfectly free from cracks and other imperfections. Ivory is also a very good material, and is, perhaps, more used than any other substance. Other woods than those named may be used, although not with such good effect. Those woods are the best which are of hard even grain, and free from natural wavy or other lines.

For blocks or plates to receive figures for printing from, boxwood, copper, steel, and a composition metal of lead and tin, are probably the best materials. The tools in each case are of the same shape, but ground in accordance with the instructions previously given respecting the angles of cutting tools for various materials. The steel plates must be thoroughly well annealed, or otherwise there will be but small chance of succeeding in cutting a good figure, or, indeed, in cutting a figure at all. Probably the better plan is, for steel plates, to use a diamond of natural fracture for the cutting tool. This diamond, which is very small, is fastened in the usual manner, into a small holder of the same shape and size as the ordinary tools, so that it may be used in the ordinary tool-holder for the instruments. I also believe this to be the cheapest tool that can be used for the purpose. Mr. H. Perigal, F.R.A.S., has informed me that he has used one diamond for cutting figures on three hundred plates, and certainly when I saw the diamond, there was no appreciable wear.

It is obvious that the use of a diamond for a cutting tool will allow of these figures being cut on glass as well as on metals. Mr. Perigal has also used it to cut patterns on steel surfaces, hardened to their utmost and very highly polished. The marks left by the tool can scarcely be called cuts, but the appearance of such patterns is very beautiful indeed, as besides the pattern itself, the iridescent colours are shown, although not so well with curved as with straight lines. There is also another advantage connected with the use of diamond tools, which will scarcely be appreciated by any but those who have had some experience with the use of the others—the diamond will cut almost equally well, whether the surface is travelling upwards or downwards, past the point of the tool, so that the surface being in motion, it does not matter which side of the line of centres the diamond is placed. Now with an ordinary tool this cannot be done, as the tool will only cut when it is on one side of the centre, and when we move it across past the centre, it no longer cuts, as the work is then moving past its point in the contrary direction.

In cutting these figures, three methods are employed :

1. The figures are cut on a moving surface by a fixed tool.

2. They are cut on a fixed surface by a moving tool.

3. They are cut on a moving surface by a moving tool.

In the first method, the work is fastened to the ornamental chuck, and the chuck driven by the lathe-spindle, the tool being held stationary in the slide-rest, whilst the figure is cut.

In the second case, the work is held on the lathe-spindle, but the spindle is not moved around, except between the cuts; the figure is produced by a tool moving over the surface, and caused to thus move by the instrument to which it is attached, and which is held in the slide-rest, the rest itself being stationary.

In the third method, the work is attached to the lathe-spindle by an ornamental chuck, moved around by the spindle, the tool being also moved over the moving surface by an instrument held in the slide-rest, the slide-rest being either in motion or stationary.

By whichever method we wish to cut our figures, the surface of the article to be ornamented must be brought perfectly true by turning in the ordinary way. The surface should be either left as smooth as possible, or it should be grained or lined with a series of light concentric circles, as will be presently described.

A very small prominence or pin of the wood should be left exactly at the centre of the turned surface, and this projection will be very convenient as a guide by which to adjust the cutting tools central.

For ornamental turning, it is usual to employ the tools of most obtuse angled points for the dark woods, and the acute tools for ivory and the lighter woods.

This is mostly a matter of taste; but it is surprising what a difference in effect is produced by altering the angle or shape of the cutting tool, and still using it to cut the same pattern.

In cutting figures, the greatest care must be taken
to have all the mechanism clean and free from oil, and
should the operator ever so slightly cut or bruise his
hands, he should tie a piece of clean rag over the
place, to prevent the annoyance of having his work
covered with drops or smears of blood.

The tools used in the slide-rest are those shown at
Figs. 168–177. The angular tools are mostly used for
ornamental engraving, the others for deeper cutting
and ornamental moulding. These tools must be kept
thoroughly sharp, and with smooth cutting edges; the
whole success, so far as appearance goes, will be spoiled
if the tools are kept dull, or with rough cutting edges.
The improved appearance of the work will generally
repay one for the trouble of taking a tool out after it
has had some little working, and the figure gone over
nearly to the required depth, and to finish it with a tool
freshly sharpened. It will be convenient to have two
other tool-holders to receive these tools, but to hold
them with their cutting edge at right angles, and also
completely reversed.

SLIDE-REST APPLIED TO ORNAMENTAL ENGRAVING.

The slide-rest bears a most important part in all
ornamental turning; this it does, however, mostly
when used with other apparatus, as by itself its uses
in this way are not great.

I will now describe its uses alone; its uses combined
will be explained hereafter. A point applied and held
against a surface in motion, during one rotation or

more, will describe a circle having for its centre the axis of rotation.

If, therefore, we have a true surface of wood on the lathe-spindle, and we put a simple point tool in the slide-rest, and apply it to the centre of the work in motion, a simple dot only will be produced ; if, however, we move the point of the tool five-tenths of an inch from the centre, by giving the slide-rest screw five entire turns, and then again apply it to the surface in motion, a circle will be produced of five-tenths in radius, or ten-tenths, equal one inch diameter. By moving the tool point farther from the centre, a larger circle will be produced, but no other figure will be described in this way. There is not much ornament, however, in a few lines arranged in concentric circles, but it is usual when a large pattern has to be made with other instruments, to first 'grail' the surface by cutting a series of concentric circles at very short intervals, and with a sharp angular tool of from 20° to 30 °.

These cuts should not be very deep, and should only be just far enough apart to bring the edges joining the cuts to a sharp edge. If the cuts be far enough apart to leave flat tops to the grooves, either they must be cut deeper, or another cut placed between every cut before made.

The darker the wood the better effect this grailing or lining has ; for light woods most amateurs prefer polishing the surface to be ornamented, and not grailing it at all ; and whether the wood be light or dark, if the pattern to be cut on it be very delicate, this lining is not applicable. There is another rather pretty pattern, which can be made with the slide-rest, and as it serves also to illustrate the effect of grailing, I will give it here, Fig. 179. The pattern is usually produced either by the straight line chuck, or the straight line movement of the ellipse cutter or geometric chuck.

1. The article to be ornamented with the pattern being held in a convenient chuck, set the lathe in motion, and bring the surface to be ornamented to a true plane.

2. Place a sharp angular tool in the slide-rest, and *grail* or line the surface as before described.

3. Remove the gut or band of the lathe—that is, throw it off its speeds—so that, were the treadle moved, the belt or gut would not communicate the motion to the lathe-spindle. Fix the dividing index or pointer in its place at one of its divided circles— say the 960 circle, and at 960.

4. Set an angular tool in the rest *on its side*, with its cutting side towards the workman.

Fix the stop of the slide-rest so as to allow the tool to traverse only so far out as will enable it to cut the longest lines of the star, and set the other stop to prevent the slide going too near the centre.

5. Screw the slide up to the last stop, and then, with the adjusting screw on the tool slide, set the tool up to its depth of cut, and draw it outwards until against the outside stop. One cut will then be made.

6. Withdraw the tool from cut by the other screw or the lever; return the slide to its place against the inside stop, move round the division-plate of lathe $\frac{1}{8}$th or 120 divisions, and make another cut in the same manner as before. Repeat this until the whole eight lines are thus cut.

7. Set the outer stop to allow the tool to cut only so far as the length of the next line of the star; the inner stop will not require altering at all.

Bring the division-plate again at 960, and then shift it twenty divisions *forwards*; make one cut, and move 120 divisions; cut again; repeat this cutting for every 120 divisions, until the eight cuts are completed.

8. Bring the plate again at 960, and move 20 divisions *backwards*, and without altering the stop of rest; make a cut, and move forwards 120; cut again, and repeat until the eight cuts are made.

9. Set the rest stop to the next line of the star; bring the plate to 960, and move forward 40 divisions; make a cut, and move 120; cut again, and repeat for the eight cuts. Bring the plate to 960; move 40 *backwards*; cut, and move 120 forwards; cut, and repeat moving 120 and cutting for the eight cuts.

10. Set the rest stop for the next line of the star; bring the plate to 960; move forward 60 divisions, and cut; move 120 and cut; continue moving 120 and cutting for the eight cuts. The pattern will then be complete, unless it is wished to cut another smaller star in the central space; if so, that can be done in a similar manner.

If it be required to make the lines of the stars get deeper as they recede from the centre, this is managed by setting the slide-rest rather out of parallel with the surface to be ornamented, so that, were the surface then turned, it would be made with a very obtuse angle.

THE ECCENTRIC CHUCK.

The instrument shown at Fig. 178 is known as the eccentric chuck. The boss (a) screws on to the spindle of

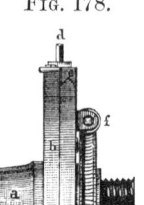

FIG. 178.

the lathe, just as an ordinary chuck; the parts (b) and (c) are slides similar to those of the slide-rest; the internal part (c) is moved along by the eccentric screw (d); this screw has ten turns to the inch, and has a small index at the end, divided into ten divisions, and marked at every other. The screw is moved by a small handle, which is only applied when required, and is removed before the lathe is set in motion. As in the slide-rest, one whole turn of the screw advances the slide (c) $\frac{1}{10}$ of an inch. In addition to this index there are other divisions marked along the side of the slide, so that by comparing them with a line on the other slide the extent of eccentricity may be seen at a glance.

On the slide (c) there is a worm-wheel (e) with 96 teeth; this is fitted on a stud to allow of its moving around, and is thus moved by means of the tangent screw (f). Some chucks are made with ordinary teeth and a spring click or catch, instead of this tangent screw motion. I think the plans are equally convenient.

The end of the tangent screw is made square to receive a suitable handle or wrench, and the collar of the screw is divided into twenty divisions, every other marked. The tangent screw is so fixed that it can be raised out of gear with the wheel. The face of the wheel is divided also into two lines of divisions, one being 96, the other 100. The slide (c) carries a small index-pointer for reading off these divisions. Both lines of divisions commence or start from the same place, and in using the chuck the index should always be started at that place.

The division-wheel has a projecting screw of the same size and pitch as the nose of the lathe-spindle; any ordinary chuck fitted to the lathe-spindle can therefore be placed equally well on this screw of the eccentric chuck. By turning the slide-screw, the slide (c) is moved along, either from or towards the lathe axis, according to the direction in which the screw is turned.

The distance the centre of the chuck-screw is from the centre of the lathe-spindle screw, as indicated by the division lines on the edge of the slides, is termed the eccentricity.

When the two centres are co-incident, the slide has no eccentricity, and in that position there are two holes, one through (b) and another through (c) which come opposite one another, so that a small steel pin may be pushed through both, and the two slides held firmly together. When this pin is in place, the work, in any holding chuck on the chuck-nose screw will run just the same as if on the lathe-spindle itself, and, if to be ornamented, may be turned in such position with advantage, as the surface is then quite true with the chuck itself. There is no absolute certainty of the work being true unless done in this way, as, if turned on the lathe-spindle and transferred to the chuck-nose, there is generally some slight degree of untruth; and it must be remembered that for good work the surface to be ornamented should be absolutely true.

Whether work has to be ornamented by this chuck or any other, the same remarks apply.

There is another more complicated eccentric chuck, called the compound eccentric chuck, but it is expensive and heavy ; and as most of the work to be done by its means can be done by simpler apparatus I have not considered it worth while to describe it particularly. In this chuck there are two eccentric slides, which can be moved around and placed at any angle to each other ; the motions of the slides are obtained in the same manner as in the simple eccentric chuck described. Other chucks of this sort are made to serve either as a combined elliptic and eccentric chuck, or compound eccentric chuck, but the above remarks apply equally to them as to the other.

When using the eccentric chuck, place it upon the lathe-spindle, and have the index of the chuck at 96. The slide being at zero, and a tool placed in the slide-rest and applied at the centre, will produce a dot.

With the eccentric slide still at zero, any movement of the slide-rest tool has the same effect as if applied to a surface direct on the lathe-spindle, that is, a circle only is produced, and that circle is larger the farther the tool is removed from the centre.

If we move the screw around five times we shall throw the slide out of centre $\frac{5}{10}$ of an inch, or give it that much eccentricity ; by applying the point of the tool to the centre as before, and setting the lathe in motion we shall produce only a dot, but that dot will be $\frac{5}{10}$ of an inch from the last centre. By shifting around the index-plate one division at a time, and applying the tool each time, we shall arrange forty-eight dots around this centre in a circle of 1-inch diameter.

If, however, we move the point of the slide-rest tool out of centre, by giving its screw five turns, and which will move it $\frac{5}{10}$ of an inch from the centre ; on again putting the lathe in motion, a circle of 1-inch diameter will be described by the tool, and the centre of this circle will be $\frac{5}{10}$ of an inch from the centre of the circle described, when the eccentric chuck had no eccentricity. The circumference of the last circle will therefore pass through the centre of the former.

Fig. 179.   Fig. 180.

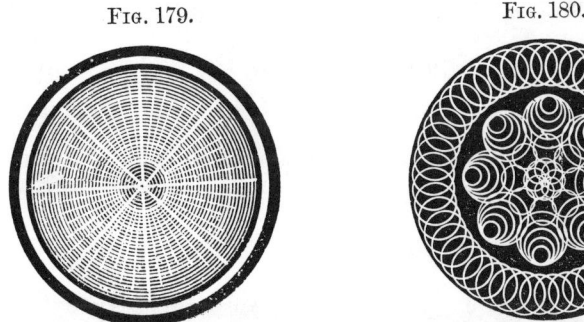

If we now turn round the index of the chuck two divisions at a time, and set the tool into cut between each, we shall make a figure of ninety-six circles, arranged equidistantly around the centre of the circle struck when the chuck had no eccentricity.

1. It will be understood that the radius of the circle is determined by the movement of the slide-rest, precisely as when turning without the chuck.

2. The eccentricity or distance the circles are from their common centre, or the centre of the figure, is determined by the movement of the eccentric slide.

3. The number of circles is determined by the movement of the division-index of the chuck.

These movements give the whole of the powers of the eccentric chuck when used alone ; its powers when combined with other motions will be described hereafter.

Fig. 180 was done with the eccentric chuck. The foregoing description of the chuck and its powers will enable the reader to understand how to cut this figure and almost any others.

THE ECCENTRIC CUTTING INSTRUMENT.

The instrument illustrated at Fig. 181 is the eccentric cutter. It is for the same work as the eccentric chuck,

FIG. 181.

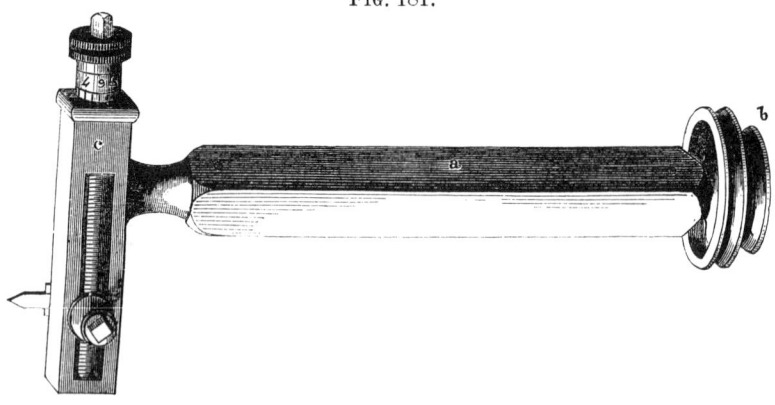

but whereas in the chuck the figures are produced on a revolving surface by a fixed tool, in the cutter they are produced by a fixed surface and revolving tool.

The shank or stem (a) is nicely fitted to the toolholder of the rest, a spindle passes through the stem, and at one end has a small brass grooved pulley (b), and at the other the eccentric slide (c), carrying the tool-holder (d), in which the various tools are held and carried.

The slide has a screw for moving the tool, with a 10-pitch thread and a small divided index on the screw-head, divided into 10, and marked at every other division. The screw end has a double milled head, which is generally sufficient for moving the slide. The screw at the back is for tightening the holder against the slide, to hold it without its shaking or throwing strain upon the threads of the eccentric screw.

The tools used with this instrument for ornamental turning are chiefly of the same shape as those shown at Figures 168 to 177 ; they are all made with bodies or stems of the same size, and should fit the tool-holder easily, but without shake. The angular tools are mostly used for line engraving, as in the case of the tools last mentioned.

The shank of the eccentric instrument is put into the tool-holder of the slide-rest, and held as an ordinary tool. Supposing the instrument to be in place, and a piece of wood having a plane surface previously put on to the lathe-spindle, and a suitable tool in the tool-holder of the instrument, we proceed as follows.

The gut is removed from the lathe-cone, and a long gut from the overhead motion placed around the small pulley at the end of the instrument, the index-pointer for the lathe division-plate is put on in place.

The eccentric instrument being in place in the rest it is applied to its work in the manner of an ordinary tool, viz. by the slide-rest screws and lever movement. All being in place and the eccentric slide at zero, on the tool being applied to any point of a surface only a dot is produced, and on shifting the slide of the rest, and again applying the tool, a dot is again produced, but eccentric to the former dot at a distance corresponding with the extent to which the slide-rest was shifted. If the slide-rest were shifted $\frac{5}{10}$ths of an inch from the centre, the dot would be made with that degree of eccentricity.

If, however, the tool of the eccentric cutter were shifted also $\frac{5}{10}$ths, corresponding to five whole turns of the eccentric slide screw, and the cutter in motion again applied to the surface, a circle of 1-inch diameter would be described by the tool of the instrument; and by shifting the division-plate of the lathe around by any number of divisions at a time, a series of such circles will be arranged around the centre of the work, and the centres would be in a circle of 1-inch diameter. It will, therefore, be seen that the same figures are traced with this instrument as with the eccentric chuck, but the method of getting the radius and eccentricity and arrangement of circles is altered.

1. In this instrument it will be seen the radius of the circle is determined by the distance the tool is shifted along the eccentric slide.

2. The eccentricity of the circle is determined by the distance the slide-rest is moved from the centre.

3. The arrangement of the circle is determined by the movement of the division-plate of the lathe-spindle.

In using this instrument care must always be taken to adjust it quite central before moving the slides. To do this it is necessary that the tool of the instrument should first be placed at its zero on the scale, any thin smooth piece of wood being then held by the hand against the surface to be ornamented, and the instrument set in motion, the tool can be brought up to touch this piece of wood so held. If the tool in revolving describe a circle on the wood, the screw must be shifted a little until the tool in revolving describes only a dot. It is then central so far as relates to its own axis of rotation, and can now be adjusted central with the axis of the lathe, by setting it in motion, and bringing it up to just touch the little knob left in the surface to be ornamented. If the dot the tool then makes be above, below, or one side of the central projection, the slide-rest must be lowered, raised, or shifted sideways until the tool makes a small dot exactly on the centre of this point. The required eccentricity and radius can now be given by moving the slides as before explained.

This instrument will describe all the figures that can be made by the eccentric chuck, but its chief use is in combination with other apparatus.

THE ELLIPSE CHUCK.

The instrument illustrated at Fig. 182 is the ellipse chuck. It screws on the lathe-mandril, the boss being fitted with a female screw fitting the mandril nose. It has slides (*b*) and (*c*), very like the slide of the eccentric chuck, but the slide is not moved by a screw, but is free to move out and in across the centre. The internal slide (*c*) has two jaws (*a*), fastened to it and going through two properly arranged grooves or slots made in the slide (*b*).

Fig. 182.

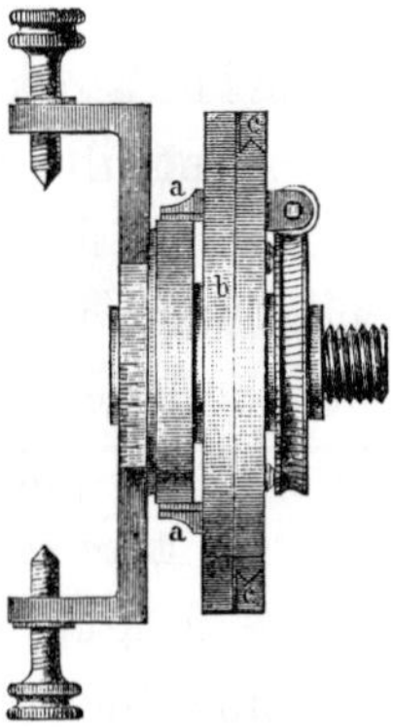

Fastened to the slide (*c*) is a tangent screw and wheel, in all respects similar to that on the eccentric chuck.

There is also another part which is fastened on to the lathe-headstock in such a manner as not to interfere with the rotation of the spindle. This part is a sort of frame, having an elongated hole through it for passing over the spindle and allowing the frame to move sideways. Attached firmly to the frame, or in one piece with it, is a circular ring, and the two jaws of the other part of the chuck are placed wide enough apart to span the ring, and fit it nicely without *play*. The top part of this frame is graduated, and when on in place comes level with the top of the headstock, where there is a line by which the graduations are read off. This scale is divided into twentieths of an inch, and generally for a distance of from $\frac{1}{2}$ inch to 1 inch from the zero point, on the left of that point only, the numbers also commencing at the zero line and going towards the left hand, supposing the operator to be facing the chuck. The frame carries two screws, which fasten it to the headstock by their conical points fitting into deep centre marks cut in the opposite sides of the headstock.

To put the chuck in position ready for use, the frame must first be put on over the spindle-nose, care being taken that the graduated side is uppermost, and that the holes or indents in the headstock which take the screw points are free from dirt. The zero point of the scale should also be opposite the line on the lathe-headstock. The other part of the chuck can now be screwed on to the spindle, the jaws being guided by hand to come opposite the ring and encircle it. On the lathe being put in motion there will be no movement of the slide (*c*), whilst the zero point of the scale is opposite the line of the headstock. The chuck may therefore be used as a receiver of any of the plain chucks, and work surfaced or turned up to a circular shape precisely as if it was directly on the lathe-spindle. When used in this way a small pin is put through a hole in both (*b*) and (*c*) to prevent any slight lateral movement of the slide.

Having a true surface on the work, remove the steadying-pin, place a point-tool in the slide-rest, and adjust it level and central with the small projecting knob left for that purpose on the surface of the work. Now if the left-hand screw of the frame be loosened and the right-hand screw correspondingly tightened, sufficient to bring the tenth divided line of the frame opposite the line on the lathe-headstock, this will move the ring ten-twentieths of an inch from its former position, where it was concentric with the lathe-spindle, and place it half an inch eccentric to it.

The lathe in revolving will carry the whole of the chuck around with it, but the jaws of the slide having to go around the eccentric ring will move the slide to which they are attached to and fro in the slide screwed on to the lathe-spindle. On setting the lathe in motion, the tool still being as left—both level and central—on applying it to the surface, a straight line will be scratched of a length equal to double the distance the ring of the chuck was placed eccentric. This line will not be *cut*, as the motion of the work past the tool's point will be in contrary directions. Thus, supposing the

R

chuck be set with the slides vertical, which is the best position in almost every case, the tool's point will then be exactly opposite the little central knob; but as the lathe is pulled round, this knob will recede from the tool's point and go towards the left; if, therefore, the point tool be placed in the holder for receiving it on edge, a tolerably clean cut will be made. This cut will have gone to its extent when the slide of the chuck is brought exactly horizontal, or has been pulled around one-fourth of a revolution. But in pulling the chuck around the next quarter of a turn, the little central knob will approach the point of the tool, so that the tool will only rub along the cut already made. At the end of this second quarter of a revolution, the chuck will again be vertical, the line will also be vertical, and the tool's point will be again opposite the little central knob.

The line cut by this half revolution has started from the centre, and is equal in length to the extent of the ring's eccentricity.

During the next quarter of a revolution of the chuck the central point will again recede from the tool's point, and the line will travel past the tool in the opposite direction. At the end of the last quarter of a revolution the chuck will be again vertical, and all the parts will have returned to the position whence they started.

If now the slide-rest screw be moved, say, five complete turns, so as to bring the tool's point outwards, $\frac{5}{10}$ths equal $\frac{1}{2}$ an inch, the ring of the chuck being left as it is, but the point tool previously placed in its ordinary working tool-holder—on the lathe being pulled round, starting from the vertical position as before, the various movements of the chuck will also be the same as before, but an ellipse will be described on the surface of the wood, with a conjugate or short diameter equal to double the extent to which the slide-rest was shifted, or 1 inch, and with its transverse or long diameter equal to double the extent of the ring eccentricity 1 inch, *plus* the length of the conjugate diameter, or to 2 inches.

By now turning the tangent-screw, and thus shifting the division-wheel of the chuck, on setting the lathe in motion, and applying the tool between each movement, a series of ellipses will be arranged equally around the central point of the wood, and the figures produced will be like those at Fig. 183.

Fig. 183.

It must be understood that each series of ellipses was cut without moving or altering the eccentricity of the ring, or the distance of the tool's point from the centre.

An ellipse having been struck on any surface attached to the chuck, if the tool's point be shifted, by means of the slide-rest screw, the same distance the *other* side of the centre, the tool being held in the reverse toolholder or the holder by which the tool may be used with its cutting edge downwards, an ellipse will also be cut, but it will be exactly at right angles to the one previously described.

In using the ellipse-chuck, it should be understood :—

1. The distance the slide travels from the centre is termed the throw of the slide.

2. The graduated scale of the ring frame being at zero, and the tool applied to the centre of the surface, a dot only is produced; but the tool applied any distance from the centre, a circle is produced, corresponding in diameter to that distance.

3. The ring being placed eccentric to the lathe-spindle, and the tool applied to the centre of the surface, a line is produced equal in length to double the extent of the ring's eccentricity; but the tool being applied a distance from the centre, an ellipse is produced.

4. The conjugate diameter of the ellipse is equal to double the distance of the tool's point from the centre; the transverse diameter is equal to double the ring's eccentricity *plus* the conjugate diameter.

5. By shifting the division-wheel of the chuck, the angular positions of the ellipses are determined.

6. By altering either the ring's eccentricity or the position of the tool, the relative length of the diameters can be altered to produce ellipses of all shapes between the right line and the circle.

7. By altering *both* the eccentricity of the ring and the tool's position to proportional extent, so as to keep the *relative* length of the conjugate and transverse diameters the same, parallel concentric ellipses are produced.

8. The tool's point must be kept at the same height of centre, or the angular positions of the ellipses produced will not be the same.

9. This chuck cannot be worked fast, as, in revolving, the eccentricity and change of position of the slide cause a great deal of shaking of the lathe, which is prejudicial to good work.

THE ELLIPSE-CUTTING INSTRUMENT.

This instrument, illustrated at Fig. 184, is for cutting ellipses and other figures upon surfaces, and is of far more service for ornamental turning than the ellipse-chuck; indeed, this instrument is one of the neatest and most convenient of any yet invented.

The stem (*a*) fits into the tool-holder of the slide-rest in the same manner as the eccentric cutting instrument.

FIG. 184.

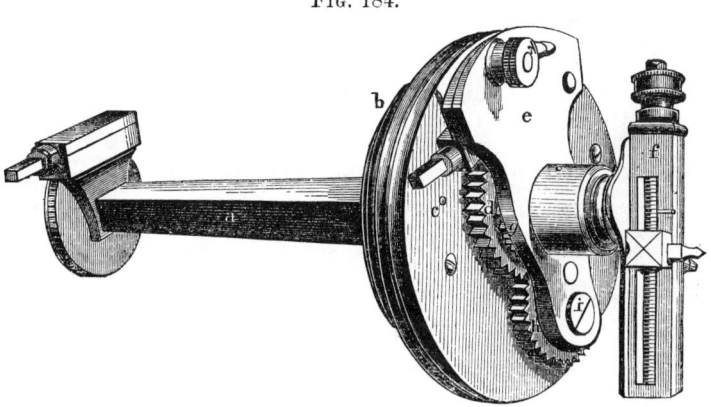

One end of this square stem is made round, and carries the pulley (*b*), which has several angular grooves, to allow of the instrument being driven by the gut from the overhead motion. The carrying plate (*c*) of the instrument is attached to this pulley, and is of course driven by it.

The stem is bored through, and a small shaft put inside it, having at one end the central wheel (*d*), and at the other a worm-wheel of 150 teeth, geared into by a tangent-screw carried by a frame fixed to the end of the square stem of the instrument. This wheel is also graduated on its edge into 72 divisions read off from a pointer on the frame carrying the tangent-screw.

Attached to the carrier-plate (c) is a radial arm (e), having on it a boss bored through, and fitted with the stem or spindle of the eccentric arm (f). This arm is precisely similar in construction to the arm of the eccentric cutting instrument. At the other end of the stem or spindle of the eccentric arm, and inside the radial arm (e), there is a brass pinion (g), geared into by the wheel (h), which, in turn, is driven by the central wheel (d). The radial arm is fastened to the carrier-plate at two points, by the screw (i) and the screw (k). The former is the centre around which the arm radiates, and is also the spindle or axis upon which the intermediate wheels revolve; the other screw goes through a curved slot in the arm, as will be seen. The arm can therefore be moved around on the centre screw (i), to the extent of this slot, and is fastened at any point of this movement by tightening the milled head screw (k.) This movement of the arm is effected by means of the small screw on (c), the square end and collar of which is seen, the extent of movement being indicated by the graduated divisions marked on the edge of the instrument. These divisions are such that a movement of one will throw the centre of the eccentric spindle $\frac{1}{100}$th inch out of place.

Now when this instrument is in the slide-rest and is set in motion by a gut from overhead passing around the pulley (b), the radial arm being fixed at the zero point of the graduated scale and the point of the tool adjusted central, a dot only will be produced. If, however, we stop the instrument, and turn around the eccentric screw to move the tool away from the centre, and again set the instrument in motion, a circle will be cut, the radius of which will depend upon the number of turns the eccentric screw was moved.

By moving the screw of the slide-rest we can place a series of circles in a row of any length and at any distance apart, and by using the index-plate of the lathe-spindle we can arrange these circles anywhere around a centre, and at any distance from that centre. It will thus be seen that the instrument, when thus only used, has exactly the same power as the eccentric cutting instrument.

This instrument is also adjusted central with the little knot left on the surface to be figured, in the same manner as was explained for the eccentric instrument. Before going further we will suppose the tool-point to have been thus adjusted central. If the screw (k) be loosed, and the radial arm shifted say 20 divisions of the graduated scale, which will throw the centre of the cutter-spindle $\frac{20}{100}$ths of an inch out of place, and the tool also shifted 20 divisions or $\frac{2}{10}$ths of an inch along the eccentric slide, on the instrument being set in motion and applied to the surface, the tool will travel across the centre of the work and produce a straight line $\frac{8}{10}$ths of an inch long, $\frac{4}{10}$ths each side of the centre.

If the eccentricity of the radial arm be now reduced 10 divisions, which will leave it $\frac{1}{10}$th inch out of centre, on again putting it into motion and applying the tool to the work, an ellipse will be produced with a conjugate or short diameter of $\frac{2}{10}$ths of an inch, and a transverse diameter of $\frac{6}{10}$ths of an inch in length.

By altering the ratio between the eccentricity of the radial arm and the cutting tool an ellipse of any proportions can be produced. So far as the shape of the figure is concerned it makes no difference whether the eccentricity of the cutter is more than that of the radial arm, or *vice versâ;* but in practice the former is to be preferred, as the cutting edge of the tool is presented to its cut in a more favourable manner.

The eccentricity of the cutter axis is caused by the movement of the arm (*e*), and this movement being around the centre (*i*), the cutter axis is evidently moved in the arc of a circle and around the wheel (*h*).

If the radial arm be moved out 10 divisions and the cutter be moved 10 also, on the tool being put in motion and applied to cut, a straight line will be produced, and if we now shift both 10 divisions more, a straight line double the former length will be produced; but this line will not come on the same place as the last, nor parallel to it, but it will be cut at an acute angle to it. We now find the use of the tangent-screw at the end of the stem (*a*); this is so graduated that, by moving it the same number of divisions as the flange, the radial movement of the cutter axis is counteracted.

We are indebted to Mr. Perigal for this neat improvement on Captain Ash's ellipse instrument.

When this instrument has cut an ellipse, any number of these figures can be arranged in a straight line by shifting the slide-rest, and if the centre of the instrument coincide with the lathe-centre, the ellipses may be placed to cut across each other in any angular position by moving the division-plate of the lathe. When, however, the two centres of the lathe and instru-

ment do not coincide, the movement of the lathe-plate
has the effect of arranging the ellipses eccentric to a
common centre; and in this case the angular position
of the ellipses is determined by moving around the
tangent-screw at the end of the instrument. The worm-
wheel having 150 teeth, if the tangent-screw be
moved around $37\frac{1}{2}$ times, the ellipse will be struck at
right angles to its former position. Any smaller
angle can be obtained by moving the tangent-screw
a less number of turns; the movement is generally
better, indicated by the division-index on the edge

FIG. 185.   FIG. 186.

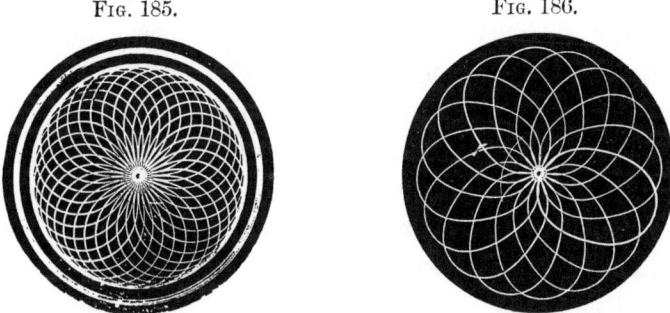

of the wheel. Fig. 185 is formed by a series of
vertical ellipses arranged around a centre by the
movement of the division-plate of the lathe. Fig. 186
is formed of a series of horizontal ellipses arranged
around a centre by the same means.

It will be well to bear in mind that, in using this
instrument, when the radial arm and the cutting instrument are both moved out of centre the same distance,
the tool will cut a straight line.

In order to produce an ellipse there must be some
difference between the eccentricities, and the proportions of the ellipse will depend upon the extent of the
two movements.

The transverse or long diameter will be equal to double the sum of the two eccentricities, and the conjugate diameter will be equal to double their difference; the straight line may therefore be looked upon as an ellipse with a conjugate diameter$=0$. This instrument cuts an ellipse when the eccentric cutter makes two revolutions, whilst the pulley and carrier-plate make one in the opposite direction. In this case there will be a 48-tooth wheel as a stationary driver, gearing with a wheel of 24 teeth on the same socket with a 36-tooth wheel gearing with another 36 on the end of the eccentric frame-spindle. When the instrument is in motion the 48-tooth wheel is still stationary and the 24 is carried around it, making two turns every time, and these two turns are communicated to the eccentric spindle by the two 36-tooth wheels.

If we remove these two 36-tooth wheels, and put a 48 on the socket with the 24-tooth wheel already on, and put a 24-tooth wheel on the end of the eccentric spindle, on putting the instrument in motion the cutting frame will no longer make only two rotations whilst the carrier-plate and pulley make one, but it will revolve four times in the same period, and instead of an ellipse a four-looped or four-sided figure will be produced.

FIG. 187.

When the radial arm is shifted the same number of divisions as the eccentric cutter the loops will all cut across the centre, as will be seen at Fig. 187.

When the arm is moved less than the cutter the loops all

pass the other side of the centre. When the arm is moved more than the cutter, the loops will all fall short of the centre. When the radial arm is moved very much more than the cutter, the figure has no loops, but becomes a four-cornered figure, as can also be seen from Figure 187.

These figures can be changed again into spirals by reversing the various wheels, so as to make the carrier plate rotate faster than the cutter frame.

In Fig. 187 the central figure is made of two four-looped figures, placed in position by moving the tangent-screw. The arrangement of the outside four-looped figures is obtained by moving the division-plate of the lathe. The intervening figure consists of three round-cornered squares so arranged by the tangent-screw.

This instrument has the advantage of being able to place these figures on surfaces of work that cannot be placed on the lathe-spindle parallel to the surface of the chuck. The flat edges of squares or polygons can be thus ornamented by means of this instrument, by merely turning the slide-rest to face the surface to be figured. The same precaution must now be taken to place it central as before, and additional care must be exercised to make sure of placing the surface exactly at right angles every way to the axis of the cutter. Should this care not be taken, the cutter in revolving will cut deeper into the surface at one part of its revolution than at the other. The surface can be readily put into position by setting it at right angles to the bed. This is done by placing the stock of a square on the lathe-bed, and shifting the division-plate by a division or by the micrometer screw until the blade of the square touches all along the surface. The stop of the slide-rest will prevent the slide being much wrong, but it is better to make sure of the surface being properly arranged by pulling round the eccentric instrument with its point *just* touching the surface to be figured. If the point of the tool touches alike all around, it *is* properly set, but if it only touches at one part of its revolution, say at the top, then the division-plate must be moved around by the micrometer screw of the index, so as to cause the top to recede from the tool just half of the difference. The instrument must then be again pulled slowly around, and re-adjusted if the movement of the division-plate was not enough or too much.

If instead of the tool in revolving touching the top or bottom, it touches one of the sides, then the slide-rest must be moved around in such direction as will bring the point of the tool from the place where it touches. This adjustment must be continued until the tool, in revolving, will touch all round equally. It is not at all necessary, in doing this, that the surface of the article should be scratched up or disfigured in any way, but a little care will have to be exercised to prevent this being the case. When thus adjusted, the figuring is conducted precisely as in the cases before mentioned.

THE ROSE-CUTTING INSTRUMENT.

The instrument illustrated at Fig. 188 is the rose-cutting instrument, the stem (*a*) is made to fit the tool-groove of the slide-rest, and has a hole bored through it in which there is a small shaft, having at one end a worm-wheel (*b*), and at the other the eccentric frame (*c*) and slide (*d*). The frame carries a small tool-box, which is moved along it, by the eccentric screw (*e*) of the same pitch as the screw used for similar purposes in the eccentric cutting instrument and the ellipse-cutter. The frame (*c*) is made with a slide to fit into the slide (*d*), and there is also a slot cut through

Fig. 188.

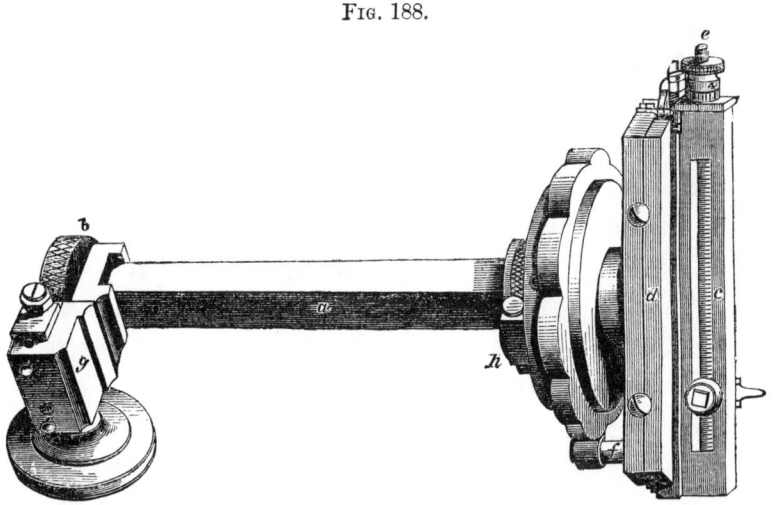

(*d*) to allow the pin (*f*) attached to (*c*) to come through and have room to move along it. This pin also carries a small steel roller.

Attached to the back end of the stem is a frame (*g*) carrying a tangent-screw with a pulley on its axis, and which screw gears with the wheel (*b*). The stem in front carries the shaper-plate or rosette, but this rosette can be exchanged for any other of different shape at pleasure, and when on is not immovably attached to the stem (*d*), but may be shifted round by turning the tangent-screw (*h*). When in work the instrument is held in the slide-rest precisely the same as the other cutting instruments, but the gut from overhead is placed around the pulley on the tangent-screw gearing with the wheel (*b*). On this pulley being set in motion it drives the shaft or spindle passing through the stem of the instrument, and consequently the slide (*a*) and frame (*c*). These, in revolving, carry round the small roller with them, and this roller is pulled against the stationary rosette by a strong spring, which cannot be seen, as it is at the back of the slide. It will therefore be seen, that as the roller is attached by the pin to the cutter slide (*c*), this slide is forced to move in and out along the slide (*d*) according to the shape of the rosette. This instrument is very simple in its use, and the patterns to be obtained by its means are exceedingly beautiful.

When a surface is to be ornamented by this instrument the chief point to be observed is, that the centre of the rosette should coincide with the centre of the place on which the figure is to be cut.

In order to adjust it central it will be necessary to raise the rubber or roller off the rosette, and then the instrument may be adjusted in two ways. By making a circle around the place where the figure is required, and then moving the tool along the eccentric slide far enough for it, in revolving, to make a circle of the same size as the guide circle ; when the instrument can be adjusted by moving the slide-rest until the circle cut by the tool, in revolving, will coincide with the circle struck as a guide. The instrument is then central, and the work can be proceeded with. It is frequently, however, inconvenient to strike a circle as a guide for the tool, and the instrument can be adjusted to a central point instead. If the figure have to be made concentric with the little central knob on the work, no other guide will be necessary; but if the figures have to be arranged eccentric to this knob, a small dot must be made with a pencil or a tool in the centre of the place where we require the figure. The tool is then moved along the eccentric frame to its zero point, so that, in revolving, it will make only a dot, and the instrument can now be easily adjusted by moving the slide-rest until the point of the tool will cut this dot precisely on the dot made for the guide.

With the rubber or roller raised off the rosette the instrument will only describe a simple circle, of a diameter corresponding with the distance the tool has been shifted along the eccentric frame; it will, therefore, be seen, that the instrument can thus be used as an eccentric cutter.

By turning back the lifting-off screw, and allowing the roller to bear against the rosette, on the instrument being put into motion and applied to the work, the tool having been previously moved along the frame towards the rubber, a figure will be cut the shape of the rosette, and of a size corresponding to the distance of the tool's point from the zero of the scale. These figures can be cut one inside the other at any intervals, by merely altering the distance of the tool's point from the centre.

If the centre of the figure coincide with the lathe-centre, the angular position of the figure may be altered at pleasure by shifting round the division-plate of the lathe and thus presenting a fresh place to the action of the cutter tool. If, however, the slide-rest be shifted and the tool applied, a rose figure will be cut at a distance from the lathe-centre depending upon the distance the slide-rest was moved, and by moving the division-plate of the lathe around so many divisions at a time, a series of these rose figures will be cut, eccentric to a common centre precisely the same as the plain circles cut with the eccentric instrument.

If now it be desired to alter the angular position of the figures, with regard to their own centre, it is obvious this cannot be done by presenting a fresh place to the tool, but it must be done by presenting the tool to a fresh place. For this it is necessary to move round the rosette on the stem of the instrument, and to enable this to be done, the tangent-screw at the back of the rosette was applied. By turning this screw the rosette is moved to a fresh position, so that upon putting the instrument in motion and applying it to the work, the same figure will be cut, but in a different angular position. By moving the tool along the eccentric frame past the centre to the side opposite the roller, and applying it in motion to the surface, a different figure altogether will be produced. In the previous position a prominence in the rosette forced the slide so as to bring the tool farther from the centre of the figure; but in this position a prominence has the effect of bringing the tool nearer to the centre, and a figure is now cut exactly the reverse of the previous one. There is the same power of enlarging these figures or altering their position as in the other.

The lifting or stop-screw also gives the means of

producing another sort of figure from any rosette. By moving the screw so as to partially raise the roller off the rosette, the full travel of the slide will be prevented, and a series of flat lines will be made at those points at which the roller is prevented touching the rosette.

Fɪɢ. 189.

Fig. 189 illustrates the uses of the rose-cutting instrument. The outside of the pattern is formed by shifting the position of the rosette between every cut. The inside part is a series of concentric rosettes, to produce which the cutter was moved further from the zero point between every cut.

Beside the chucks and instruments described there are several others, but they are little used and are comparatively unimportant. Among these are the epicycloidal chuck, the straight-line chuck, the rose-engine, &c.

The first is rather a complicated instrument for producing epicycloidal figures, most of which can be obtained by the other apparatus. It goes on to the mandril end in the same manner as the others. The straight-line chuck is an instrument placed on the mandril end for getting the right line motion—some varieties of this chuck are made to work with the continuous rotation of the lathe-spindle, others require the motion of the lathe to be alternate. The rose-engine is a lathe in which the rose figures already described are obtained by moving the work instead of moving the tool.

This is done by making the whole of the lathe-headstock rock to and fro under the guidance of rosettes placed on the lathe-spindle and which in revolving rub against fixed points or rollers, and so give the rocking motion to the work. It is a clumsy and complicated piece of mechanism, expensive, and of comparatively little service.

The geometric chuck is the most complicated of all the ornamental turning chucks, but that is correspondingly useful. Almost the whole of the figures which can be produced by the chucks described, either alone or combined, can be obtained by the geometric chuck. I shall therefore reserve the description of it and its uses until after I have given a few explanations of the modes of combining the various chucks and instruments already described.

COMBINATIONS OF ORNAMENTAL APPARATUS.

Hitherto I have explained only the simple uses of the various chucks and instruments used by the ornamental turner; enough has been said, however, to convey a good impression of the uses of each; and the instruction given, if attended to, can scarcely fail to enable the operator to be tolerably successful in his attempts at ornamental engraving.

The first great step to success is to understand thoroughly the simple uses of the instruments, and not attempt more complicated combinations of instruments until acquainted with their separate uses and capabilities. Without this knowledge their combined action would be conducted blindly, and appear to be dependent upon chance only for success.

I may mention that the figures given have been

chosen as the ones best adapted to show the combined action of the instruments. These may be modified, and other patterns be obtained with but slight alteration, many of which will almost equal in beauty those obtained by the geometric chuck. It will not be necessary for me to explain every step and movement required to

FIG. 190.　　　　　　　　　FIG. 191.

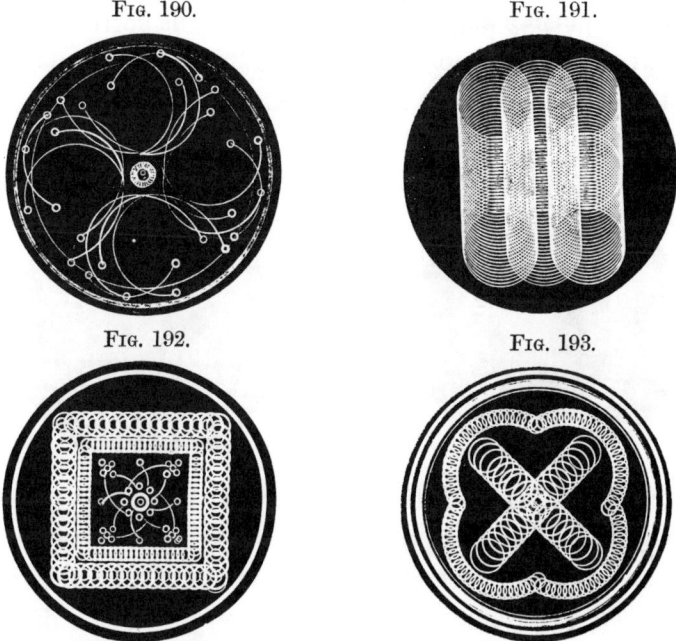

FIG. 192.　　　　　　　　　FIG. 193.

produce the patterns, as, after the instruction already given, the reader will have no difficulty in seeing for himself.

Fig. 190 was produced by a combination of the segment-wheel and excentric chuck, with a fixed tool in the slide-rest.

Fig. 191 was produced by the excentric cutter and excentric chuck, the cutter being shifted by the screw of slide-rest between every cut.

Fig. 192 was produced by the same instruments and in a similar manner.

The inside curved lines were made by the segment-wheel.

Fig. 193 was made by the excentric cutter and excentric chuck, the circles of the cross being spaced by the slide-rest screw, the circles forming the border by the division-plate of lathe.

Fig. 194 was produced by the excentric cutter, which made the small circles. The ellipse shape can be

FIG. 194.　　　　　　FIG. 195.

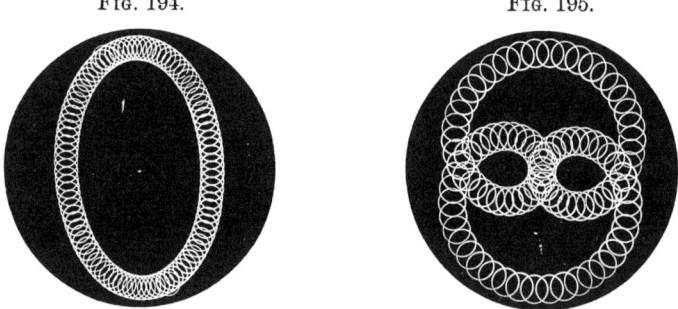

obtained either from the ellipse-chuck, or by using the excentric chuck, with the division-plate of the lathe. If the latter mode be employed, any amount of excentricity is given to the chuck, and between every cut the index-wheel of the chuck and division-plate of lathe are moved any number of divisions, in the proportion of 1 to 2 in *opposite* directions.

In the figure there are 96 circles. To obtain these, between every cut the chuck-wheel was moved $\frac{1}{96}$th and the lathe $\frac{2}{96}$ths of a revolution; this had the effect of causing the lathe to move around twice in one direction, whilst the chuck-wheel was moved once in the other direction. This is usually termed ' double counting.

To produce Fig. 195, the counting was the same, but the movements were both in the *same* direction.

Fig. 196 was produced by the same instruments, but the movements were such as to cause the lathe to make three revolutions, whilst the chuck-wheel made one in the opposite direction. To make that figure the chuck had an excentricity of $4\frac{1}{2}$ turns of its screw, the rest was moved $1\frac{1}{4}$ turns towards the operator.

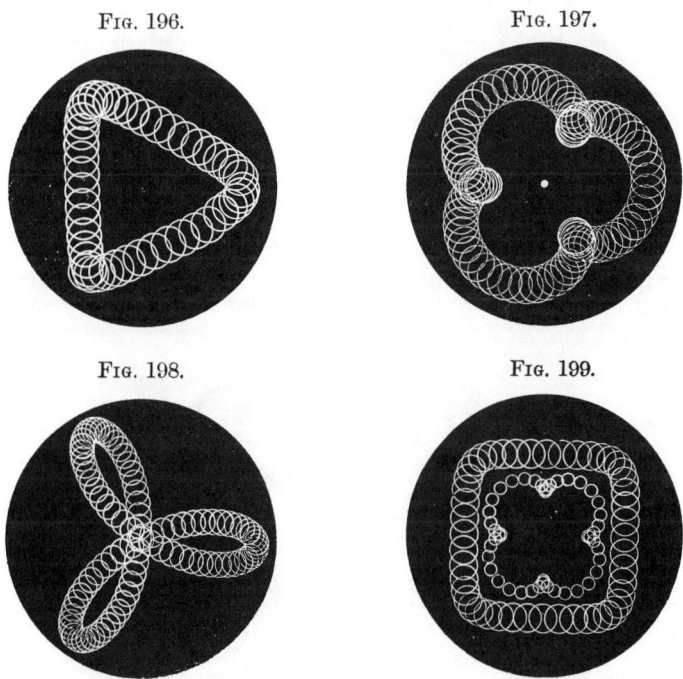

FIG. 196.   FIG. 197.

FIG. 198.   FIG. 199.

Fig. 197 was made with the same relative velocity, namely 3 to 1. The excentricity and movement of rest were also the same, but the lathe and chuck-wheel were both moved around in the same direction.

Fig. 198 was made in the same manner, with a velocity ratio of 3 to 1. The movements were in opposite directions, and the excentricity of the chuck and movement of the slide-rest were equal.

Fig. 199. This figure had a velocity ratio of 4 to 1. For the inside the movements were in opposite directions, the excentricity was equal to 5 turns of the screw, and the movement of the rest $1\frac{1}{10}$ turns of its screw.

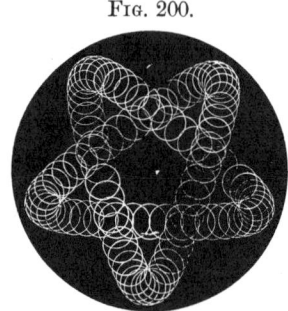

FIG. 200.

For the inside the movements were in the same direction, the chuck's excentricity was 3 and the rest's movement $1\frac{1}{10}$ turns.

Fig. 200 was produced by a velocity ratio of 5 to 2 in opposite directions. The excentricity was $4\frac{1}{2}$ and the movement of the rest 2 turns of the screw.

FIG. 201.

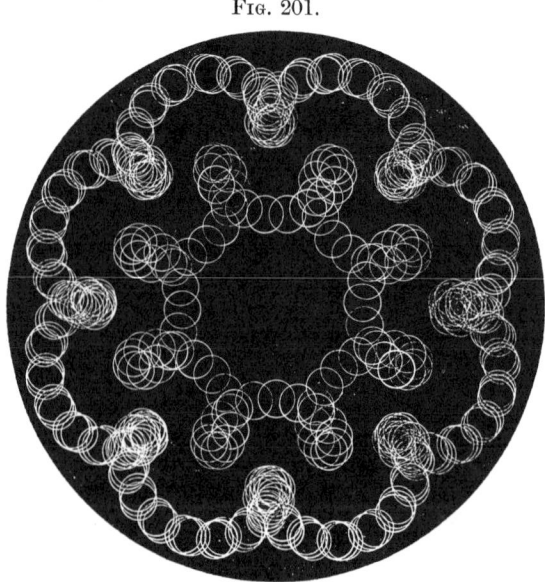

Fig. 201 had a velocity ratio of 8 to 1. For the outside the direction of motion was the reverse of what it was for the inside pattern.

By altering the relative velocity of the lathe-wheel and chuck-wheel, figures of almost any number of sides or loops can be obtained by these instruments; and by substituting the ellipse instrument for the excentric instrument, the same figures are produced in ellipses instead of circles. The ellipse patterns are, as a rule, much more beautiful than the others, but they are no more difficult to produce. Indeed, there is no great difficulty in producing a pretty pattern with any instrument; but when the system of double counting is employed, the movements of the required divisions become exceedingly tedious, and require considerable patience.

I may here say a word on the ornamental uses of the vibrating saddle, or apparatus for irregular shape turning, shown at Fig. 130.

If we have a true surface attached to the lathe-spindle, and we cut a line on it with a tool held in the slide-rest, while the sliding clutch is in gear with the worm-wheel on the surface-screw, an Archimedian spiral will be described, the pitch of which will depend on the relative velocity of the lathe and surface-screw. The circular spirals in the inside of Fig. 202 are spirals of that sort, and were so described.

FIG. 202.

The outside spiral of the same figure was cut by the combined action of the last motion, and the vibration of the saddle caused by an eccentric circle for a shaper-plate. The shaper-plate made four revolutions whilst the lathe-spindle made one. So also in Fig. 203, the outside is formed of two of the same spirals, the

FIG. 203.

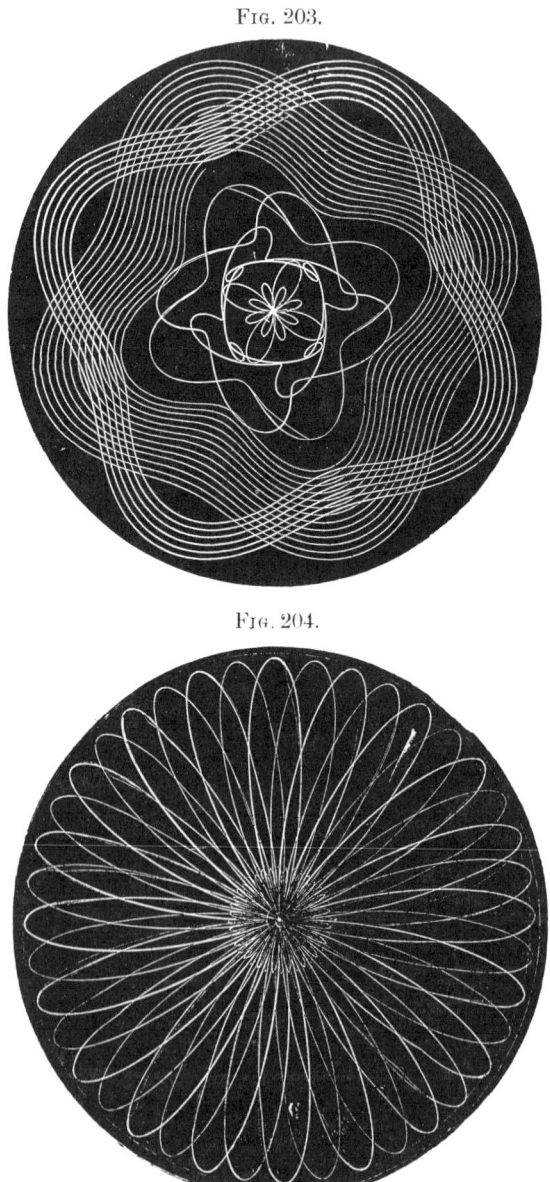

FIG. 204.

internal figures were all produced by the same shaper-plate and with the same velocity ratio, but with the tool's point at smaller distances from the centre.

FIG. 205.

Fig. 204 was produced by the motion of the slide, but the shaper-plate was a crank-pin, having a throw equal to half the diameter of the figure.

Fig. 205 was produced also by a crank-pin, having a throw equal to the width of the figure, the velocity ratio being expressed by a mixed number or a whole number and a fraction.   The figure produced is formed of one continuous line.

By combining the movement of the saddle with the excentric instrument or ellipse instrument, the figures produced are very beautiful.

Figs. 206, 207, 208 were produced by the vibrating saddle and excentric instrument.

In Fig. 206 the shaper-plate was a crank-arm, making five revolutions, whilst the lathe-spindle made two.

FIG. 206.

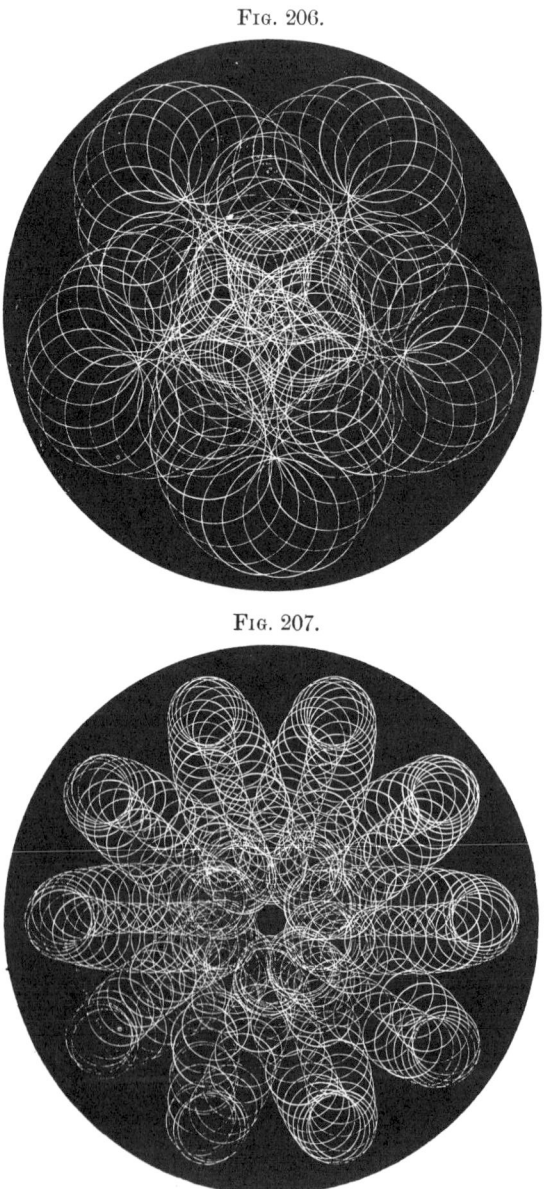

FIG. 207.

In Fig. 207 a crank-arm made ten revolutions to one of the lathe-spindle.

In Fig. 208 the shaper-plate was an excentric circle moving sixteen turns to one of the lathe.

The interior rose-work had very little excentricity, and the movement of the slide-rest was consequently but very slight. The roses of the border were produced in the same manner, but were so placed by the

Fig. 208.

excentric chuck. The main figure is, I think, very fine, the circles forming it were cut by the excentric instrument.

In using the various instruments with the moving saddle, it will be understood that the movement of the lathe is not continuous, but the circles or ellipses formed by the instruments are spaced by the division-plate of the lathe. In this case the movement of one or more divisions not only moves the lathe a certain distance around, but the shaper-plate and slide carrying the instrument are also moved a corresponding distance.

The figures to be produced by the various combinations of apparatus are practically endless, but I cannot afford more space to their further explanation.

COMPENSATING INDEX, OR ELLIPSE DIVIDER.

In using the ellipse-chuck in conjunction with the excentric cutting instrument, and in using the excentric chuck and excentric instrument for ellipses or other figures obtained by double counting, it necessarily occurs that the ellipses or other figures are not equally divided. The angular velocity of the figure is continually changing—in the ellipse the circles cut by the excentric instrument are crowded together at the ends of the long diameter. It will be seen that this is precisely the same whether the ellipses are cut by the ellipse-chuck or by double counting, and that the same unequal spacing of the circles occurs in the looped and other figures. It will also be hereafter seen that the same peculiarity occurs with the ellipses and other figures cut by the geometric chuck. In order to obviate this—which is by some considered a defect—a very neat and ingenious instrument was devised, I believe by Mr. Ibbetson, and which is usually called the compensating index, and by him considered the third part of the geometric chuck. This, however, is a misapprehension, as, although the instrument may be used in conjunction with the geometric chuck, it is equally applicable to the ellipse-chuck and to double counting.

In using the ordinary index-pointer and division-plate, although the same space is passed at each movement of the division-plate, still the spaces between the circles cut on the figure are not equal.

This instrument performs its purpose by keeping the angular velocity of the figure constant.

When used with the ellipse-chuck or for double counting, it is applied and used in place of the ordinary index-pointer or spring. As its construction and action are simple, an illustration will be unnecessary.

It consists of a thin plate or arm carrying a crank-plate with adjustable throw, and the wheels necessary to drive the crank-plate from the lathe-spindle. The thin plate fits against the lathe-spindle just inside the headstock, and is also kept firm by a link which connects it to the lathe-bed so as to hold it with the line joining the centres of the wheels, quite horizontal.

The wheels are small brass wheels and are changeable, with the exception of the one on the lathe-spindle, which is fixed. When used with the ellipse-chuck, wheels are put on to cause the crank-plate to rotate twice whilst the ellipse is generated, or during one revolution of the lathe-spindle.

The throw of the crank-arm is regulated by a screw with a divided head, the throw must be the same as that of the chuck. The crank arm works in a small block, which slides in a slot cut in another arm fastened against the lathe-spindle, but not directly affected by the movement of the spindle, although it is so through the media of the wheels and crank arm, because as the crank arm rotates it causes the slot arm to oscil-

late through an arc, struck from the centre of the
lathe-spindle. Attached to this oscillating arm is a
short index-pointer for taking into the holes on the
division-plate in place of the one generally used.

The ellipse-chuck must be exactly upright, whilst the
spindle centre, the crank-plate centre, and centre of the
crank-pin, are all in one line and horizontal. The
crank-arm is then at the extreme outward end of its
stroke in the slot. The excentric instrument would
be cutting at the flat lines of the ellipse, where the
circles would be farthest apart if they were cut without the compensating index.

The instrument is used in a similar manner for
double counting, but with the geometric chuck it is
placed differently.

THE GEOMETRIC CHUCK.

The geometric chuck is an arrangement of mechanism for producing two or more circular movements in
parallel planes. The combination of these movements
with different velocity ratios and different radii results
in the formation of a great variety of highly interesting
curves and geometric figures. Two of these movements are combined in double counting or counting
with the lathe division-plate and excentric chuck-wheel,
but in this case the motions are intermittent, whereas
with the geometric chuck they are continuous. In
double counting, the various parts of the figure are
separately worked out by tedious motions of the hand
and counting, which, even when care is taken, are very
liable to be done incorrectly, whereas the figures pro-

duced by the geometric chuck are generated automatically by continuous motions, requiring no attention after the chuck is properly arranged and the lathe set in motion.

There has been a great deal of controversy as to who was the inventor of these instruments. The chuck usually goes under the name of Ibbetson's Geometric Chuck, and Ibbetson himself says he derived the idea and the name from the geometric pen of Suardi, who published an account of it in 1752.

The rectilinear movement of the slide was the first plan for getting the excentricity, and this was evidently derived from the ordinary excentric chuck. With this arrangement every movement of the slide required a fresh adjustment of the wheels to gear with the wheel on the slide. It appears that after contriving his chuck, he saw in the 'Manuel du Tournour' a description of 'La Machine Epicycloide,' and this instrument had a flange motion, of which the excentricity was obtained without throwing the wheels out of gear. Ibbetson altered his chuck to work on this plan, which he states to be the best plan. It did not occur to him that the wheels might be kept in gear by linking them, as was the plan afterwards adopted by Mr. Perigal. A writer in the 'Mechanic's Magazine,' September 26, 1859, stated that he had 'possessed geometric chucks and compound geometric chucks, but that the ideas of them came so easily, and must have occurred to many others besides myself, that they did not appear to be worth communicating.' This and the assertion that the geometric chuck would describe spirals, seems to have rather disturbed Mr. Ibbetson's equanimity, and to

have evoked a reply in the shape of a pamphlet entitled
' A Brief Account of Ibbetson's Geometric Chuck.' This
was published at five shillings, but contains but few specimens, and little information on the chuck or its action.
The jealousy with which he guarded his chuck may be
seen from his assertion that he had ' never made any
particular communication of the mechanism of the instrument, but to four gentlemen, who gave me their
word and honour, under their handwriting, that they
would not divulge any part of it in any way whatever.'
It was certainly an ingenious contrivance, but its importance for preventing forgery of bank notes appears
to have been much overrated by the inventor. With
regard to the chuck being able to generate spirals, it
can most certainly do so, but, as Ibbetson says, they
must sooner or later return into themselves ; they
are nevertheless spirals, although not the spirals of
Archimedes.

H. Perigal, Esq., F.R.A.S., who has devoted a great
deal of time to the study of the curves generated by
the geometric chuck, has materially improved it by
reverting to the rectilinear movement, and applying
means whereby the wheels are caused to follow up
the slide and keep in gear. This is accomplished by
mounting the wheels on double radial arms, as will be
seen hereafter. By simplifying it he hoped to render
it less costly, so as to facilitate its adoption and use by
most amateur turners, but the makers persisted in
charging a prohibiting price for it, so that very few
have hitherto been sold.

The geometric chuck is shown at Fig. 209, the illustration is too plain to render much explanation neces-

sary. It is there, however, shown on a frame devised by Mr. Perigal, and by which amateurs may arrange all their figures upon paper placed in the tracing chuck, at the same time making a note of their adjustment previous to executing a fac-simile with the same combinations and conditions in the lathe. This apparatus is convenient for use upon the table either in the library or workshop.* A flange chuck for holding paper is shown on the geometric chuck-nose, but this can be

FIG. 209.

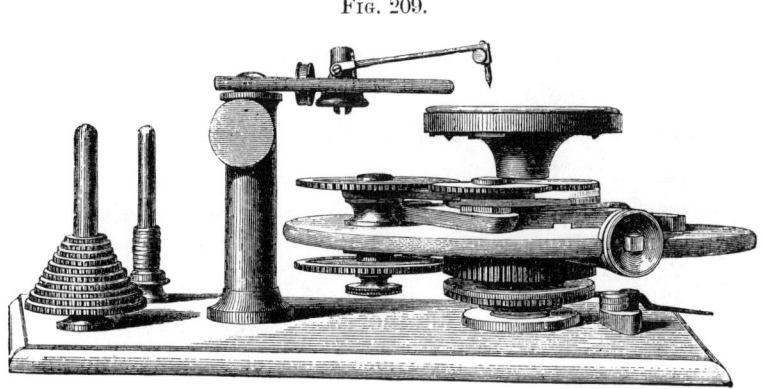

removed, and any other substituted. On the boss of the chuck is a socket, which carries two wheels, one of which is narrow, with ninety-six teeth, and is the stop or index-wheel; this wheel is fastened against a flange of the same size as the top of the wheel teeth, and which is divided into ninety-six, each division-mark being at the top of a tooth.

When the chuck is on in place, there is a small spring

* This apparatus is manufactured by Mr. E. Baker, of 13 Mount Street, Grosvenor Square, who furnished me with the photograph, and of whose work I can speak very favourably.

index, for taking into the teeth of the index-wheel. The second wheel on the socket has also ninety-six teeth, but is much wider. This is the driving wheel of the chuck.

The train of wheels to communicate motion to the excentric axis are varied according to the nature of the figure the chuck is to produce. Some of them, it will be seen, are carried upon double radial links, which keep them in gear with the excentric wheel in every position of the slide. The slide screw is of ten pitch two threads, its index is divided into twenty, and numbered every two. The slide chiefly throws out one way —towards the index; when central a pin may be put through the slide to keep it steady and allow work on the chuck to be surfaced or turned up.

The excentric index-wheel has ninety-six teeth and a spring catch, it is also divided on its flanged edge. Some chucks can be caused to revolve in contrary directions by moving another wheel into gear; but the simplest plan is to interpose another arbor with an intermediate wheel, as a less costly expedient.

In using the geometric chuck, it is first screwed on the nose of the mandril, the stop released, and the chuck pulled round a few times by hand to be certain there is no binding of the axles or dirt between the wheels. Should there be any unusual resistance to this pulling around, the operator must ascertain and remove the cause before setting the lathe in motion.

The mechanism of the chuck being rather delicate, and the whole success of the instrument dependant upon the absolute truth in all respects of the mechanism, it is manifestly of importance to keep the instrument

free from dirt when not at work, to protect it as much
as possible from dust and grit when at work, and also
to keep the whole of the bearings and slides well oiled
and quite free from abrasion.

The number of figures to be obtained with the
chuck, and their variety, is so great that it is necessary
to use the chuck systematically, and to obtain the
various figures by rule and not by repeated chance
trials. I don't mean to say that it is advisable—
although certainly possible—to calculate beforehand
the exact nature of the curve or figure certain wheels
and certain excentricities will produce, or to lay down
the figure and calculate the exact conditions of the
instrument necessary for its generation. This much,
however, should certainly be done. All the conditions
or parts affecting the shape of the figure should be each
known by a name, which should also be as expressive
as possible. The share each part of the instrument has
in generating a figure should be understood, and also
the extent to which varying conditions of a certain
part affect the figure generated. Thanks mainly to
the researches of Mr. Perigal, the laws governing the
motion of the geometric chuck and the production of
figures by it are tolerably well known, and I here hope
to convey to the reader sufficient information on these
points to enable him to judge with considerable accuracy both of the figures produced by certain motions
and of the motions necessary to produce known figures.

Hitherto, except amongst a few who have thoroughly
studied the action of the chuck, it has been looked
upon as a most complicated and wonderful piece of
mechanism, so difficult to understand as to be uncertain

in use. But by thus working systematically, it no longer appears fortuitous in its effects, but the figures generated by its movements are found to follow certain and unalterable laws, which can be calculated upon beforehand with perfect surety, and no great difficulty.

I will now give the most important laws, and strongly advise those who desire to be well acquainted with this beautiful instrument to read them attentively, and try them over by aid of the chuck itself, as by this means they will not only be easier remembered, but their practical applications will be better understood.

1. The axis of the first motion of revolution, or the axis of the lathe mandril carrying the geometric chuck, is termed the 'deferent axis.'

2. The axis of the second motion of rotation, or the axis carried by the first slide of the chuck, is termed the 'epicyclic axis.'

3. The axis of the third motion of rotation, or the axis carried by the second excentric slide, is termed the 'compound epicyclic axis.'

4. The distance from the deferent axis to the epicyclic axis is termed the 'deferential radius.'

5. The distance from the axis of the lathe to the point of the tool describing the figure, when the first part or simple geometric chuck is used, is termed the 'epicyclic radius;' but when the second part, or compound geometric chuck, is used, the distance from the epicyclic axis to the compound epicyclic axis is termed the 'epicyclic radius.'

6. The distance from the axis of the lathe to the point of tool in the slide-rest delineating the figure is termed the 'compound epicyclic radius.'

7. The proportion or ratio the deferent radius bears to the epicyclic radius, or the epicyclic radius bears to the compound epicyclic radius, is termed the 'radial ratio.'

8. When both the deferent axis and the epicyclic axis are rotating in the same direction, whether left to right like the hands of a watch or the reverse, the motion is said to be

direct, and the same term is applied to the same conditions of the epicyclic and compound epicyclic axes.

9. When the deferent axis and the epicyclic axis, or the epicyclic and the compound epicyclic axes, rotate in contrary directions, their motion is said to be inverse.

10. The ratio or proportion the number of evolutions of the deferent axis bears to the number of rotations of the epicyclic axis is termed the ' velocity ratio.' The same term is applied to express the ratio between the number of rotations of the epicyclic and compound epicyclic axes.

11. The terms 'rotation' and 'revolution' must be understood according to their kinematic meaning, and not their dictionary or popular meaning. According to the latter, they both mean the same state of motion, and are used indiscriminately one for the other; but according to the former, they each have a separate signification, and must not be confused the one with the other. [When a body turns round its own centre it rotates, when turning round any other centre it revolves.]

12. Curves or figures generated by one circular motion or simple rotation are true circles or circloids. These are the figures generated by a point applied to a surface in motion on the lathe-spindle.

13. Figures generated by two circular movements, or double rotation or revolution, are termed bicircloids. These are the figures delineated by a point applied to a surface attached to the geometric chuck in motion.

14. Figures generated by three circular movements, of rotation and revolution, are termed tricircloids ; and so on, according to the number of generating movements. Tricircloids are generated by the compound geometrical chuck.

15. Figures generated by the same velocity ratio, but reversed direction of motion, are termed 'twin curves.' Thus the velocity ratio of 2 of the deferent axis to 1 of the epicyclic axis will, when the motion is inverse, produce an ellipse, but when direct will produce a two-looped figure. The ellipse and two-looped figure are termed ' twin figures' or twin curves.

16. Figures generated with a constant direction of motion, but reversed velocity ratio, are termed ' reciprocal figures.' Thus a velocity ratio of 2 to 1 inverse will produce an ellipse

but a velocity ratio of 1 to 2 inverse will produce a one inside-looped figure. The ellipse and the one-looped figure thus produced are reciprocals.

17. With constant velocity ratio and direction of motion, but variable radial ratio, many varieties of the figure, due to the constant conditions, are produced. The changes thus produced are termed the 'phases of the curve.'

18. The apocentres are the points farthest from the centre of the figure. They all are contained in the circumference of a circle equal in radius to the sum of the radii of the deferent and epicycle.

19. The pericentres are the points nearest to the centre of the figure, they are contained in a circle of a radius equal to the difference between the two radii.

20. The number of both apocentres and pericentres is the same as the number of loops or branches in the figure.

21. Figures with their loops all meeting or cutting through the centre are termed 'centric.' Those having each of their branches or loops wholly on one side of the centre are termed 'ciscentric;' and those having loops which circumscribe the centre are termed 'transcentric figures.'

Ciscentric phases of a figure may be looped, cusped, orthoidal, or wavy.

With the exception of two figures, the annuloid and ellipse, the transcentric and centric phases are all looped.

22. Complemental curves are the two similar figures generated by inverse motion, with complemental velocity ratios.

Supplemental curves are the two similar figures generated by direct and inverse motion with supplemental velocity ratios.

23. When the angular velocity of the deferent is less than that of the epicycle, or the number of rotations of the epicyclic axis is greater than the number of its revolutions, the curve or figure produced is a double spiral or volute going from the centre with a gradually increasing speed, and then returning to the centre with a speed as gradually decreasing.

24. When the angular velocity of the deferent is greater than that of the epicycle the figure produced is looped or cusped.

25. The deferential velocity determines the number of loops which will be produced.

26. The epicycloidal velocity determines the order of their arrangement.

27. When the velocity ratio is expressed by a fraction in its lowest terms, the number of rotations of deferent axis being the numerator, and the number of rotations of the epicyclic axis the denominator—the numerator will show the number of loops to be obtained from the combination, and the denominator will show their arrangement, whether consecutive or alternate, &c.

28. Other conditions being constant, the direction of motion determines the placing the loops inward or outwards.

29. Direct motion will only generate curves or figures with inward loops.

30. Inverse motion will generate all figures with loops, both inside and outside, centric, ciscentric, or transcentric.

31. The radial ratio determines the position of the loops with regard to the centre of the figure, whether they will be centric, ciscentric, or transcentric.

32. If the radial ratio is as 1 is to 1, or if the radius of the deferent and epicyclic circles be of the same length, the loops of the figure produced will be centric, and the pericentres will all be situated in one point—the centre of the figure.

33. When the epicyclic radius is less than the deferent radius the loops of the figure generated will be ciscentric.

34. When the epicyclic radius is greater than the deferent radius the loops will be transcentric.

35. The motion being direct, the figure is cusped when the radius of the epicycle is to the radius of the deferent in the same ratio as the epicyclic velocity is to the sum of the epicyclic and deferent velocities.

The motion being inverse, the figure is cusped when the radius of the epicycle is to the radius of the deferent in the same ratio as the velocity of the deferent is to the difference between the velocities of epicycle and deferent.

36. The motion being direct, the curve is orthoidal when the radius of the epicycle is to the radius of the deferent as the square of the deferential velocity is to the square of the sum of the deferential and epicyclic velocities.

The motion being inverse, the curve is orthoidal when the radius of the epicycle is to the radius of the deferent as the square of the velocity of the deferent is to the square of the difference between the velocities of the deferent and epicycle.

37. With the exception of the annuloid and the ellipse all figures resulting from two circular movements may be generated by two different velocity ratios.

38. The motion being inverse, the same figures are generated by a velocity ratio expressed by a fraction having the deferent velocity for a numerator and epicyclic velocity for its denominator as by a velocity ratio expressed by a fraction (in its lowest terms) having the velocity of the deferent for a numerator and the velocity of the deferent minus the velocity of the epicycle for a denominator. These are complemental figures.

39. With direct motion and a velocity ratio expressed by a fraction having the velocity of the deferent for a numerator and the velocity of the epicycle for a denominator, the same figure is produced as with inverse motion and a velocity ratio expressed by a fraction having for its numerator the deferent velocity and for its denominator the sum of the two velocities. These are supplemental curves.

The capabilities of the geometric chuck are illustrated by the Figs. 210 to 225. The blocks by which

Fig. 210.

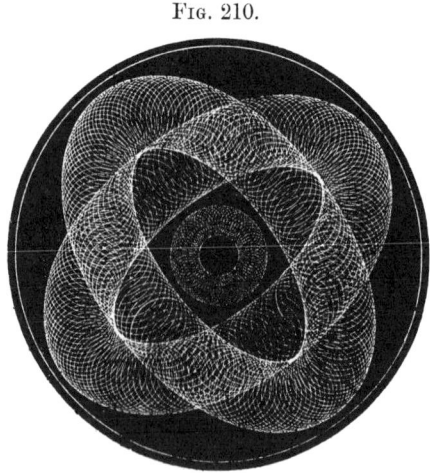

these impressions are printed are practical examples of the chuck's uses and powers, as they were cut in the

lathe entirely by its aid.* These illustrations will, however, give but a small idea of the immense variety of
figures the geometric chuck will execute, as the figures

FIG. 211.

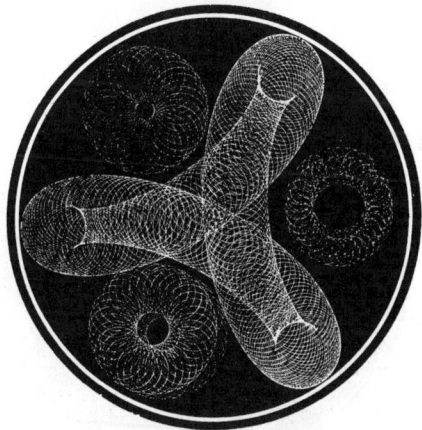

FIG. 212.

that can be generated by the simple and the compound
geometric chucks are literally endless.

* These blocks were furnished me by Mr. G. Plant of Alsager,
Cheshire—their beauty will cause them to be admired. They were cut
by one of Mr. Plant's own chucks.

By comparing these figures with those which illustrate the effects of double counting, the difference will
be at once perceived.

FIG. 213.

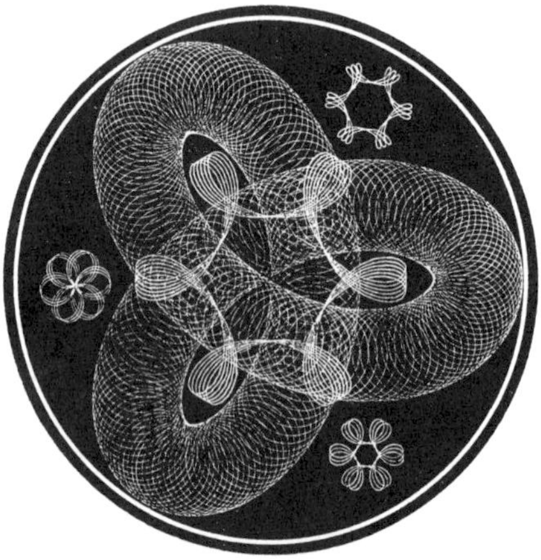

FIG. 214.

The figures shown are the result of two sun and
planet motions, those to be obtained by the simple geometric chuck are comparatively uninteresting, and their

form will easily be understood, without any examples. The compensating index, sometimes called the third part of the geometric chuck, has been explained

Fig. 215.

Fig. 216.

already. By applying it to the chuck, the ellipse and other figures are divided equally, as has been explained. The ellipses shown at Fig. 210 are not so divided, as

they were cut without the compensating index. The
third part of the geometric chuck in reality is another
excentric motion, with wheels similar to the second

FIG. 217.

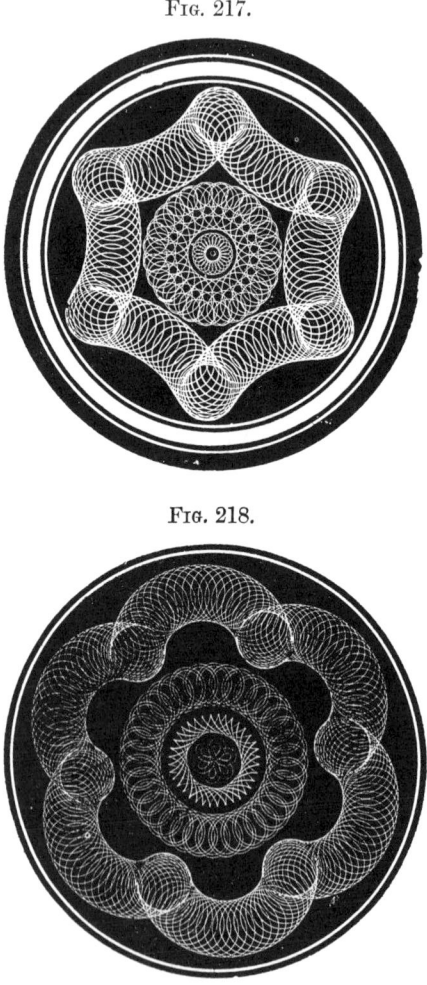

FIG. 218.

part. When all three parts are used there are three
sun and planet motions, and a much greater variety and
number of figures may be produced, although many of

them are almost indistinguishable from the number of
lines.

FIG. 219.

FIG. 220.

ORNAMENTAL CUTTING AND CARVING.

It is not always necessary that the various patterns
should be merely cut with angular tools. For very

intricate patterns, very fine lines are required, but
other patterns produced by the same apparatus can

FIG. 221.

FIG. 222.

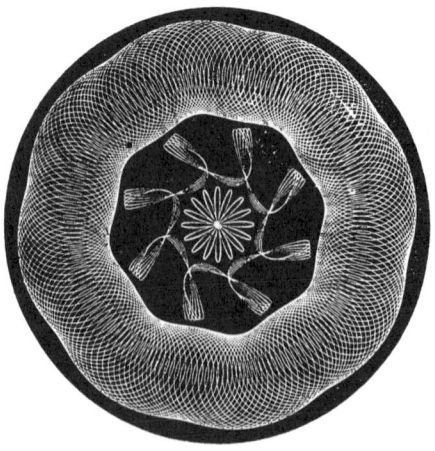

be rendered highly ornamental by being cut in relief,
cut very deep, or with beaded and curved tools.

A very effective ornamental pattern is obtained by using a veneer of a dark wood on light wood or ivory,

Fig. 223.

Fig. 224.

and then cutting the pattern through the veneer to expose the light surface underneath.

The various rose-engine patterns are very fine when cut deeply with a bead or moulding tool. In all these cases, however, the pattern should be simple, and composed of not too many overlaying lines.

When thus cut they have a totally different appearance from that when cut by simple angular tools.

Nor are these the only uses of the apparatus, for the excentric chuck and the ellipse chuck both have their uses in turning ornamental solids. The forms to be

Fig. 225.

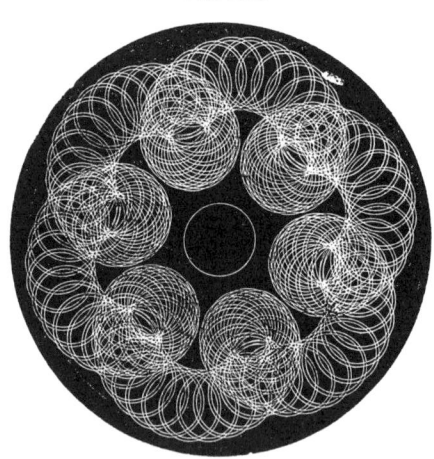

produced by them are apparent from their uses in figure engraving. The tools used for such turning are the same as those for plain turning, and are similarly used. The slide-rest tools are in most cases to be preferred to hand tools.

An apparatus is also frequently applied to the slide-rest to enable it to turn and ornament with precision various curved articles. This contrivance goes under the name of a curvilinear apparatus, and performs its

work by means of various profile plates, which, being
affixed to the lathe, cause the tool to follow their curves.
But for turning ornamental solids, the ordinary slide-
rest is frequently replaced by another more convenient
and comprehensive contrivance, of similar nature, and
called a spherical slide-rest.

FIG. 226.

The instrument shown at Fig. 226 is the spherical
slide-rest as made by Mr. Evans, the old-established
amateur lathe-maker of Wardour Street, Soho. This
rest is used, as its name indicates, for turning spherical
work, which it will do with greater ease and exactitude
than by the hand operation previously described. This
instrument, it will be seen, has four slides, which are
necessary to obtain the various movements and adjust-

ments required for this style of turning. Each of these
slides of course requires to have the usual strength, and
as these are four, it becomes necessary to make them
of steel, and to fit them together with a great regard to
stiffness as well as exactness. The tool slide has a tool
receptacle with holding-down screws, two setting-up or
adjusting screws, and a lever handle; all arranged the
same as in the ordinary slide-rest already described.
The tool-slide altogether fits into a socket attached to
the radius-slide next below it, and it may be turned
round to any position in the socket and fastened there
by tightening the screw at the side, as will readily be
understood by referring to the illustration. The two
lowest slides are also arranged like the slides of an
ordinary rest, at right angles to each other, and they
are both moved by two screws, the ends of which are
squared to receive small winch handles. The other
slide is also moved by a screw and a handle, but this
one, besides carrying the socket for the tool-slide, is
fixed upon a worm or tangent wheel, which in turn is
placed upon the slide below, but in such a manner that
both the worm-wheel and its slide may be moved
around upon it. This is done by means of a tangent-
screw fastened to the lower slide, and rotated by a
handle, as shown in the illustration. This handle is
made long to allow the top, or radius slide, to pass
over it without interfering with the operator's fingers.
The various handles are shown in place, but, of course,
they are removable.

The manner of using the slide-rest is very simple,
and its successful using is entirely a matter of adjustment. The centre of the worm-wheel must come in

a vertical line passing down through the centre of the sphere to be turned, and the two bottom slides afford means for so adjusting the worm-wheel. The size of the sphere is determined by the distance the point of the tool is placed from the same vertical line by means of the third, or radius slide. The tool-slide screws are more for the convenience of putting the tool into cut than for any adjustment for the size of the sphere.

The various adjustments having been made, the tool's point is caused to travel around and describe the required curve by turning the handle on the tangent screw. By the suitable relative arrangement of the centres of the work and worm-wheel, and the tool's point, the rest will cut both concave and convex curves; it will also cut a great variety of other figures, such as lemon, orange, and egg shapes, and, besides this, the rest is applicable to any of the ordinary slide-rest purposes.

FIG. 227.   FIG. 228

The traversing spindle is also used for turning a screw, and also oblique turning or 'swash' work, by substituting a pumping socket for the screw socket on the spindle end. These pumping sockets are merely grooves so cut in the socket as when running around in contact with a stationary pin, the spindle of the lathe is caused to traverse endwise in its bearings once or more during each rotation. Figs. 227 and 228 illustrate the work produced in this manner by pumping sockets, which cause the lathe-spindle and work to travel once forward and back in each rotation.

The bottom part of Fig. 228 is an illustration of the style of work produced when the spindle makes several strokes each revolution.

Of course, in this style of turning, the work must not be supported by the screw centre, but must be treated in the manner mentioned under screw-cutting with the traversing spindle.

The most intricate works are, however, produced by instruments held in the slide-rest, the cutters of which are set in very rapid rotation.

The drilling instrument is very similar to the one already described and illustrated, but it is made much slighter, and, having to rotate much faster, is fitted with smaller pulleys.

The drills used are made like Figs. 229, 230, 231, 232, and of many other shapes of cutting edge.

FIG. 229.   FIG. 230.   FIG. 231.   FIG. 232.

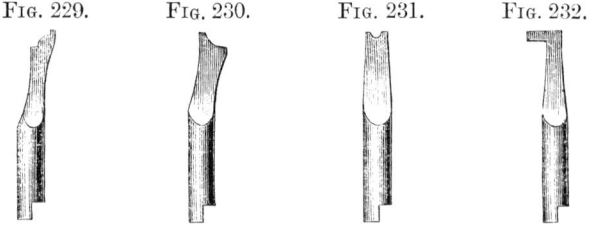

This instrument only allows the drill to be applied horizontally, and as it is often necessary to use them in other positions, various modifications of the instrument are made, one of which, called the vertical drilling instrument, allows the drills to be applied vertically. Another, called the universal instrument, allows them to be used in any required position.

There is another instrument, called the excentric drill, very like the excentric instrument, but stronger made, and using similar drilling instruments.

Fig. 233 is a cutting instrument; its shank is square, and fits the receiver of the slide-rest. It has a hole, through which the cutter-head spindle passes, and is fastened by a nut, which allows it to be placed at any

FIG. 233.

angle. The cutters used are similar to Figs. 168 to 177, and they are driven at a great speed, generally with the cutting edge running downwards, so that the shavings may go down, instead of being thrown up into the operator's face.

There are also various modifications of this instrument; of which the universal cutting instrument allows the cutter to be used in any position, and the internal cutting instrument is for reaching into long recesses or holes where the other instruments are not applicable.

Fig. 234 is the spherical chuck. It screws on the lathe-spindle end, and is generally used in conjunction with the segment divider for orna-

FIG. 234.

menting spheres, which are held in an ordinary chuck screwed on to the nose of the spherical chuck. By moving round the screw-head the position of the work on the spherical chuck is determined. The chuck-nose may also be swivelled and fixed at

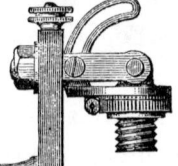

any angle by means of the quadrant slot and screw.

The divisions of the figures or ornament on the work,

is obtained by means of the tangent screw and wheel, as will be easily understood.

Fig. 235 is the spiral chuck. It is a sort of false nose

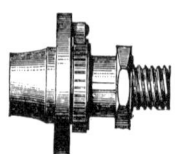

FIG. 235.

screwing on the spindle end, and carrying a screwed nose to receive any of the ordinary chucks. This nose forms part of a socket which may be shifted round without altering its centrality, it also carries an index-plate and catch, and is fitted to receive one of a series of change-wheels.

The chuck itself forms part of a set of apparatus for spiral turning. Through the medium of this contrivance the lathe-spindle is connected with the slide-rest screw by change-wheels, which act in precisely the same manner as in the self-acting lathe already described. The slide-rest screw when used in this manner acts in the same way as the leading screw of a self-acting lathe.

The remaining parts of the apparatus are a radial arm and studs, which fasten on against the headstock, just behind the spiral chuck. This arm has a long slot hole for receiving the various spindles used to carry the intermediate change-wheels.

For screw-threads of ordinary pitch the lathe is driven as usual, and its motion sets the rest-screw in motion and traverse the tool. When coarse-pitched spirals are required for cutting Elizabethan ornaments, twisted pillars, and such work, the lathe-spindle and slide-rest screw are, as before, connected by a set of change-wheels, which will produce the required pitch, but the gut is thrown off the driving cone, and the cone and work are driven by turning the handle of the rest-screw.

The ordinary slide-rest tools are not applicable to this style of work, as the motion is too slow to enable them to cut properly; but by using revolving drills or fly cutters driven at a great speed, the work may be driven as slowly as may be necessary without inconvenience. These spirals are generally cut upon cylinders of wood or ivory, but the apparatus is so made as to allow the spirals to be cut upon cones and surfaces. This is done by using wheels of such a shape as will gear with each other when their axes are at an angle to each other. Some of the wheels are ordinary spur-wheels, others are bevel-wheels, and others are rounded upon the driving edge.

By slightly modifying this apparatus it will act so as to cut wavy lines longitudinally on articles. For this sort of work the wheel on the chuck socket is removed, and a lever put on in its place. This lever is prevented moving by a key, unless the lathe-spindle moves also. Throughout its length it is furnished with about a dozen holes. The slide-rest screw is, as before, connected by wheels to the intermediate socket, and this socket has upon it an excentric, the excentricity of which may be altered. The excentric is connected to the lever on the chuck at one of the holes by means of a link. It will, therefore, be seen that on turning the slide-rest screw the tool or cutter in the rest will be traversed, and the intermediate socket being driven the excentric will cause the lathe-spindle and work to oscillate, and these oscillations will cause a wavy line or groove to be cut on the work.

The number of these waves in a certain length will depend upon the change-wheels. The depth of the wavy line will depend upon the extent of oscillation, and this may be altered by altering the extent of excentricity and by placing the connecting link into another hole of the lever on the chuck.

When more than one spiral or wavy line is required they are spaced, not by altering the wheels but by means of the index-plate on the spiral chuck.

FIG. 236.

Fig. 236 is a vase, the top part of which is formed of an egg shell. The pedestal is best made of African black wood; it is first turned to the outside shape, the fluting is then done with the drilling instrument, the spacing being managed by the division-plate of the lathe. The beads or little spheres are also cut with a properly shaped revolving drill.

Fig. 237 is an illustration of another style of work done by the drilling instrument or excentric drill.

FIG. 237.   FIG. 238.   FIG. 239.

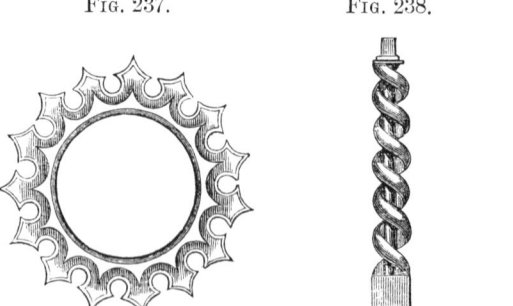

This is meant for a small picture frame. It can be cut circular as shown, or elliptical, but in the latter case the spacing of the holes must be done by means of the division-plate and the compensating index or ellipse divider.

Figs. 238 and 239 are specimens of hollow spiral work. Sometimes these are cut out of the solid, but generally the interior is bored out first, and the tube thus formed put upon a mandril of soft wood. The spiral and spaces between the spirals are then cut out by fast running fly-cutters of proper shape, used in the cutting instrument. The internal spindle is inserted when the spiral work is mounted in place, in the ornament of which it forms a part.

The spindle may be plain, or may itself be spiral, or ornamented in any other manner. When this style of work is properly done, it forms one of the prettiest ornaments that can be made.

SHARPENING TOOLS, ETC.

The ornamental lathe, rest, and chucks, require even more attention and care than the others described. The running parts go much faster, and should never be allowed to get hot or abrade, as the absolute truth of every part must be retained, if good work be desired.

The ordinary turning tools are not ground every time they become dull, but are rubbed a few times over an oilstone. After a time, however, the tools become too blunt to be thus sharpened, and then they must be reground; this should be done with care, and the tools afterwards nicely honed to remove the stone scratches from their cutting edges.

The flat and angular tools used for polishing and for line engraving with the ornamental chucks and instruments require to be very nicely sharpened. Some do this by eye, but amateurs generally use an instrument, called a goniometer, and which is contrived for the purpose.

This contrivance has two graduated arcs, one of which is adjusted to the angle of the tool, and the other to the angle of its bevel or chamfer. The tool to be ground is fixed in the instrument, and held by a tool-holder, provided for the purpose. When properly fixed and adjusted, the edge of the tool to be ground, and the two legs of the goniometer, form a tripod, which is moved over a flat surface, formed of a slab, in which is a grinding plate. The grinding plates are usually three, all fixed into the slab. The first is an oilstone plate, which is used for grinding, the second a brass plate used with very fine emery powder or oilstone powder, for smoothing the tool, and the third is an iron plate used with crocus for polishing the fine cutting edges.

I do not wish to encourage carelessness, but may mention that this process is not in all cases followed, being somewhat too refined and tedious.

The bead and circular tools and drills are generally ground by conical or moulded grinders of brass and iron, and used with the polishing powders just mentioned. These grinders are sometimes rotated in a small frame attached to the slide-rest, and sometimes are held in a chuck attached to the lathe-spindle, the tools being held in a tool-holder in the slide-rest.

SPOTTISWOODE AND CO., PRINTERS, NEW-STREET SQUARE AND PARLIAMENT STREET.